Catholic Modernists, English Nationalists

Catholic Modernists, English Nationalists

Timothy J. Sutton

DELAWARE

Newark: University of Delaware Press

Associated University Presses
2010 Eastpark Boulevard
Cranbury, NJ 08512

The paper used in this publication meets the requirements of the American National Standard for Permanence of Paper for Printed Library Materials Z39.48-1984.

Library of Congress Cataloging-in-Publication Data

Sutton, Timothy J., 1978–
   Catholic modernists, English nationalists / Timothy J. Sutton.
      p.   cm.
   Includes bibliographical references and index.
   ISBN 978-0-87413-077-5 (alk. paper)
   1. English literature—Catholic authors—History and criticism.   2. English literature—20th century—History and criticism.   3. Modernism (Literature) —Great Britain.   I. Title.
   PR120.C3S87   2010
   820.9′921282—dc22   2009026746

To Michael and Barbara Sutton

Contents

Acknowledgments

I WOULD LIKE TO THANK THE FACULTY AT THE UNIVERSITY OF MIAMI who have contributed to my intellectual development and made this project possible, particularly Patrick A. McCarthy, Frank Palmeri, and Zack Bowen. I do not have enough space to express how grateful I am to have been molded as a scholar by such professional and generous teachers. I also would like to extend a special note of gratitude to Michael Patrick Gillespie of Marquette University and Michael Sinowitz of DePauw University, who yielded some of their valuable time to contribute to this project. Thanks also to my colleagues at the University of Miami, especially Amanda Tucker, who has read chapters and offered valuable advice. I am grateful to the faculty members at Auburn University who have offered proofreading services, including Jonathan Bolton, Will Spates, Brendan Balint, Kellie Dawson, and Sunny Stalter. I send warm thanks to my younger sister Amanda Aitken, who helped proofread various chapters, and my twin sister Jamie Shifley, who listened to my complaints and laughed at my jokes when I needed a break from research. Thanks to Adam McMahon for his creative cover ideas and Rafael Egües for taking the book jacket picture. Numerous friends have also provided proofreading and research assistance, including J. K. Wall, Lt. Carey McIntyre, Dominic Buckley, and Fr. James Nowak.

I would be remiss if I did not mention the moral and spiritual support of the Catholic Student Association at the University of Miami and the Catholic Student Organization at Auburn University. Writing is a rewarding but occasionally isolating endeavor, and the love and strength you have provided has been essential. Finally, I send thanks to my parents, who have supported me in innumerable ways as I have pursued this project.

Quotations from the poems and prose of Gerard Manley Hopkins are reprinted from *Major Works* by G. M. Hopkins, edited by C. Phillips (1986), *Further Letters* by G. M. Hopkins (1956), and

9

Selected Prose by G. M. Hopkins (1980) by permission of Oxford University Press on behalf of the British Province of the Society of Jesus. Excerpts from *The Good Soldier* by Ford Madox Ford (Carcanet) are reprinted with kind permission from David Higham Associates Limited. Quotations from *T. S. Eliot: Collected Poems, The Complete Plays of T. S. Eliot, For Lancelot Andrewes, The Idea of a Christian Society, After Strange Gods, The Letters of T. S. Eliot: 1898–1922, Notes Towards the Definition of Culture, The Sacred Wood,* and *To Criticize the Critic and Other Writings* are reprinted with kind permission of Faber and Faber Ltd. Excerpts from *T. S. Eliot Collected Poems, 1909–1962, Four Quartets, The Cocktail Party, Murder in the Cathedral, Notes Towards the Definition of Culture; After Strange Gods: A Primer of Modern Heresy; The Idea of a Christian Society;* "Lancelot Andrewes," "Thoughts After Lambeth," "Andrew Marvell," and "Dante" (in *Selected Essays* by T. S. Eliot); and "Richard Aldington 15 November 1922," "Eleanor Hinkley 8 September 1914," "Vivien Eliot to Charlotte C. Eliot Easter Sunday 8 April 1917" (in *The Letters of T. S. Eliot, 1898–1922*) are reprinted by permission of Houghton Mifflin Harcourt Publishing Company. Excerpts from *Black Mischeif* and *Decline and Fall* are reprinted by permission of Little, Brown & Company. Quotations from Graham Greene novels *Brighton Rock, The Comedians, A Burnt-Out Case, The End of the Affair, The Lawless Roads (Another Mexico), Our Man in Havana, The Power and the Glory, The Heart of the Matter, The Man Within,* and *The Quiet American* are reprinted with permission from Penguin Group USA and David Higham Associates Limited. Excerpts from Graham Greene's *The Lost Childhood and Other Essays* are reprinted from Penguin Group USA. Excerpts from *Black Mischief* and *Decline and Fall* by Evelyn Waugh are reprinted with permission of Little, Brown & Company. Excerpts from *A Sort of Life, Ways of Escape,* and *Monsignor Quixote* by Graham Greene are reprinted by permission of Simon & Schuster, Inc. All rights reserved.

Catholic Modernists,
English Nationalists

Introduction

What are the roots that clutch, what branches grow
Out of this stony rubbish?

—T.S. Eliot, *The Waste Land*

THE DECLINE OF THE BRITISH EMPIRE IN THE COURSE OF THE twentieth century does not merely stand as a correlative event in relation to the movement of literary modernism, with its aesthetic themes of fragmentation, loss, and divergent and competing voices. In fact, these themes can be directly connected to England's fragmenting empire, the loss of its international dominance, and the expanding global audience listening to the independent voices of the colonies. But England did not discard its colonial and imperial sense of itself willingly, and this resistance moved beyond military force (as does every stage of colonization). In *Culture and Imperialism*, Edward Said warns of the backlash of an empire's "nostalgia for imperialism," a nostalgia that pervades English modernist art.[1] *Catholic Modernists, English Nationalists* discusses the extent to which conversion to Catholicism provided literary modernists in England an answer to their desire for a return to Western hegemony, authority, and security under a justifying transcendental myth, and, more importantly, it traces how this impulse is reflected in each modernist's work.

With the exception of T. S. Eliot, the authors whose work comprises the focus of this book—Gerard Manley Hopkins, Ford Madox Ford, Evelyn Waugh, and Graham Greene—were educated as Anglicans and had to abandon the national church in order to convert. The transnational character of the Catholic Church would prove to be in some degree an appealing as well as alienating factor in each of their conversions and lives as Catholics. T. S. Eliot was an American born in St. Louis and educated at Harvard, but his self-selected national identity was English. Eliot is also dif-

13

ferent from the other four because, although he considered himself an "Anglo-Catholic" with a theology and spirituality that would seem profoundly Roman Catholic today, he never left the Anglican Church after he joined it in 1927. Eliot's decision may explain why some of his contemporaries were willing to abandon their national ties and become Catholics, while others, like C. S. Lewis, remained somewhat uncomfortably Anglican.

Although the doctrinal and political divide between the Anglican Church and the Catholic Church has grown increasingly wide in the late twentieth and early twenty-first centuries, the differences in the nineteenth and early twentieth centuries, especially between the High Anglicans and Catholics, were fewer if still insurmountable. Over the last two decades, scholars of literature and history have contributed substantially to the study of the popular depiction and political presence of the Catholic Church in England and its relationship with High Church Anglicanism in the nineteenth century, but less work has been done on the Catholic influence in England in the twentieth century. However, in the past half decade, Ian Ker's *Catholic Revival in English Literature, 1845–1961,* Joseph Pearce's *Literary Converts,* and Adam Schwartz's *Third Spring: G. K. Chesterton, Graham Greene, Christopher Dawson, and David Jones* have focused on Catholic writers in twentieth-century England, with an emphasis on their conversion narratives and their lives as practicing Catholics. Although *Catholic Modernists, English Nationalists* is in debt to these works, this book is focused to a greater extent on each artist's relationship to the aesthetic and political tenets of English literary modernism and to the way conversion altered their own form of English nationalism and attitude toward British imperialism. Furthermore, implicit in each of these previous studies is the spiritual link between the modernist converts and John Henry Cardinal Newman and the Oxford Movement members who eventually converted to Catholicism. While drawing such a connection is tempting, it overlooks an important strain of English Catholicism—that of the old recusant English Catholic families who had remained in northern and western England since the Reformation. It is my contention that the Catholic genealogy of the modernist converts points to their connection with these recusant Catholics, who were distinguished by their lack of evangelical zeal, simple but intellectual liturgies, minimal clerical leadership or Roman influence, and, in part owing to their landowning status, pro-empire political views. The Newman Catholics, on the other hand, could never quite shake their associations with contemporary Catholic and High Anglican or Anglo-Catholic movements such as the Ritualists, whose interest in Catholicism was primarily aesthetic, or the ultramontane Catholics, who emphasized the importance of the papacy and its authority over the English church.

THE NINETEENTH-CENTURY ENGLISH CATHOLICS AND NEWMAN

The 1851 census in England revealed that, out of a population of just under 18 million people, less than half (5.3 million) of 12 million Anglicans regularly participated in weekly services.[2] Considering that two-thirds of 6 million dissenters attended services, these statistics suggest the Church of England's loss of spiritual influence, which can be attributed primarily to the rise of the urban middle class. Industrialization in England during the nineteenth century interfered with the central organizing body of the Anglican Church: the county parish, where the Anglican Church constituted a vital part of the social fabric. But in industrialized cities like Manchester and London, social identity was typically divorced from religion. In 1896, popular Anglican clergyman A. F. Winnington-Ingram unequivocally insisted, "It is not that the Church of God has lost the great towns; it has never had them."[3] The Irish-Catholic immigrants, who comprised a majority of the Catholics in mid-Victorian England and worked in urban areas, had equally poor attendance numbers as urban Anglicans, with only about half of approximately 600,000 Catholics attending Mass regularly.[4] This relatively low percentage compared to the higher Mass attendance rates in Ireland speaks to the Irish immigrants' adaptation of English urban culture, a process accelerated by the absence of a language barrier. However, the eventual influx of converts and additional Irish immigrants in the second half of the nineteenth century substantially raised the number of Catholics in England; aided by greater solidarity and a more visible social and political place in English cities, percentages of attendance at Mass among Catholics eventually rose in the early twentieth century.

I noted earlier that the Catholic converts in this study were at-

tracted to a specifically English version of the faith, and their Catholicism was distinct from the faith of the Irish Catholics.
Although historically significant, parliamentary acts such as Catholic Emancipation in 1829, which gave Catholics the right to hold
political office in England, were actually pushed forward by Irish
politicians like Daniel O'Connell, who wanted to gain political
power for Ireland in Great Britain after the 1801 Act of Union.
Ultimately, O'Connell's work did little to improve the social position of Catholics in England. But this ineffectual political result
came as little surprise to the recusant Catholics, who quietly opposed the law not only because it was promoted by an Irishman,
but also because it gave the clergy more power over the Catholic
people in England and, thus, the Roman hierarchy more influence
over the English Catholic church. Despite his eventual disagree-
ments with the recusant Catholics, Newman likewise resisted
O'Connell's influence, although his views may have been shaped
by an early anti-Irish prejudice that he would later revise. According to historian Christopher Hollis, when Newman was contemplating conversion around 1840, one of his central objections to
members of the Catholic hierarchy was that they "did not unequivocally condemn O'Connell, whom he looked upon as a wicked
agitator and a wanton disturber of the peace."[5] Newman later supported Rome's decision to reinstitute bishoprics in England in
1850, but the recusant Catholics withheld support for this action
for the same reasons they opposed the Catholic Emancipation Act
in 1829: fear of tighter control from Rome. The 1850 decision was
inspired by Cardinal Nicholas Wiseman, eventual Catholic archbishop of Westminster, who was known for his extremist ultramontane views. Anglicans likewise reacted vehemently against the
1850 decision, calling it the "Act of Papal Aggression," although
the decision had very little influence on the religious temperament
of the country. Their response was primarily an emotional one
arising from a centuries-old anti-Catholic paranoia. Nevertheless,
it seems recusant Catholics and Anglicans could agree on their desire to limit Roman influence on Christianity in England.

The character of the recusant Catholic faith in England can be
described as resilient and independent, and necessarily so in a hostile environment where the Roman hierarchy would not have had
much control even if the recusant families had welcomed it. Unlike
in Ireland, where the faith of the masses was poetic and nationalis-

tic but intellectually underdeveloped, Catholics in England belonged primarily to the upper classes and were well educated and
sufficiently catechized.[6] The recusants' loyalty was to the Catholic
tradition of their family, although they were typically conservative
and nationalistic. The English Catholic Mass was often held at
country estates, in multi-purpose buildings, and even outdoors.
Inevitably, the aesthetic disparity with the Continental Catholics,
whose ceremonies often took place in ornate cathedrals, led to a
sense of spiritual disunity. According to English Catholic historian
John Bossy, "Mass in this environment was, in reality as in theory,
very much a private Mass for a private congregation; outsiders
came to it by invitation."[7] Historically, the simple and secluded
worship space and lack of evangelical zeal among English Catholics arose as survival strategies after the English Reformation,
when public knowledge of their faith could have cost them their
lives.

Considering the very private and reticent religious behavior of
the Catholic modernists, the link with the recusant Catholics
seems much firmer than any with other Catholic groups in England. In fact, the recusant Catholics were more or less hostile to
Newman and other nineteenth-century Catholic movements. The
major spiritual leaders of the recusants were less historically significant men than Newman, such as Bishop Richard Challoner,
whose popular eighteenth-century prayer book *The Garden of the
Soul* (1740) helped to model the English devotional style until the
twentieth century.[8] Similarly, Challoner's many pamphlets on
apologetic issues that would be relevant to nonclergy, such as explaining papal infallibility (before it was pronounced doctrine in
1870) or how to defend the Catholic Church in conversation with
Anglicans, had widespread influence on the English Catholic community. Challoner's work in some respects imbued the English
Catholic church with practices popular in the European church.
The Reverend George Stenning, a Catholic priest writing in 1921
on the condition of Catholics in England, commented on these
new expressions of the faith: "The piety of the faithful of our day
is more stirred by such services as Benedictions, processions, popular hymns, expositions of the Blessed Sacrament, and many other
forms of devotion unknown to the mediaeval Catholic," but the
English assimilated these practices while retaining their reserved
character.[9] Essentially, it was the style of Catholicism advocated

by Newman and other nineteenth century converts that disgusted the recusant Catholics and not the substance of their beliefs, since both groups were more or less doctrinally orthodox. According to historians Nicholas Atkin and Frank Tallett, "Many 'old' Catholics, who were already disturbed by the wide-scale Irish immigration, were suspicious of the papalism and sincerity of the new converts [of the Oxford Movement], and found their proselytizing fervour distasteful."[10]

Of course, the idea that the Catholic Church in England was a defender of conservative aesthetics and stripped-down liturgies seems entirely inconsistent with portrayals of Catholicism in Victorian novels such as Charles Dickens's *Barnaby Rudge* or Charlotte Brontë's *Villette,* where Catholics are portrayed as superstitious fanatics following clergy who engage in diabolical rituals, and the Mass is often portrayed as a melodrama conducted in opulent churches. However, these inaccuracies often were derived not from observations of English Catholics but from stereotypes of Continental expressions of the faith rooted in ill-informed anti-Catholic sentiments.[11] It is true that some groups like the Ritualists were attracted to Catholicism because of its potentially more extravagant liturgy, but this group and others like it were actually High Church Anglican movements that produced few Catholic converts. Conservative Anglicans also opposed the Ritualists, partially because it was rumored that they promoted homosexuality.[12] The controversy these groups stirred prompted the passing of the Public Worship Regulation Act, signed by Benjamin Disraeli in 1874, which exercised greater control over extravagant liturgical practices.

As their reaction to the passing of the Catholic Emancipation Act and the reinstitution of the Catholic hierarchy indicates, the recusant Catholic families feared change in part because they wanted to protect their independence from Roman influence. According to historian Edward Norman, "Opposition to the new devotional styles came from those traditional English Catholics who correctly discerned that they were an external and popularized sign of a great shift in emphasis within the Church—the remoulding of English Catholicism according to the vision of the ultramontanes."[13] The recusant Catholic mistrust of such groups and of Continental Catholics seems consistent with their distinct style of Catholicism, but the more intriguing rift separated the recusant

Catholics and politically conservative intellectuals like Newman who converted primarily for doctrinal reasons. Newman's Catholicism, at least at the point of his conversion, was similarly "English"—meaning he likewise preferred a simple liturgy, did not emphasize the use of icons or veneration of the saints, and initially challenged the Vatican on matters such as papal infallibility (although after the latter belief became doctrine, Newman became more obedient to Rome). The natural adversaries for both Newman and the recusant Catholics were the ultramontanes—especially Wiseman and Henry Edward Manning, also an English Catholic bishop and eventual cardinal—who criticized the isolated nature of English Catholicism and approached political problems from a more European and less English perspective.

Possibly the recusant Catholics, familiar with the patterns of converts and seasoned by defense of their particular brand of the faith, were wise to be cautious with Newman, who would become increasingly sympathetic to a global vision of the contemporary Catholic Church and some aspects of liberal politics. Newman likewise did little to ingratiate himself with the recusant Catholics and chastised their behavior throughout his career. In his widely read sermon "The Second Spring," Newman condescendingly calls the recusant Catholics "a mere handful of individuals" who "merely happened to retain a creed which in its day was the profession of the Church."[14] Although the recusant Catholics certainly made no widespread public effort to spread their faith or communicate with any sort of solidarity, Newman's derisive language is not entirely fair or accurate. For centuries, the landed Catholic families maintained and passed on their faith through intermarriage among other Catholic families and by encouraging sons and their families to live on or near the original family land. One reason the concentration of Catholics was in the north and west of England was that, after the Reformation, their land in that area of the country was positioned on high ground where they could more easily defend their estates and thus their Catholic identity.[15]

However, industrialization, intermarriage with Irish Catholics and Anglicans, and agricultural modernization eventually caused many of these families to lose their English Catholic traditions in the twentieth century.[16] But in 1852, when many of these families were still organized and faithfully Catholic, Newman unjustly described them as only being "found in corners, and alleys, and cellars, and the housetops, or in the recesses of the country . . . as ghosts flitting to and fro."[17] What Newman initially desired, as the title to his "Second Spring" address indicates, was a revitalized Catholic movement in England that was neither grounded in the elite families that survived the Reformation nor tied slavishly to Rome. Ian Ker explains that the converted Newman thought there should be "lay speakers and public meetings in the big towns. Young Catholics should band together as the Tractarians had."[18] The recusant Catholics, of course, would have cringed at such a development.

Like the recusant families, the novelists and poets in this study rarely spoke about their faith publicly, but their Catholic spirituality was interwoven into their life and work in an indirectly evangelistic manner. Waugh's romantic depiction of the Brideshead estate and Greene's portrayal of the heroic Mexican priest in *The Power and the Glory* are tools of evangelization as valuable as any of Newman's sermons in defense of the faith. Newman dreamed of a revival in Catholic literature, but he probably would have been disappointed with the Catholic modernists' disillusioned realism and their lack of solidarity with other Catholic authors of the modernist movement. Ultimately, Newman's only potentially valid criticism of the established Catholics centers on their evangelical apathy rather than the authenticity of their faith. Ironically, Newman himself was often criticized for his lack of evangelical zeal after the initial excitement surrounding his conversion, but he still refused to find common ground with the recusant Catholics.[19]

What is arguably even more ironic is that the particularly English brand of Catholicism that Newman hoped to instill inadvertently helped revive a form of the faith inevitably derivative of the Catholicism preserved by the pre-Reformation remnants. In *Catholic Devotion in Victorian England,* Mary Heimann writes that, despite Newman's "second spring propaganda . . . it was an invigorated English recusant tradition, not a Roman one, which was most successful in capturing the imagination of Catholics living in England from the middle of the nineteenth century to the early years of the twentieth."[20] Although Heimann's account is accurate, she is somewhat dismissive of Newman's influence. The revival was made possible by Newman's work and the public attention surrounding his conversion and subsequent career, but

Newman did not anticipate that a great number of these converts would assume the character of the recusant Catholic faith that he considered irrelevant. The nationalistic, reserved, aesthetically simple, and independent Catholicism of the modernist converts attests to this pattern. Meanwhile, the more aggressively evangelical and ultramontane converts who cited Newman as a central influence, such as G. K. Chesterton and Christopher Dawson, had less influence on the nature of English Catholicism in the twentieth century.

MODERNIST POLITICS IN THE TWENTIETH CENTURY

The work of the most visible nonmodernist Catholic converts of the early twentieth century, such as Chesterton and Hilaire Belloc, added to the sense that there was a reactionary Catholic position fomenting in England. However, the modernists had no meaningful collaboration in political or artistic spheres with the other Catholic converts of the period. Unlike the modernists, Belloc was neither sentimental nor nostalgic; instead, he employed a polemical rhetoric that envisioned a return to precapitalist and even pre-Reformation European society. In works such as *Europe and the Faith* (1920) and *Essays of a Catholic* (1931), Belloc identifies the Reformation as the key event in the decline of European power and therefore argues that reconversion to Catholicism represents the only remedy to modern social challenges. In *Europe and the Faith,* he blames Protestantism for the "abomination of industrialism" and "the loss of land and capital by the people" and for igniting World War I.[21] One common theme of Belloc's work is that the Europeans, and Englishmen in particular, must choose loyalty to the church over nationalistic allegiances, which, considering the recusant Catholic tradition discussed above, was not a popular position among English Catholics. Even as a writer, Belloc's polemical vision was fundamentally different from the Catholic modernists; he sought a social and political unity that went far beyond personal submission to church authority, the reinvigoration of Catholic culture, or the relatively abstract bonds of myth and tradition.

Belloc both admired and promoted Chesterton's writing, but Chesterton's lighthearted tone and his excitement about his con-

version (which seemingly never waned) distinguish his objective
from that of the controversial Belloc. Chesterton's art cannot be
deemed modernist, although his literary standing was not negligible. The "Father Brown" novels mix mystery and plot in a manner
best classified as Victorian; even *The Man Who Was Thursday*,
a fragmented theological/psychological thriller, concludes with an
explicit moral that rarely if ever occurs in modernist texts. Chesterton valued his moral message over artistic complexity or origi-
nality, and that message was closely aligned with Newman's in his
call for the English church to find a unified voice that expressed
solidarity with Rome. The combination of this aesthetic and religious difference with the English modernist converts distances
Chesterton from the central points of analysis in this book. Nevertheless, as Hugh Kenner points out in *Paradox,* his book on Chesterton, the author's use of paradox and his critique of the modern
world through philosophical and mythical works influenced the
modernist movement, even if his work is not necessarily part of it.

Although Chesterton's aesthetic may have been similar to that
of the Victorians, his conservative politics, like Belloc's, were not.
Almost every artist associated with modernism likewise moved
politically to the right of the great Victorian novelists, such as
Dickens, George Eliot, and Thomas Hardy. A relatively simplistic
yet persuasive explanation for the shift to the right is that the liberalism of the Victorians failed to cure the social evils it vowed to
eradicate. Furthermore, the English liberal agenda, resistant to
overtly nationalistic rhetoric and opposed to granting the Anglican
Church a predominant place in politics, did not provide a moral or
spiritual center for English artists. Still, this conservatism led the
modernists to very different paths. For example, Ezra Pound, and
to a lesser extent W. B. Yeats, moved toward the political conservatism of fascism, while the authors in this project turned to orthodox Christianity. Eliot and Waugh mocked the Victorian's
moral hypocrisy, but Yeats wanted to be free of leftist socialism
and what he perceived to be the constraining religiosity of the
more conservative Victorians. In his introduction to *The Oxford
Book of Modern Verse,* Yeats mocks the Socialists "disturbing Tra-
falgar Square on Sunday afternoons," as well as conservative
poets like Lionel Johnson and Francis Thompson who converted
to Catholicism.[22] Yeats then offers his own description of the difference between Victorians and the modernists. "Then in 1900

everybody got down off his stilts; henceforth nobody drank absinthe with his black coffee; nobody went mad; nobody committed suicide; nobody joined the Catholic Church; or if they did I have forgotten. Victorianism had been defeated."[23] Although Victorian aesthetics were dying by 1900, Yeats's alleged reasons for "Victorianism's" demise would all resurface in later modernists: Pound and Eliot mounted very high stilts; various American and British artists from F. Scott Fitzgerald to Malcolm Lowry had problems with alcohol; Hemingway did commit suicide, and Waugh and Greene confessed to making attempts; finally, this book is made possible by the fact that a number of modernists became Catholics.

Yeats's misinterpretation of the forces behind the modernists' rise against the Victorians is symptomatic of the lack of agreement among modernists as to what they were reacting against or seeking to promote. A similar divergence in understanding of the purpose of the movement proved to be one crucial element in the rift between Pound and Eliot. Before Pound knew of Eliot's conversion, he had asserted, "Christianity has become a sort of Prussianism, and will have to go."[24] After their relationship ended, Pound criticized Eliot's faith and concluded that his "diagnosis is wrong. His remedy is an irrelevance."[25] The break between Pound and Eliot is paradigmatic of the split between modernists who turned to right-wing political systems for transcendental meaning and those who turned to faith.

Michael Levenson's *Genealogy of Modernism* notes the modernist movement's initial objective to create an exciting and provocative approach to art in the first decade of the twentieth century—a line of development I will soon trace to the historical avant-garde—to the more cautious aesthetic and foreboding tone the high modernists assumed as the Great War neared. Levenson claims that, despite its aesthetic innovations, liberal humanism was still the dominant sentiment of the poetry of that first decade. But many modernists, Pound most notably, disliked this approach; with the Vorticists, Pound determined to resist the humanism that made the arts "dull and complacent" in order to follow, as the manifestoes in *Blast* proclaim, an art meant for "THE INDIVIDUAL" that has "nothing to do with 'The People.'"[26] It would be easy to attribute this turn toward a less egalitarian aesthetic (embraced by both the later historical avant-garde and modernists) to the psychological strain of the Great War. But a sense of disillusionment pervaded English literary circles before that catastrophe. For example, Levenson notes that just before the war began in 1914, Ford lamented, with a trace of irony, that what is lacking in literature "is religion, is intolerance, is persecution, and not the mawkish flap-doodle of culture, Fabianism, peace and good will."[27] The reality of the war would yield a fertile environment for such an aesthetic reformulation.

A renewed nationalistic fervor swept through all of England at the dawn of the Great War, and the Vorticists and other members of the avant-garde were not exempt from this patriotic social environment. According to Paul Peppis, the Vorticists "played a role in encouraging English intellectuals to greet the advent of the European war in August of 1914 by rushing to their nation's cause."[28] In fact, Eliot biographer Lyndall Gordon recounts that Eliot once visited a recruitment officer after the United States joined the Allied effort. Pound responded by writing a letter to the U.S. Embassy requesting his friend be denied, in which (according to Gordon's paraphrase) Pound explained that "if this were a war for civilisation, not merely for democracy, it was folly to shoot one of the six or seven Americans capable of understanding the word."[29] Considering the immense number of seemingly senseless deaths, Pound's reservations proved wise. While England drudged through the war, the futility of the trenches wore on the morale of civilians and soldiers alike, and the initial nationalist push and ideological motivation slowed considerably.

As often happens in times of prolonged distress, religion played a role as both a moral answer and provider of comfort. In *The Great War and Modern Memory*, Paul Fussell emphasizes the ubiquitous use of Crucifixion and Resurrection imagery among soldiers of all nations because of the themes of self-sacrifice and renewal.[30] He even notes that "roadside calvaries were not likely to go unnoticed by British passerby, not least because there was nothing like them on the Protestant rural roads at home," where the cross did not include the Christ figure.[31] Such seemingly inconsequential details reflect the difficulty of sustaining any cohesive religious revival in England during World War I. Because the Anglican Church was (and is) a state religion, nearly every religious act and symbol was inherently tied to the divisive political world. Even in domestic politics, High Church Anglicans typically allied themselves with the Tory Party and Low Churchmen and Dissenters maintained liberal sympathies; the smattering of Catholics, although generally conservative, historically had been barred from playing any meaningful role in the government and did not maintain strong party identifications.

For this reason, it would not be fair to say that each of the artists in this study had the same politics. Though all were more or less conservative, what that designation signified from man to man or decade to decade was in constant flux. Similarly, each of the artists in this book traveled a different road to conversion. With these factors in mind, it is important to underscore my argument that historical and biographical evidence does not support the notion that these conversions point to the existence of a coherent movement or some sort of Catholic "literary revival," as scholars have implicitly and sometimes explicitly suggested. Nevertheless, I do mark a political difference between these conservative converts and the increasingly right-wing leaning Yeats and Pound, and an aesthetic difference between these English modernist converts and Belloc and Chesterton.

Therefore, this book focuses on conservative and Catholic artists who avoided any official relationship with the Tory/Conservative Party or the Vatican, a distance that once again suggests the modernist converts' link with the recusant Catholics. The modernists' political writings were rarely done in the name of a party, and the modernist Catholics showed a relative disregard for their relationship with the English church hierarchy or for Vatican-sponsored criticisms of their work. Even faithfully practicing converts like Hopkins and Waugh (and Eliot in the Anglican community) expressed only mild concern with their standing among church officials, while the more doctrinally liberal Ford and Greene quite openly ignored official Catholic social or moral teachings and scoffed at clerical criticisms of their novels. Nonetheless, these converts proudly considered themselves Catholic, and their work helped to reintroduce a Catholic literature into English culture. If any unifying characteristic exists among them, it is that they conceived of their Catholic faith in relation to their modernist aesthetics, and that the effect of their faith on their art in turn influenced both the cultural place of Catholicism and the path of modernism in England.

Joint Tenets of Modernism and Catholicism

My conception of English literary modernism in this book is rel-atively broad, but distinguished from the historical avant-garde movement—Futurists, Vorticists, Gertrude Stein, HD, and Pound (who straddles the divergence)—in the early twentieth century. Andreas Huyssen outlines one helpful understanding of the differ-ence between the modernist and the historical avant-garde atti-tude toward high and low art in *After the Great Divide: Modernism, Mass Culture, Postmodernism*. "The culture of modernity has been characterized by a volatile relationship between high art and mass culture" while "the historical avantgarde aimed at develop-ing an alternative relationship between high art and mass culture and thus should be distinguished from modernism, which for the most part insisted on the inherent hostility between high and low."[32] In addition to maintaining Huyssen's characterization of modernists in relation to the avant-garde (even if artists such as James Joyce and Eliot invoked and parodied examples of popular fiction, music, painting, and sculpture), I also separate the two groups because the modernists, according to Stephen Spender in *The Struggle of the Modern*, "feel responsible to a past which had been degraded" and abandoned its sense of tradition, while the historical avant-garde embraces the possibilities of the technologi-cal, global future.[33] When E. M. Forster wrote in *Aspects of the Novel* in 1927, "every institution and vested interest is against" modernism's objectives, including "organized religion, the State, the family in its economic aspect" because these institutions "have nothing to gain," he spoke more precisely in the name of the his-torical avant-garde rather than in the name of the high modernists, most of whom were very much invested in reforming political, reli-gious, and local/familial institutions.[34] Although the distinction between the modernists and the historical avant-garde is impor-tant, the inherent subjectivity of modernist aesthetics and Catholic spirituality makes it necessary for me briefly to outline where I see the systems converging in the work and faith of the artists con-cerned in this project. Each of these connections between the ten-ets of modernism and Catholic spirituality can only be drawn, admittedly, on correlative and not causal grounds, but important sociopolitical factors explain the attraction of Catholicism for many modernists.

The first and most consistent connection between English modernists and Catholics is their recognition of and respect for tradition. Although the modernists certainly stimulated new developments in aesthetics, they did so with a conscious understanding of the literary tradition out of which their new aesthetic grew. The most explicit delineation of this notion is found in T. S. Eliot's essay "Tradition and the Individual Talent." Even artists who clearly wanted to break with the Victorian tradition drew connections between their work and earlier English or even European literary movements. For example, Hopkins's metrical experiments were undoubtedly innovative, but his effusive tone and the natural subjects of much of his work link him to the early Romantics; Eliot's deliberate citing of the seventeenth-century metaphysical poets or the French symbolists as his primary influences serves as a more self-conscious example. In Yeats's controversial introduction to *The Oxford Book of Modern Verse,* he explains how the modernists conceived of their aesthetics in relation to tradition, even if they wrote specifically against their Victorian predecessors. "Poetry was a tradition like religion . . . and it seemed that [the modernists] could best restore it by writing lyrics technically perfect."[35] Yeats underscores the technical aspects of modernism, which were innovative yet often influenced by the formal traditions of pre-Victorian or foreign poets.

The posthumous publication of much of Hopkins's verse likewise brought new attention to the modernists' technical differences from their immediate predecessors. Furthermore, Hopkins's influence demonstrates that the modernists, unlike many artists of the historical avant-garde, hardly abandoned a concern with strict form. What Yeats and most modernists particularly disliked was the overtly didactic and moral aspects of Victorian literature. For Pound and the young Eliot, the modernist poet's message must resist a straightforward moral that would not reflect accurately the complexity of humanity's experience in the modern world. In "The Metaphysical Poets," Eliot explains, "Poets in our civilization, as it exists at present, *must* be difficult. . . . The poet must become more and more comprehensive, more allusive, more indirect, in order to force, to dislocate if necessary, language into his meaning."[36] Of course, Eliot here promotes the "comprehensive," "allusive," and "indirect" nature of his own verse, but this self-serving criticism nonetheless characterizes the style of many modernist poets who followed Eliot's and Pound's lead. The allusive and comprehensive nature of the modernists' verse was a means to invoke tradition from which they developed aesthetic innovations.

The modernists' quest for tradition was also historical and spiritual as well as aesthetic. Therefore, joining the Catholic Church represented one way a modernist could lay claim to a more thorough connection with the Christian tradition than was offered by any Protestant denomination. The Catholic Church considers its message to be that of two millenia of tradition, but during the early twentieth century, the provocative tenets of the modernist theologians (led by George Tyrrell of England and Alfred Loisy of France) ignited widespread controversy in the Vatican and throughout the Continent. This conflict culminated in Pope Pius X's encyclical *Pascendi*, in which Rome condemned the theological modernists for their questioning of the authenticity of the Gospel narratives (although elements of their historicist approach to biblical scholarship would influence the documents and theological assumptions of the Second Vatican Council). However, English Catholics in the early twentieth century practiced their faith seemingly unaffected by the Vatican's theological turmoil. In addition to underscoring these modernist converts' connection with the recusant Catholics of previous generations, who likewise generally stayed clear of Vatican censure, this condition can be attributed to other more immediate factors. The logical reason most English Catholics were never entangled in this controversy is that the modernist theologians were essentially challenging biblical research and pedagogy as it was conducted in Catholic academic circles, seminaries and schools, but England had few Catholic schools and even fewer Catholic seminaries. It also attests to the fact that, like the recusants, the literary modernists were not a unified body—if the hierarchy wanted to criticize their work, it would have to be done on a case-by-case basis.

One element of Pius X's encyclical against the theological modernists that did mirror the attitude of many literary modernists was the sense of frustration and alienation with the increasingly urban and dehumanizing global world, which is the second major connection I make between Catholicism and literary modernism (and another factor that distinguishes the modernists from the artists of the literary avant-garde). The Catholic Church had a difficult time adjusting to new technological developments and the sociological conditions these advances propelled; ideological changes in art, production, and trade (especially of intellectual material) also exasperated the hierarchy's defense of orthodox theology. At the beginning of the *Pascendi* encyclical, Pius X warns the church that the theological modernists "lay the ax not to the branches and shoots, but to the very root, that is, to the faith and its deepest fibers."[37] But while the Vatican met this sociocultural conflict with fear and a paranoia that for decades stunted the potential intellectual benefits of what it perceived to be a comprehensive error, the literary modernists expressed their disillusionment in significant works of tragic realism and irony. Ford assumed a jovial voice in describing their approach. "I am in the London of the 1910's, and I am content to endure the rattles and the bangs—and I hope to see them rendered."[38] A sense of alienation owing to the moral emptiness and secularism in the modern world is in some way evident in nearly every work in this project from Hopkins's desperate "Terrible Sonnets" to Waugh's social satirical novels. However, because of its historical tradition and assurance of a more important kingdom to come, the Catholic Church itself offered modernists another answer to the morally destitute world; the Church's tradition permits the response of frustration and irony, but simultaneously yields a reason for hope.

Yet, behind the ironic tone of many modernists lies nostalgia for a more ordered and universal culture, which marks my third and final correlation between Catholicism and English literary modernism. In the introduction to *Postmodernism, or The Cultural Logic of Late Capitalism,* Fredric Jameson claims that a major distinction between postmodernists and their precursors is the "pain of a properly modernist nostalgia with a past beyond all but aesthetic retrieval."[39] But converts found that, within the Catholic tradition, their nostalgia could be allayed by spiritual retrieval as well as an aesthetic one. The word *catholic* means "universal," and because the Catholic Church (unlike the Anglican Church) had to adapt to diverse societies in many continents, it was forced to at least attempt to define theological distinctions and liturgical practices that were compatible with various cultures. Similarly, the Catholic modernists desired to create a literature that demonstrated an awareness of the traditions of various nations and cultures in the increasingly global modern world. This characteristic at least partially accounts for the fragmentation in the narrative voice, plot, and/or theme that characterizes modernist aesthetics. The extent to which this universality is achieved by either the Catholic Church or by the modernists is debatable, but the intent is evident. It is also worth noting that the Catholic modernists in England attempted to retain their pro-empire political stance while making room for new voices, just as the Catholic Church before the Second Vatican Council strained under its effort to control the diversifying church with a strong, hegemonic European hierarchy.

A desire to find order in the twentieth century's socially fragmented landscape also parallels the modernists' preoccupation with myth systems, a movement spurred by Sir James Frazer's publication of *The Golden Bough*, which was released in its complete twelve-volume form between 1907 and 1915. Modernists from Yeats to Joyce to Eliot made explicit use of this text.[40] The modernists were not the first to revive myth as an aesthetic ordering device; in fact, at the close of the nineteenth century, politicians, artists, and intellectuals frequently depicted the British Empire in mythical terms, which in part helped form the strong nationalism of late nineteenth-century poets like Hopkins. Yeats and the Irish Revivalists also used myth to propel their nationalist movements by drawing political and thematic parallels to Ireland's pre-Catholic, Gaelic history. But with the evident decline of the empire in the twentieth century, the modernist converts' allegiance to the Catholic Church provided a substitute myth system that is in its conception both transcendental and multicultural. The jump to conversion for Englishmen meant abandoning nationalistic ties at least in terms of religion, but the nature of the English Catholic Church, with its recusant history, was such that it allowed them to continue to belong to an organization that at least attempted to function and express itself in distinctly English terms. Furthermore, the Anglican Church's social and political power declined considerably with the passing of each decade in the twentieth century. Anglicanism's difficulty maintaining relevance in the twentieth century partially explains why Hopkins's conversion constitutes a much more dramatic step than it did for Waugh or Greene.

Hopkins's conversion is also the most tumultuous of those considered in *Catholic Modernists, English Nationalists* due to his emotional nationalism, in addition to the strain it imposed on his relationship with his High Church Anglican family. The effect conversion had on Hopkins's nationalism and his poetry will be the major focus of the first chapter. In his precociously modernist forms and tone, Hopkins expresses his difficulty in balancing his strong sense of nationalism with his loyalty to the Jesuit Order, especially during his exile in Catholic Ireland. Ford's conversion also took place in the late nineteenth century, but in Germany, not England, and the character of his faith was cultural rather than doctrinal. In the second chapter, I examine Ford's portrayal of Catholics in his novels *The Good Soldier* and *Parade's End* and his stress on preserving national and cultural traditions. The chapter also discusses Ford's deliberate use of his two short-lived journals, *The English Review* and *The Transatlantic Review*, to define the central tenets of the modernist movement in England. In chapter 3, I trace how T. S. Eliot's poetry and prose reflect his movement from a self-proclaimed "Anglo-Catholic" to a mystic with somewhat revised attitudes toward the Anglican Church and the British Empire. Chapter 4 analyzes the novels of Waugh, who regularly portrayed the recusant, landed Catholic families that still remained in England in the twentieth century. I also account for Waugh's caustic response to the liturgical changes instituted at the Second Vatican Council just before his death. The fifth and final chapter considers the works of Graham Greene, whose novels after the Second World War reflect a move from a modernist to a postmodernist Catholic literature in England.

1

Gerard Manley Hopkins:
A Royal Catholicism

If I should die, think only this of me:
That there's some corner of a foreign field
That is forever England.

—Rupert Brook, "The Soldier"

BECAUSE GERARD MANLEY HOPKINS WAS RAISED IN A STRICT HIGH
Church Anglican home, his conversion to Catholicism at the age
of 22 in 1866 did not require him to acclimate to a completely unfamiliar form of liturgical practice or system of doctrine. However,
Manley Hopkins, Gerard's father, studied and took pride in Anglicanism's history and theology, which made Gerard's conversion a
dramatic and contentious affair that might have caused little disturbance in a less-observant home. Manley Hopkins demanded an
explanation from Gerard for his conversion, fearing that his son
had been seduced by the Ritualists—High Church Anglicans
concerned more with ornate ceremonies and architecture than
theology and dogma—and that his conversion was propelled by
Catholicism's aesthetic appeal. Hopkins responded, "I am surprised you sh[oul]d. fancy . . . aesthetic tastes have led me to my
present state of mind: these w[oul]d. be better satisfied in the
Church of England, for bad taste is always meeting one in the ac-
cessories of Catholicism."[1] Hopkins's point highlights the fact that
the style of Catholicism preserved by the recusant Catholics since
the Reformation was stripped-down aesthetically and liturgically.
Hopkins was hardly seduced by Catholicism, despite the popular if
generally unsubstantiated fear of many devout nineteenth-century
Anglicans that Catholicism's aesthetic appeal attracted young Englishmen. Instead, Hopkins's intellectual motives for conversion
aligned closely with those of Newman, although Hopkins did not

share Newman's animosity toward the recusant Catholic families in England. As Hopkins later told his father, he primarily was convinced by "simple and strictly drawn arguments, partly my own, partly others' . . . common sense . . . reading the Bible . . . an increasing knowledge of the Catholic system (at first under the form of Tractarianism, later in its genuine place)."[2] Like Newman, Hopkins more or less read his way into the faith without influential evangelization from lay or religious Catholics. His conversion narrative follows a pattern of many English converts in the late nineteenth and early twentieth centuries: they were inspired to conversion by Newman's work, but then adopted a more independent and nationalistic form of Catholicism than that of Newman.

Hopkins's decision to join the Jesuit order may have been driven by his attraction to drama and risk in his spiritual life, as he chose an order known for its evangelization and the one most feared by Anglican intellectuals.[3] The Jesuits in England primarily came from the recusant Catholics, a pattern established well before the Oxford Movement. The recusant Catholics' and Jesuits' resistance to the ultramontane movements, which emphasized papal authority, and their particularly English style of faith suited the nationalistic Hopkins well. Despite Newman's relative distance from the Jesuits, he supported Hopkins's arduous decision and wrote, "Do not call 'the Jesuit discipline hard,' it will bring you to heaven."[4] Although Hopkins never publicly regretted his decision to convert or to join the Jesuits, he had difficulty reconciling his adopted faith with the beliefs of his friends and family, his own aesthetic tastes, and especially his strong English nationalism.

THE ROMANTIC TEMPTATION: HOPKINS'S EARLY VERSE

W. B. Yeats, who once met Hopkins through Yeats's father, wrote in the introduction to *The Book of Modern Verse*, "I read Gerard Hopkins with great difficulty, I cannot keep my attention for more than a few minutes; I suspect a bias born when I began to think. He is typical of his generation where most opposed to mine. . . . My generation began that search for hard positive subject matter, still a predominant purpose. Yet the publication of his work in 1918 made 'sprung verse' the fashion, and now his influence has replaced that of Hardy and Bridges."[5] Yeats characterizes

Hopkins as a Victorian poet because of what Yeats perceived as his abstract religious subjects, while acknowledging only Hopkins's metrical influence on the modernists. But like the modernists of the twentieth century, Hopkins's verse often uses concrete description to express spiritual themes. Of course, throughout the introduction, Yeats slants literary history toward the biases of his own memory and aesthetic sympathies; for example, he describes himself as a strict modernist, choosing not to recall his sometimes effusive, sentimental early verse. Much recent critical work follows Yeats's lead and focuses on Hopkins's close relationship to his Victorian peers. For example, in *Gerard Manley Hopkins and the Victorian Temper,* Alison G. Sulloway notes Ruskin's influence on the young Hopkins's aesthetic and social views; however, Sulloway overemphasizes Hopkins's identification with his fellow Victorians when she argues, "[Hopkins] suffered the classic religious traumas for which the age was famous. In his case he resolved his religious crises by submission to Rome."[6] Despite Ruskin's influence on Hopkins's aesthetic views on painting or architecture, no evidence exists that Hopkins, whose early High Church Anglican beliefs were hardly typical among the great Victorian prose writers and poets, questioned his Anglican faith before he began studying Catholicism. Instead, it was his intellectual encounter with Catholic thought that caused him to sever his ties with his Anglican faith; Hopkins earns his reputation as a Victorian because of his politics and nationalism.

Efforts to classify Hopkins as a prototypical Victorian in his poetics and faith have arisen in reaction to the well-established view that his verse represents a precocious example of modernism, with its innovative rhythm and difficult diction and syntax. Hopkins's later work, especially the "Terrible Sonnets," is best characterized as modernist, but his early poetic subjects and themes contain many similarities with the Romantics. Like each of the modernist Catholic converts, Hopkins's Catholic faith provides him a complex answer to the challenges of the modern world and drives him to apply a modernist aesthetic still influenced by previous literary traditions. In "The Linguistic Moment," J. Hillis Miller classifies Hopkins as a Romantic and contends that the primary reason for Hopkins's conversion was his belief in the "Real Presence" of Christ in the Eucharist. Although the Eucharist was one of many biblical and historical reasons for Hopkins's conversion, Miller accurately notes that, for Hopkins, "In that [Eucharistic] Presence nature, God, self, and Word come together. Poetry, if it is to have value, must repeat that magical assimilation of the dispersed into one."[7] But Miller fails to specify that each of these elements must be ordered properly in the work of a Catholic: God must always rule over man, who takes precedence over nature and the word (in the linguistic sense), the last two of which man properly uses as a means to God, the theological/biblical Word or *Logos*. The Romantics had little regard for this order, but an orthodox Catholic like Hopkins had to preserve it.

Miller claims that Hopkins disliked the Romantics' "irrevocable splitting apart" of man, nature, and God, but the problem was quite the opposite: the real danger for Hopkins was the Romantic temptation to conflate God and nature rather than split them apart.[8] Wordsworth, an exemplary early Romantic, demonstrates this pantheistic tendency in book 8 of *The Prelude*, where he frequently ignores these boundaries, and speaks of "the Spirit of Nature" or "the sanctity of nature" in much the same terms that a Catholic might speak of the third person of the Trinity.[9] Later in the same book, Wordsworth recalls his unwillingness to yield man, with his "weight of meanness, selfish cares,/Coarse manners," and "vulgar passions," the same level of respect and love he gives nature.[10] Throughout his writing career, Hopkins remained painstakingly conscious of what is, from a Catholic perspective, the Romantic's pantheistic error so as to maintain the proper relationship between the created object—be it a natural scene or the human body—and the Creator, God. Newman similarly felt the need to remind himself not to equate the beauty of the natural world with God; he once wrote in a diary, "Dear Mary seems embodied in every tree and hid behind every hill. What a veil and curtain this world of sense is! beautiful, but still a veil."[11] Hopkins recognized that his sensitivity to the natural world ran much deeper than the more scholarly Newman's and therefore felt more threatened by his attraction to it.

When Hopkins entered the Jesuit novitiate, he temporarily ceased writing verse because he felt that it might lead him to idolize the aesthetic objects that inspired his poetry. He explained the situation to his boyhood friend, A. W. Baillie. "I want to write still and as a priest I very likely can do that too, not so freely as I sh[oul]d. have liked, e.g. nothing or little in the verse way, but no doubt what w[oul]d. best serve the cause of my religion."[12] Although there was no formal edict from his superiors banning him from writing verse, Hopkins anticipated the Jesuits' pragmatic approach to spiritual work. In the introduction to *The Spiritual Exercises,* Jesuit founder Ignatius Loyola emphasizes the active life of a Jesuit, whose spiritual activity functions as a "way of preparing and disposing the soul to rid itself of all inordinate attachments."[13] Although he would revise his position later, Hopkins initially applied this teaching by restricting his writing of verse and contemplation of nature. One of Hopkins's novice educators clarified how to form the proper Jesuitical character. "Deeds, not words, are insisted upon as proof of genuine service, and a mechanical, emotional, or fanciful piety is not tolerated."[14] Only by re-conceiving his verse as a form of action, rather than merely a linguistic exercise, could Hopkins feel justified in writing verse as a Jesuit.

A sensitive poet like Hopkins would find much reason to censure himself in the intense spiritual environment of a Jesuit novitiate house. Not surprisingly, Hopkins's first poem after a five-year hiatus, "The Wreck of the *Deutschland,*" did "serve the cause" of Catholicism, but in it Hopkins does not abandon his Romantic love and respect for nature, a balance maintained more confidently after his self-imposed moratorium on writing poetry. Considering these postconversion works, Miller concludes that "in spite of Hopkins' Catholicism, he may be seen as a poet in the Romantic tradition."[15] But it ultimately was Hopkins's understanding of God in Catholic terms (and not in spite of it)—with its focus on the immanence of God in the Real Presence, and also in the natural world—that freed him to explore God's presence in the natural world through his verse.

Hopkins's impulse to celebrate nature, especially while at Oxford before his conversion, also frequently inspired his nationalism. But as joining the Catholic Church became a more likely possibility, Hopkins consciously tried to distance himself from identifying too strongly with England, whose national church he was leaving. For example, in "The Alchemist in the City," written in 1865 just months before Hopkins became a Catholic, he describes the beauty of the natural world surrounding Oxford's towers, but then halts in the middle of the poem to remind himself:

> No, I should love the city less
> Even than this my thankless lore;
> But I desire the wilderness
> Or weeded landslips of the shore.
>
> (21–24)[16]

Conversion will lead him away from Oxford, so he cannot become too attached to the school he loves, and Hopkins's metaphorical "wilderness" represents his somewhat romantically conceived spiritual future—challenging, unknown, but promising—in the Catholic Church. Similarly, in his poem "See How Spring Opens," which celebrates his conversion, Hopkins compares his final years in the Anglican Church to the end of winter with its "hunting winds and the long-lying snow" (2). Hopkins's connection between the "Spring" and his Catholic conversion echoes Newman's 1852 sermon "The Second Spring," on the expected cultural and intellectual revival of Catholicism in England. Newman, however, applies the metaphor in a much more abstract manner, while Hopkins follows the Romantic pattern wherein a concrete reflection on the natural world leads to an intuitive spiritual and emotional self-understanding.

Hopkins wanted to stress the spiritual insight gained from his contemplation of nature, but like the Romantics, he was aware of how his aesthetic surroundings might affect his emotions. Just as Wordsworth writes in *The Prelude,* "From Nature doth emotion come, & moods / Of calmness equally are Nature's gift," the aesthetic beauty of Hopkins's natural environment directly influenced his disposition and therefore the tone of his verse (as well as his productivity as a poet).[17] This correlation explains Hopkins's contentedness at St. Beuno's College at a beautiful setting in Scotland despite the tedium of his theological studies there, and it contributed to his unhappiness while holding a somewhat prominent teaching position in sordid nineteenth-century Dublin the last five years of his life. Well before his time in Dublin, Hopkins lamented the urban and industrial growth throughout Europe, a common complaint of many Romantics and Victorians.

In "God's Grandeur," Hopkins describes his frustration with England's abuse of nature, but he nonetheless assures himself, in a way the Romantics did not, that the natural world is not eternal and industrialism cannot soil God. Hopkins composed the poem in 1877 while he did menial parish and teaching work at Mt. St. Mary's College in Chesterfield. The first octave emphasizes the division between the glory of nature and the tarnish of development:

> The world is charged with the grandeur of God.
> It will flame out, like shining from shook foil;
> It gathers to greatness, like the ooze of oil
> Crushed. Why do men then now not reck his rod?
> Generations have trod, have trod, have trod;
> And all is seared with trade; bleared, smeared with toil;
> And wears man's smudge and shares man's smell: the soil
> Is bare now, nor can foot feel, being shod.
>
> (1–8)

Hopkins emphasizes the mortality of "God's grandeur" as expressed through nature in a concrete manner that is likewise suggestive of the sacramental language of the church, wherein God's presence is not just spiritual but physical and immanent. God "charges" the world with beauty that shines spontaneously as the reflection of light from "shook foil." The gift will pass, although the Giver remains. Yet Hopkins nostalgically laments that "man's smudge" and "man's smell," which allude to sins that stain the soul, as well as the "trade" that drives the industry, which renders the purity of the natural world "seared" and "bleared," accelerate the loss of God's revelation in nature. In the first stanza, Hopkins rhetorically doubts whether man can remove the stigma of sin or reverse the destruction of the natural world. Only God possesses power over sin and the natural world he created, and Hopkins wonders why men do not "reck his rod." The question can obviously refer to any person in need of salvation, but the pleading tone is likely directed at his beloved England, which refuses to convert back to the Catholicism of its past—a call that resurfaces in "The Wreck of the *Deutschland*." The answer that "Generations have trod, have trod, have trod" suggests mankind's inability to return to God and possibly alludes to the ineffectualness of Catholics in England to reconvert the nation.

Hopkins reverses this pessimistic tone in the sestet. Despite man's abuse of nature, God preserves it. "And, for all this, nature is never spent" (9). The verb *spent* points to economically motivated industrialism, which still has not ruined the "freshness deep down things" (10). Similarly, God renews the "freshness" of the spirit of mankind through his forgiveness, despite humanity's sin. Both the natural world and man's nature are preserved because "The Holy Ghost over the bent / World broods with warm breast and with ah! bright wings" (13–14). No longer afraid that praising the natural world will lead to idolatry, in "God's Grandeur" Hopkins's aesthetic contemplation induces worship of God's creativity and forgiveness. Hopkins's use of the natural world as a means to understanding God fits Catholic spirituality more closely than most forms of Protestant spirituality that, partially owing to the early reformers' stress on humanity's "depravity," often view any aspect of the physical world as something divorced from God. In *The Spiritual Exercises*, St. Ignatius contemplates why "the heavens, sun, moon, stars, and the elements; fruits, birds, fishes and other animals . . . have all been at my service" and been given to humanity as a gift and responsibility.[18] The founder's words reveal why the Jesuitical emphasis on the immanence of God in the natural world permitted Hopkins to embrace his aesthetic interests, when he thought Catholicism might mean he would have to flee them.

In "To What Serves Mortal Beauty?" written in Ireland in 1885, Hopkins returns to this subject and more consciously describes how natural beauty can be a means to God and not a distraction from him. In the first lines, Hopkins calls mortal beauty "dangerous" because it "does set danc- / Ing blood" (1–2), a response that likely refers to Hopkins's attraction to the male body, a desire he feared in his youth.[19] But Hopkins has matured spiritually and sexually, and he admits that admiration for the body's or nature's beauty "keeps warm / Men's wits to the things that are" (3–4). He states that Catholic teaching (or possibly Hopkins refers specifically to the Jesuit rule) liberates him to enjoy the world's beauty. "Our law says / love what are love's worthiest . . . / World's loveliest—men's selves" (10–11).

Of course, Hopkins will not cultivate lust or worship nature's beauty above God; instead, when encountering natural beauty, he aims to:

> Merely meet it; own,
> Home at heart heaven's sweet gift; | then leave, let that alone.
> Yea, wish that though, wish all, | God's better beauty, grace.
>   (12–14)

The first half of each line celebrates God's creation, while the second half counsels how to view it in light of Catholic thought. When Hopkins commands, "leave, let that alone," it sounds as if he counsels himself as much as the reader. Again, this emphasis echoes St. Ignatius's "First Principle and Foundation," where he explains, "The other things on the face of the earth are created for man to help him in attaining the end for which he is created. Hence, man is to make use of them in as far as they help him in the attainment of his end, and he must rid himself of them in as far as they prove a hindrance to him."[20] Because the aesthetic object and the emotions Hopkins derived from it were crucial to his verse, he always remained conscious of the Jesuit teaching on the proper order of the relationship between man, God, and his creation.

Yet it is this focus on the object that connects Hopkins to both the Romantics and the modernists. For example, Wordsworth criticized his eighteenth-century literary predecessors' verse because of the lack of evidence that "the eye of the poet had been steadily fixed on his object."[21] Over a century later, T. S. Eliot similarly censured his Victorian contemporaries because, in the case of Swinburne and others, "the object ceased to exist."[22] The difference is that the Romantics inherently valued the object to a greater degree and focused on the immediate effects of its beauty, while the modernists described the object with almost pessimistic realism and valued it equally and possibly more immediately for its symbolic function. As Hopkins's personal spiritual struggle became the central theme of his later verse, his treatment of the aesthetic object more closely followed the modernist tradition, as he regularly used the object or natural scene as a symbol, metaphor, and reflection of the workings of an abstract God in his own demanding life.

Hopkins's Verse and Nationalism

Along with Hopkins's more modernist approach to the subjects of his poetry, his postconversion verse became increasingly concerned with politics, a poetic subject that distances Hopkins from the early Romantics and moves him closer to the modernist tradition. As he promised in his letter to Baillie just before conversion,

Hopkins returned to verse to "best serve the cause" of Catholicism. But in his evangelizing efforts, Hopkins had no desire to abandon his nationalism, which proved a tough balance to maintain. In *Imagined Communities,* Benedict Anderson discusses the difficulty of keeping mixed religious and national allegiances in the modern world. He marks the fifteenth century as the point in history where social identity ceased to be found primarily in religious faith and was instead grounded in geographic and political commonalities. "For all the grandeur and power of the great religiously imagined communities, their *unselfconscious coherence* waned steadily after the late Middle Ages," mainly as a result of "explorations of the non-European world."[23] According to Anderson, without religious faith as the central binding element among men, "unchosen" characteristics provide the basis for identification. "[N]ation-ness is assimilated to skin-colour, gender, parentage and birth-era—all those things that one can not help."[24] But for a firmly believing Catholic like Hopkins, such superficial identifications of unity frequently conflicted with the church's emphasis on the unity of the "Body of Christ." Anderson notes the predicament of the modern Catholic and the tension created by these often opposed notions of identity. He describes one relevant case. "The deliberate, sophisticated fabrications of the eighteenth century Catholic mirror the naïve realism of his thirteenth-century predecessor," but arguments for territorial unity through religious faith were rendered "utterly selfconscious, and political in intent."[25] Once the common bond of all Europeans, the practice of religion carried a more specific nationalistic significance in eighteenth-century Europe—and it is so with Hopkins in nineteenth-century England.

To remain a loyal English nationalist without compromising his Catholic faith, Hopkins consistently looked to the glorious past of England before the Reformation or to the future where he hoped it would reconcile its differences with the Catholic Church. According to Anderson's notions of nationalism, Hopkins's reaction is not uncommon. "The fact of the matter is that nationalism thinks in terms of historical destinies."[26] The term *historical destinies* suggests a preoccupation both with the past as understood by the nation itself (and deliberately put into legendary terms) and the future as the nationalist believes it is destined to be fulfilled. Similarly, for Hopkins, only post-Reformation England presents an environment where his Catholicism displaces him politically, a historical determination that explains why he found solace in emphasizing England's Catholic past and, at least in Hopkins's imagination, its potentially Catholic future. Furthermore, this sense of a "historical destiny" frequently caused nationalists to become full-fledged imperialists, and Hopkins's attitude toward the Irish at the end of his life assumed an imperial tone.

Initially, Hopkins willingly risked alienating his countrymen by begging them to return to their Catholic roots. The sinking of the German passenger ship *Deutschland* in December of 1875, in which five nuns drowned, provided Hopkins an opportunity to urge his fellow Englishmen to conversion. Hopkins particularly sympathized with the nuns because of their dedication to their Catholic faith in spite of persecution in their native Germany, which they were forced to leave when its first chancellor, Bismarck, suppressed Catholics in the country. But the first eleven stanzas of "The Wreck of the *Deutschland*" actually concern Hopkins's own spiritual dedication to God. His language invokes the Catholic notion of God's immanence: "Since, though he is under the world's splendour and wonder, / His mystery must be instressed, stressed" (39–40). God's presence permeates the physical world, even in the destructive storm, but his "mystery" goes beyond the merely physical world. "Instressed, stressed" refers to Hopkins's application in "*Deustchland*" of his self-styled "sprung rhythm," a metrical form that kept the rhythm as close as possible to regular speech by adding stressed syllables. Hopkins also used the term *instressed* in contexts outside of his verse, where it was related to his notion of *inscape*. Although Hopkins did not always use the terms consistently, *inscape* generally refers to the inner nature of something that can be sensed only after complete knowledge of its physical aspects is mastered. *Instress* frequently describes the nearly uncanny feeling derived from contemplating inscape. For example, in a journal entry, Hopkins claims that a comet induced in him "a certain awe and instress, a feeling of strangeness."[27] Similarly, in "*Deutschland*," Hopkins tells how contemplation of God's mystery will lead one to experience the "instress" derived from his presence. Hopkins's notions of "inscape" and "instress" correlate with his theological sympathies for Duns Scotus, who emphasized the particularity and uniqueness of created things, rather than their universal attributes (a connection discussed more fully below). It is also worth noting that the complexities of these terms and other elements of Hopkins's diction and syntax, not to mention his rather unfamiliar metaphors, kept the poem from being accessible to the general public and explain why Hopkins's postconversion verse influenced the experimental formal elements of modernist poetry.

But the unfamiliar language does not mean Hopkins believed that the natural world or God's presence is inaccessible, although it takes diligent prayer and refined faith to comprehend. Through much of the long first section of *"Deutschland,"* Hopkins depicts the world in a storm much like the ship was, but he still worships God whose presence sustains "Whether át ónce, as once at a crash Paul, / Or as Austin, a lingering-out sweet skill" (77–78). To show the many available roads to conversion, Hopkins refers to Paul's sudden conversion as depicted in the Acts of the Apostles and to Saint Augustine's methodical march through many philosophies and heresies before God finally led him to the Catholic Church. In the second part of the poem, Hopkins praises the nuns' holy conduct during the sinking: they stayed in their cabins and prayed that others might survive. But in stanza 21, he temporarily ceases praising their heroic actions in the drama and laments their exile: "Loathed for a love men knew in them, / Banned by the land of their birth, / Rhine refused them, Thames would ruin them" (161–63). The lines clearly echo Hopkins's own sense of rejection in England. The verb *would* not only refers to the fact that they eventually drown in the Thames, but it also suggests that, were they to attempt to practice their Catholic faith in England as Hopkins does, it would "ruin them."

The veiled biographical themes that can be discerned when Hopkins discusses others' trials are characteristic of Hopkins's later verse, as is the tendency to invoke slightly melodramatic religious metaphors to emphasize the spiritual significance of his subjects. For example, Hopkins associates the nuns' sacrifice with Christ's five wounds on the cross. "Five! the finding and sake / And cipher of suffering Christ" (169–70). One of Hopkins's primary attractions to conversion was the personal risk involved that would affect him on a private and intellectual level, and this desire for spiritual adventure explains his sometimes sensational language in describing Catholic sacrifice. While a defense and promotion of Catholic spirituality in *"Deutschland"* beckoned Hopkins out of his self-imposed restriction from verse, he does not forget his native country in the poem. By the final stanza, Hopkins focuses his attention on unconverted England, asking that "Dame," the Virgin Mary, will remember "English souls" and that Christ may begin a new "easter in us" (273, 274–75). The "easter" Hopkins desires is the resurrection of Catholicism in England, a wish that became the central theme in his other shipwreck poem, "The Loss of the *Eurydice*," which laments the death of proud British soldiers who drowned in the ship in 1878 after an unexpected storm during training off the Isle of Wight.

"The Loss of the *Eurydice*" is not nearly as technically experimental nor as popular as *"Deutschland."* It focuses primarily on how even the glorious British navy cannot withstand the will of God. In the final stanza of *"Eurydice,"* Hopkins suggests that only the prayers of Catholics might help save the souls of the Anglican dead. He prays for the young soldiers, "for sculs sunk in seeming / Fresh, till doomfire burn all, / Prayer shall fetch pity eternal" (118–20). Without his prayers to convince God to grant "pity eternal," these "Fresh" Anglican souls would burn in hell. Predictably, these works were not well received by Hopkins's own family, friends, or the British public. Bridges summed up the response best when he complimented the artistic achievement of *"Deutschland,"* yet still claimed, "But I wish those nuns had stayed at home."[28]

Hopkins's tone toward his fellow Englishmen, especially Anglicans, is somewhat condescending in *"Deutschland"* and even more so in *"Eurydice,"* while his nationalism was uncharacteristically silent in the former and veiled in the latter. Some critics mistakenly consider his zealous Catholic rhetoric in these works as evidence of a developing ultramontane position in Hopkins's faith and politics.[29] But his Catholicism was too English in its expression and too politically concerned with England to be identified with Edward Manning's Vatican-centered faith. Yet while Hopkins's pride in the empire, which surfaced so strongly when its authority was challenged, as well as his strong dislike of Gladstone, aligned him with Tory conservatism, he did follow the pattern first set by the recusant Catholics by refusing to profess loyalty to a political party. Not surprisingly, ultramontanes like Manning, while defending extremely conservative positions in the church, stressed that English Catholics must avoid identification with political parties so as to "be Catholics first, and citizens afterward."[30] Hopkins never would have articulated his stance in those terms, but he generally concealed his political sympathies immediately after his conversion, in part because his loyalty to the Catholic Church was for a time more firm than his patriotism.

Hopkins made few political comments in his journal or letters before or just after his conversion. Once in the Jesuit novitiate house at Stonyhurst, however, he became more vocal on such issues, probably because of the broader range of his study and his increased exposure to England's political situation. In a letter from Stonyhurst to his longtime friend, Robert Bridges, Hopkins confessed that his economic views had moved left of the typical Victorian or English Catholic. "Horrible to say, in a manner I am a Communist. . . . England has grown hugely wealthy but this wealth has not reached the working classes."[31] These thoughts reveal the tension between Hopkins's desire to preserve the aristocratic classes that represent England's tradition and history and his recognition that, in the modern world, the older social system cannot be kept without sacrificing the integrity of those who perform the indispensable manual labor of industry.

Hopkins's conflicted attitude toward the working classes was inconsistent rather than ambivalent. For example, Hopkins's mildly serious profession of communism is motivated by his sincere sympathy for the poor; yet their lack of faith, education, and respect for England's history could not be easily overlooked for a man of Hopkins's intellect, religion, and nationalism. He encountered a similar situation in Ireland, where he sympathized with the economic plight of the Irish Home Rule advocates but was disgusted by their lack of respect for the British Empire and ready recourse to violence to overthrow it. In fact, Hopkins usually employs his most emotional rhetoric when defending the British Empire, not in supporting the church or working classes, where he typically uses a more patient, logical style. He may have intellectually recognized the problem of working class poverty, but his heart lay with the fate of the British Empire.

A letter to Baillie in 1888 demonstrates the difference: Hopkins speaks of the poor as merely an aesthetic and moral problem, but then (without notice) begins to express heartfelt disappointment at the British army's failure against the Dutch in the Boer Wars:

What I most dislike in towns and in London in particular is the misery of the poor; the dirt, squalor, and the illshapen degraded physical (putting aside moral) type of so many of the people, with the deeply dejecting, unbearable thought that by degrees almost all our population will become a town population and a puny unhealthy and cowardly one. Yes, cowardly. Do you know and realise what happened at Majuba Hill? 500 British troops after 8 hours' firing, on the Dutch reaching the top, ran without offering hand to hand resistance before, it is said, 80 men. Such a thing was never heard in history. The disgrace in itself is unspeakable. Still it might have been slurred over by pushing on the campaign. But Gladstone was equal to himself and to the occasion. . . . What one man could do to throw away a continent and weaken the bonds of a world empire he did. . . . He is, without foresight, insight or resolution himself, the bright form of the thoughts and wishes of the Liberal masses.[32]

After lamenting the existence of the poor without discussing the need for governmental reform, Hopkins suddenly complains about the failure and cowardice of the British army without any discernable transition (unless "Yes, cowardly" is a transition. But who is "cowardly" but the British army he has not yet begun discussing?). In recounting the army's trouble, his less-tempered rhetoric demonstrates his deeper emotional investment. Hopkins specifically blames Gladstone, whom he always disliked, because his errors helped "throw away a continent and weaken the bonds of a world empire." If Africa has been "thrown away," is the loss England's or Africa's or both? In his late career, Hopkins usually understood the British Empire's rule as one that also benefited the colonized, a belief that explains his difficulty accepting Home Rule. Therefore, Hopkins's use of the term *bonds* probably did not mean to suggest "chains," but rather the supposed mutually beneficial ties of the colonizer and colonized.

Although Hopkins's nationalism is evident even before conversion, he seems increasingly imperial and concerned with the fate of the British Empire in his late career. One explanation for this focus is that the Boer Wars and other sporadic colonial disturbances revealed the vulnerability of England's imperial control. Hopkins's experience in Ireland no doubt kept him attentive to the issue, but he showed concern even before he moved to Dublin. As his career moved him farther from his boyhood home near London and, more importantly, away from Oxford, Hopkins tempered the criticism of England he levied in the pro-Catholic shipwreck poems. Living in England kept Hopkins aware of England's failings, but once in Ireland he sentimentally glorified his home country.

One way Hopkins managed to support England without harping on its refusal to convert was by recalling a time when his glorious nation was still Catholic, a psychological strategy that matches the form of nationalism proposed by Anderson. Hopkins employs this strategy while reflecting on his alma mater and favorite church father in "Duns Scotus' Oxford," a poem that praises the fourteenth-century Catholic theologian who once taught at Oxford. Hopkins wrote the poem during his brief assignment at his alma mater, and the first two stanzas celebrate the aesthetic beauty of Oxford. The third stanza gives the natural scene added importance as Hopkins reflects on the fact that Scotus once walked the grounds: "Yet ah! this air I gather and I release / He lived on; these weeds and waters, these walls are what / He haunted who of all men most sways my spirits to peace" (9–11). Scotus's theology stressed man's need to experience God in physical and not merely spiritual form, meaning Christ's incarnation was intended for more than the sacrifice on the cross. Constantly concerned with the relationship between aesthetic beauty and spiritual obedience, Hopkins found support in Scotus's writings for his use of the natural world to guide him to God. Furthermore, contemplating the success of a Franciscan in Catholic England meant Hopkins need not criticize his beloved nation. In the final stanza, he exalts Scotus's "not / rivalled insight," which he believes is not surpassed by "Italy or Greece"—signifying Thomistic thought, as well as the Aristotelian framework out of which Aquinas defined his systematic theology. However, Hopkins metonymically refers to them by their nations to stress that it is also England that conquers.[33]

Occasionally, Hopkins could actually find hope for a Catholic England in the present, not only by thinking in terms of history and destiny. When an English soldier requested a blessing from him while he still served at the Oxford parish, Hopkins predictably used the scene as inspiration for a poem, "The Bugler's First Communion." The event proved the perfect occasion for Hopkins to unite his nationalistic (and imperial) and religious notions without the usual strife. Hopkins imagines the young soldier as being born "of Irish / Mother to an English sire (he / Shares their best gifts surely, fall how things will)" (2–4). The playful tone does not conceal the fact that the "best gift" of the Irish mother was most likely the Catholic faith—Hopkins had not yet experienced his difficulties in Ireland and possibly still sympathized with the predominately Catholic country—while the father passes on the bravery and pride necessary for Hopkins's model English soldier. In the sixth stanza, Hopkins, who was hardly a successful preacher, rejoices that he has influenced this young infantryman:

> How it does my heart good, visiting at that bleak hill,
> When limber liquid youth, that to all I teach
> Yields tènder as pùshed pèach,
> Hies headstrong to its wellbeing of a self-wise self-will!
>
> (21–24)

As he does when observing a natural scene, Hopkins exaggerates nearly every aspect of the encounter, thereby creating a rather condescending tone toward the young man whom he calls a "liquid youth" and compares to a "tender peach" because he directs his will to serve God as both a Catholic and an English soldier. But the underlying emotion in these lines is self-satisfaction: Hopkins finally achieves a moment of success in England as a preacher and admits that the encounter causes him to "trèad tùfts of consolation / Days after" (25–26).

The lines following this self-reflection prove even more striking regarding the national-religious themes that the poem invokes when Hopkins imagines his role as a preacher not unlike a soldier in the British army. "I in a sort deserve to / And do serve God to serve to / Just such slips of soldiery Christ's royal ration" (26–27). The young soldier's Catholicism makes possible the conflation of God's will and England's success as a nation. By calling Christ "royal," the adjective most immediately identifiable with imperial England and its armed forces, Hopkins further emphasizes the connection. As Hopkins's nationalism grew more virulent in his later career, he frequently employed imperial and militaristic rhetoric in his spiritual reflections. For instance, in 1879, the same year he wrote "The Bugler's First Communion," Hopkins emphasizes Christ's triumphant purpose in a sermon: "Our Lord Jesus Christ, my brethren, is our hero, a hero all the world wants. . . . He is a warrior and a conqueror; of whom it is written he went forth conquering and to conquer."[34] The Jesuits, who have called them-selves "God's foot soldiers" since the founding of the order, em-phasize the biblical notion of the spiritual battle. In *The Spiritual Exercises*, St. Ignatius counsels that his brothers must be valiant soldiers of Christ because the devil himself engages in the fight like an enemy combatant, who "will encamp, explore the fortifications and defenses of the stronghold, and attack at the weakest point."[35] But Hopkins quite consciously reinterprets the metaphor of the spiritual battle and conflates the expansion of his faith with the expansion of the British Empire, despite the fact that the advance-ment of one was incompatible with the advancement of the other.

Once Hopkins began writing verse again, he showed a greater willingness to voice his opinion on political topics, and his diffi-culty maintaining loyalty to both church and nation was com-pounded by his numerous reassignments ordered by his Jesuit superiors. To complicate matters further, besides a brief, unex-pectedly successful stay at a parish near Manchester, Hopkins's ministry and mental and physical health were in intermittent de-cline after his stint at Oxford. In January of 1880, he was removed to the industrial slums of Liverpool where he suffered from de-manding parish work and wrote few poems. From there he was yet again relocated in 1881, this time to Glasgow, Scotland, where he at first resisted the idea of being out of England, but eventually adjusted to the people and even began to learn Scottish dialects, some of which influenced the diction and rhythm of his later verse. Hopkins's final two years in England were spent at Stonyhurst, where he taught classics to secondary students.[36] This assignment opened the door to his being hired as a classics professor by the Jesuits then presiding as administrators at University College Dub-lin (UCD). In 1884, Hopkins traveled west to Dublin, where he assumed his post under a cloud of controversy that had almost nothing to do with Hopkins personally, but directly implicated him in the Irish political scene that would challenge and dismay him throughout his final five years of life.

NATIONALISM AND MODERNISM: HOPKINS IN IRELAND

Fr. William Delany, president of UCD, visited Hopkins at Stony-hurst in 1883 to convince him to go to Dublin to teach at the school the Jesuits had recently acquired. Delany's motives in selecting Hopkins were strategic: the relatively inexperienced and eccentric Hopkins may not have been his first choice, but Delany was determined to hire a Jesuit so the £400 annual salary might be retained to help the struggling school. Delany's selection met much resistance, especially by the school Senate leader, Rev. Dr. William Walsh, eventual archbishop of Dublin, who felt that other Catholic schools in the University College system should hire Irish professors to appease the nationalistic sentiments of the students. The dispute was not kept from the public as is evidenced by Hopkins's own statement in a postscript to Bridges briefly after arriving in Dublin. "There was an Irish row over my election."[37] Hopkins's offhanded tone (and placement of the line at the end of his letter) makes it seem as if he found the circumstance at least mildly entertaining. However, the divisions between nationalistic Irish Catholics and foreign Catholics in Dublin would become problematic for Hopkins.

The struggle over Hopkins's appointment was a microcosm of the larger intra-Catholic battles in late nineteenth-century Ireland. While Delany desired to assign foreign Jesuits to the school's faculty so they could institute an educational system based on successful universities on the continent and in England, Walsh and many other administrators felt that the failure of the school before the Jesuits took control was due to its lack of appeal to the nationalistic Irish youth. Appointing Englishmen to these posts would further alienate the university from the Dublin Catholics who provided its undergraduate body. Dublin lacked London's international character, nor was it a central industrial European city, which contributed to its distinctively Irish citizenship. Most of the wealthy English families had already moved to the Dublin suburbs. A Catholic school like UCD would have to accommodate the nationalistic fervor of Dublin's youth if it had any chance of filling its classrooms, but it could not compromise its Catholic faith (and, in this case, its Jesuit spirituality). Delany won the battle over Walsh in the instance of Hopkins's election, leading to the powerful clergymen's resignation from involvement with the school; however, the nationalistic Irish were winning the war for the character of Irish Catholicism during Hopkins's stay in Dublin.

Catholic Irish nationalism maintained a different character than the Protestant or sometimes secular national-cultural movements

in Ireland, such as the twentieth-century groups later followed by
Yeats and the other members of the Irish Theater, or even the
champions of the Gaelic League (although the latter had many
Catholic members). The late nineteenth-century Catholic students
and families that Hopkins encountered consciously defined themselves against what they saw as the moral degradation of Protestant and secular culture, despite the non-Catholics' claim to be
reviving Ireland's Gaelic past. One reason for their resistance was
that the Catholic Church still controlled the elementary and secondary levels of education throughout Ireland, while Trinity College Dublin, run by the Anglican Church of Ireland, monopolized
university-level education in the city. At the local level, the Catholic clergy had more influence on politics than the upper-echelons
of the church hierarchy who historically have maintained a less
revolutionary nationalistic posture in Irish politics.

In the face of the often-violent Fenian groups, the church hierarchy kept a watchful eye and, at times, leveled unequivocal indict-
ments. Cardinal Paul Cullen, one of the most powerful church
leaders in late nineteenth-century Ireland, once remarked, "If ever
an attempt is made to abridge the rights and liberties of the Catholic Church in Ireland, it will not be by the English Government,
nor by a 'No Popery' cry in England, but by the revolutionary and
irreligious Nationalists of Ireland."[38] This fearful prediction arose
partly out of Cullen's frustration with his inability to convince his
priests not to support radical nationalist movements, which would
only grow more ungovernable with clergy support. History would
prove Cullen's prophecy erroneous, as the Irish Free State established in 1922 proved to be welcome ground for the Catholic
Church. Nevertheless, in the nineteenth century, there is little evidence that the Catholic hierarchy or foreign Catholics (Hopkins
included) distinguished the Fenians—some of whom would form
into the Irish Republican Army (IRA), the military wing of Sinn
Fein—from the nonviolent Catholic Home Rule supporters, a
trend that continued in political and mass media circles throughout the twentieth century.

Despite the historical collusion of the Catholic hierarchy and
the British government ruling in Ireland, the Irish people still saw
the Catholic faith as the primary distinction between them and
their colonizers, and Hopkins found himself in an uncomfortable
position with the Catholic nationalist students and faculty at

UCD. The strength of Walsh's position in the Irish Free State is partly owed to the fact that the slow but definite success of UCD nearly tripled the number of young Catholic men receiving university-level education between Hopkins's term there and the Great War. Hopkins no doubt sensed this pattern and feared his work might be contributing to the dismantling of the British Empire. As late as 1888, he wrote to Newman, "This poor University College, this somehow-or-other manned wreck of the Catholic University, is afloat and not sinking; rather making a very little way than losing any" because of the efforts of "good and really patriotic people" who preserve the institution.[39] One suspects Hopkins wished the school ("wreck") would sink like the *Deutschland;* the tension in this letter to Newman reveals Hopkins's difficulty balancing his own Catholic faith and English nationalism in Ireland.

When Newman first arrived in Dublin, he possessed a similar view toward the Fenians and also toward the Home Rule advocates: the British Empire must be allowed to rule for the mutual benefit of both nations. However, Newman quickly revised his stance when presented with a more accurate picture of the Irish political environment. In 1887, when Hopkins complained to him about the unruly Irish political scene, Newman counseled, "The Irish Patriots hold that they never have yielded themselves to the sway of England and therefore have never been under her laws, and have never been rebels. . . . If I were an Irishman, I should be (in heart) a rebel."[40] Ever the scholar, Newman's view of the situation hinges not on an emotional defense of the British Empire or on passionate Irish efforts for independence, but on the appropriate use of the term *rebel.* For Newman, the Irish could not betray an institution to which they never offered allegiance, but Hopkins's more mythical conception of the importance of the British Empire prevented him from accepting such a tempered view of the Irish nationalists.

The longer Hopkins worked in Dublin, the more inflated his notion of the importance of the British Empire became, and he began to think of his verse as an imperial apology for the empire rather than as a tool of Catholic evangelization. For example, in a letter from Dublin Hopkins wrote three years before his death to his closest friend and fellow poet Robert Bridges in London, Hopkins explicitly stressed the tie between art and nationalism, writing, "We must then try to be known, aim at it, take means to it. And this without puffing in the process or pride in the success. . . . Besides, we are Englishmen. A great work by an Englishman is like a great battle won by England. It is an unfading bay tree. It will be even admired by and praised by and do good to those who hate England (as England is most perilously hated), who do not wish even to be benefited by her. It is then even a patriotic duty."[41] His bold imperial tone surfaces conspicuously in this letter. The "great battle" that is won by writing well profits those "who do not even wish to be benefited by" England's intellectual might. Hopkins implicitly favors the mission of the empire rather than that of the church and suggests that British colonization benefits all mankind regardless of the national will of the colonized; it is "perilous" to hold any animosity toward Great Britain. The passage is especially surprising when considered in light of Hopkins's earlier comments about his potential fame as a poet. In 1879, he explained to his friend, poet Canon Dixon, "The life I lead is liable to many mortifications but the want of fame as a poet is the least of them."[42] In an 1881 letter to Dixon, Hopkins framed his refusal to seek fame in a spiritual context: "For genius attracts fame and individual fame St. Ignatius looked on as the most dangerous and dazzling of all attractions."[43] Hopkins's conception of the purpose of his verse underwent dramatic progressions: First, he avoided writing poetry entirely as a novice Jesuit, only to return to it to "serve the cause" of his faith without seeking personal fame. Ultimately, he argued that his fame as a poet might be used to help spread the ideologies of the British Empire, and therefore he believed it should be sought to serve his nation.

Hopkins's revised attitude toward his own potential fame and his more vocal patriotism in Ireland likely stem from a need to compensate for his inability to establish a common identity with other Catholics in Ireland. "To Seem the Stranger," the first of a group of poems now commonly referred to as the "Terrible Sonnets" or "Sonnets of Desolation," reveals Hopkins's overbearing sense of isolation in Ireland.[44] In the first stanza, he reflects with melancholy:

> To seem the stranger lies my lot, my life
> Among strangers. Father and mother dear,
> Brothers and sisters are in Christ not near
> And he my peace/my parting, sword and strife.

(14)

The language is less concrete than his other postconversion verse, and the tone and voice more desperate. "Father and mother" and "Brothers and sisters" refer to his family as well as to his other English compatriots, who were mostly Anglicans, and therefore "in Christ not near." But because Catholicism in Ireland was directly related to the Home Rule movement that frustrated Hopkins, he can find no sense of community with other Catholics there and considers them mere "strangers." The second stanza also underscores his distress in exile. "England, whose honour O all my heart woos, wife / To my creating thought, would neither hear / Me, were I pleading, plead nor do I" (5–8). He calls his homeland "wife" to stress the poetic tradition out of which his work grew, but it is especially striking because the metaphorical relationship is typically used by Catholics to describe the church's relationship to Christ. (On various occasions in his late verse, Hopkins invokes other traditional Catholic metaphors to express the nature of his nationalistic loyalties.) Hopkins consciously attempts to find spiritual solace in his trying position. "I am in Ireland now; now I am at a thírd / Remove. Not but in all removes can I can / Kind love both give and get" (9–11). Finally, he laments that his "word," his poetry, must be "heard unheeded" by others. Hopkins questions whether his lack of success is due to "heaven's baffling ban / Bars or hell's spell thwarts" (12–13), meaning God's will or the devil's interference. He also implies a contrast with Mary, the Mother of God through whom the Word became incarnate, and his own unfruitfulness.

Hopkins's uncertainty reveals that, in Ireland, he endured the arduous spiritual-psychological quagmire of interpreting the source and purpose of suffering: if the suffering was sent by God and meant for his purification, then Hopkins would willingly portray himself as a sort of martyr sacrificing his comfort, and eventually his life, in the name of the Catholic faith. However, in part because of the sense of alienation from the church Hopkins experienced in Ireland due to his poor relationships with other Jesuit faculty, as well as from the Irish's use of the church as one ideological basis for their reasons to rid themselves of England's rule, he sometimes showed reluctance to conceive of his suffering in Catholic terms and chose instead to accept his affliction in the name of his country. The Terrible Sonnets reveal Hopkins's confusion and internal strife in Ireland, but this was not the first period in his life in which he expressed his spiritual frustrations in his verse. For instance, his preconversion poem "My Prayers Must Meet a Brazen Heaven" fits the tone and themes of the Terrible Sonnets. In the poem, he fears that his prayers to God "fail and scatter all away" (2) because of "the long success of sin" (8). In the final couplet, Hopkins again uses the Jesuitical motif of depicting the spiritual life in military terms: "A warfare of my lips in truth / Battling with God, is now my prayer" (15–16). However, in those earlier works, Hopkins demonstrates fortitude in confronting the challenge set forth by God, a determination that wavers in the Terrible Sonnets.

The classics assignment at UCD was intended to be permanent, and this situation added to Hopkins's sense that this trial would not likely give way to a more fruitful and joyful spiritual period. Hopkins laments the indeterminacy of his exile in another of the Terrible Sonnets, "I Wake and Feel." The first stanza metaphorically illustrates the sense of his life in Ireland being spent in a permanent night:

> I wake and feel the fell of dark, not day.
> What hours, O what black hours we have spent
> This night! what sights you, heart, saw; ways you went!
> And more must, in yet longer light's delay.
>
> (1–4)

The tone in the Terrible Sonnets waffles between desperate and despairing, and in these lines the description is relatively abstract and even vague. Still, the numerous caesuras, alliteration, and form are characteristic of earlier Hopkins. With the exception of providentially returning to England or finally achieving heaven in death, he knew there was little chance of closing the endless night, "light's delay." The following stanza underscores this notion, where Hopkins corrects himself. "But where I say / Hours I mean years, mean life" (5–6). His quick revisions emphasize the downward plunge of his spirit in the face of the endlessness of his assignment. Hopkins's challenge of remaining in Ireland turned into an endurance test only death might end. In the fourth and final stanza, after describing his psychological struggle in increasingly concrete terms, Hopkins states, "I see / The lost are like this, and their scourge to be / As I am mine, their sweating selves; but worse" (12–14). Apart from Christ, Hopkins might become like those who choose not to follow Christ—"their sweating selves"—and the "lost" are "worse" because they are cut off from Christ completely. Despite the self-comparison to those damned and abandoned by God, these lines express a certain hope that Hopkins's resilience in these trials will not lead him to the pain of eternal isolation in hell.

As a whole, the Terrible Sonnets are not necessarily despairing in the sinful Catholic sense of disbelieving in God's ability to guide one through the period of trial. The works depict Hopkins's attempt to convince himself of the significance and efficacy of his sacrifices and to request God's assistance in withstanding them. In "Carrion Comfort," Hopkins describes his efforts to fight off the temptation to despair that haunted him while in Ireland. He valiantly defies this temptation in the first stanza, in a search for hope:

> Not, I'll not, carrion comfort, Despair, not feast on thee;
> Not untwist—slack they may be—these last strands of man
> In me ór, most weary, cry *I can no more.* I can;
> Can something, hope, wish day come, not choose not to be.
>
> (1–4)

In these powerful lines, Hopkins returns to the more concrete, symbolic, and fragmented language that earns him the precocious modernist label. He resists his self-pitying wish to "cry *I can no more*" and even commit suicide, a possibility Hopkins suggests by the desire to "untwist . . . these last strands of man" and "choose not to be." Hopkins evinces the struggle for affirmation by claiming he can "something" before asserting that he can always "hope" for the coming of "day," a dream that could only be realized by his leaving Ireland. In the middle two stanzas, Hopkins's determination turns into a desperate questioning of why God insists on putting him through such a test. Yet he truly knows the answer. "Why? That my chaff might fly; my grain lie, sheer and clear," because the chaff, his sins, must be purged so that he may be made worthy of Christ's harvest. Hopkins remembers "I kissed the rod" (10), a sacramental act signifying his willingness to carry his own cross and endure suffering in the name of Christ. The final stanza concludes in a manner similar to "My Prayer Meets a Brazen

Heaven" (written two decades earlier), and Hopkins depicts himself, like Jacob, physically battling God. "I wretch lay wrestling with (my God!) my God" (14). Once again, the image does not signify despair for Hopkins, but fortitude and perseverance; after all, Jacob overcame the angel.

Complicating Hopkins's spiritual battle in Ireland was his need to defend his British nationalism in the face of the strong push for Irish Home Rule. In his nationalistic verse, however, Hopkins does not assume the alternating hopeless-then-resilient tone so prevalent in his spiritual works. Instead, Hopkins employs a consistently bold and proud nationalistic rhetoric, as he draws on increasingly militaristic depictions of England's greatness. This aggressive defense of the British Empire—despite its incompatibility with his faith—is likely compounded by his sense of isolation in exile. In Edward Said's essay "Reflections on Exile," he discusses the tendency for exiles to seek a more aggressive national identity while in a foreign land, even if this identity is based on mythical or imaginative conceptions. Said explains, "Exile, unlike nationalism, is fundamentally a discontinuous state of being. Exiles are cut off from their roots, their land, their past. They generally do not have armies or states, although they are often in search of them. Exiles feel, therefore, an urgent need to reconstitute their broken lives, usually by choosing to see themselves as part of a triumphant ideology or a restored people."[45]

Hopkins's verse in Ireland reflects a similar condition. When he discusses his Catholic faith in the final five years of his life, he emphasizes the personal spiritual struggle without establishing the political contexts that were so central to "The Wreck of the *Deutschland*" and most of his postconversion poetry. Somehow, he never quite came to terms with the incompatibility of his faith and imperial views. But with the "urgent need to reconstitute [his] broken life" while in Ireland, Hopkins stressed his identification with England and its empire independently of his religion.

Hopkins also matches Said's observation that exiles are "in search of armies," or in Hopkins's case, in search of identity through the British Empire's militaristic conquests. As is evident in "The Bugler's First Communion," Hopkins relished the rare opportunity to praise both the British military and his Catholic faith. In Ireland, Hopkins composed "The Soldier," which again focuses on the connection between the conquering British soldier and

Christ as "conquering hero," as he emphasizes in the earlier sermon. Hopkins first questions his own instinct to constantly "bléss /
Our redcoats, our tars" (1–2), especially since they are merely
"frail clay . . . foul clay" (3). But Hopkins believes their work is
modeled on the work of Christ: "Mark Christ our King. He knows
war, served this soldiering through; / He of all can reave a rope
best" (9–10). Hopkins here invokes the disciple-soldier formula-
tion not to depict a spiritual battle, but to commend expansion of
the British imperial army. Needless to say, this construction is
hardly an orthodox one for a Catholic. The Jesuitical notion of
Christ's foot soldier is, after all, metaphorical, and the Jesuits
would not likely have approved of its use in championing dubious
colonial endeavors.

By 1886, Hopkins began to call himself a "Home Ruler," but the
context of this profession alters its implications somewhat. For example, in a letter to Baillie on June 1, 1886, Hopkins praises
Matthew Arnold's diatribe against Gladstone, whose poor man-
agement as prime minister made Home Rule inevitable. He then
explains, "[Home Rule] is a blow at England and may be followed
by more, but it is better that sh[oul]d. be by peaceful and honourable means."[46] Hopkins's ominous tone suggests that his support
for Home Rule is reluctant and motivated by his fear of worse violence in Ireland (which would prove, tragically, to be a legitimate
fear). The next year he warns Baillie that because Home Rule is
possible for the Irish, the nationalists will intensify their revolt:
"Now the nearer passion is to its attainment the fiercer it is."[47] The
word *passion*, especially from the mouth of a clergyman, suggests
a desire unchecked by reason. That this was Hopkins's view of
Home Rule is clear from a letter written that same year to Baillie
in which he insists, "Home Rule of itself is a blow for England and
will do no good to Ireland."[48] His revised attitude toward Home
Rule was very different from that adopted by Newman, who truly
felt that the Irish nationalists were just in their cause once he became familiar with the political climate in Ireland. Hopkins's only
justification for supporting Home Rule was to prevent violence. In
his final months, he writes with disgust, "If you knew the world I
live in! Yet I continue to be a Home Ruler: I say it must be, and let
it be."[49] In a tone of resignation similar to when he gave up on the
hope of England's reconversion to Catholicism, Hopkins's decision to support Home Rule is much less a choice than a political

necessity. By calling himself a "Home Ruler," he intended to emphasize the bitter irony of his political quandary.

Hopkins reacted to this objectionable situation by composing some of his most explicitly patriotic poems. For instance, "What Shall I Do for the Land That Bred Me," written in 1888 just months before his death, also underscores Hopkins's nationalism and continues to formulate an association between his evangelical project and the duty of an English soldier. The work is a patriotic war song with a refrain sung at the end of each stanza. In the first stanza, he wonders if he might yet help his beloved England:

> What shall I do for the land that bred me,
> Her homes and fields that folded and fed me?—
> Be under her banner and live for her honour:
> Under her banner I'll live for her honour.
> Chorus: Under her banner [we] live for her honour.
>
> (1–5)

The fervent criticisms Hopkins once issued at non-Catholic England have completely disappeared. He praises England for its "homes and fields" that inspired his earlier verse and proclaims his undying loyalty. In the third stanza, he awkwardly connects his nationalism to his faith. "Call me England's fame's fond lover . . . / Spend me or end me what God shall send me, / But under her banner I live for her honour" (12,14–15). In his final months, Hopkins was still resiliently determined to accept God's will, even if his vocation should "end" him, but now that sacrifice seemed to be accomplished in the name of England rather than in service to the Catholic Church. This is not to say that Hopkins abandoned his faith, but that he emphasized that the purpose of his conversion was to return England to its Catholic roots. He accepted that his effort has failed, but he maintained a pride in his country he could not conceal, even if it compromised the political attitudes of most of his fellow Catholics. The final stanza again demonstrates that Hopkins understands his ministry in the terms of an English soldier, rather than as a Pauline or Ignatian one:

> Where is the field I must play the man on?
> O welcome there their steel or cannon.

> Immortal beauty is death with duty,
> If under her banner I fall for her honour.
>
> (11–15)

With his health diminishing and death looming, Hopkins promises to endure "death with duty," which he seemingly would owe to his Jesuit order, but he here gives it in the name of imperial England.

Hopkins's somewhat melodramatic self-portrayal in his final years possibly has its seeds in the dreams of his youth for a daring life of faith, which likely propelled his conversion to Catholicism. In Ireland, Hopkins was overloaded with menial tasks, primarily consisting of grading innumerable exams. On New Year's Day 1889, a distraught Hopkins wrote in his journal, "What is my wretched life? Five years wasted almost have passed in Ireland. I am ashamed of the little I have done, of my waste of time, although my helplessness and weakness is such that I could scarcely do otherwise."[50] Without the means to live a dramatic life of faith or to carry out the triumphant evangelization of his beloved England, Hopkins instead imagines himself as both a religious and national martyr, attempting to spread a faith to England that she already rejected. According to Anderson, such a desire makes sense in the psychology of nationalism. "Dying for one's country, which usually one does not choose, assumes a moral grandeur which dying for the Labour Party, the American Medical Association, or perhaps even Amnesty International can not rival, for these are all bodies one can join or leave at easy will."[51] The Catholic Church could easily be added to Anderson's list of organizations one may freely leave or join, which may explain why Hopkins determined to emphasize the sacrifices he made for his country, rather than those he made for his faith, as his death drew near.

2

Ford Madox Ford:
Le Maître Catholique of Modernism

If you are good, Fordie, you will go to a place on the clouds; and there will be harps. You will sit on a cloud and sing praises unto the Lord, and that is what you will do for ever and ever. You will wear a kind of white dress. And there will be creatures like mama but with great wings. But, if you are bad, you will go to a much worse place.

—Rudyard Kipling

FEW CRITICS CONSIDER FORD MADOX FORD A CATHOLIC NOVELIST IN the vein of Evelyn Waugh or Graham Greene. Although Ford would have been as uncomfortable with the designation as was Greene or Waugh, his major works—*The Fifth Queen, The Good Soldier,* and *Parade's End*—are no less concerned with the social dynamics of English Catholicism than Waugh's most heralded novels, and Ford embraced his Catholic identity more willfully than Greene ever did. Ford's last mistress, Janice Biala, probably articulated what many critics already suspected when she claimed, "I don't remember any talk about religion. . . . It didn't play any role in our life," even though she also admitted Ford "believed in Catholicism philosophically."[1] For a man of Ford's historical sensitivity to insist on professing a faith even "philosophically" deserves more critical attention than it presently has received. He certainly conceived of himself as a genuine Catholic; for example, Ford reacted both jubilantly and defensively to meeting Pope Pius X in 1911. "He was the kind and dear head of my family—of my own family. I was listening. I never felt so at home. We are a great family, we Catholics, and I was in the private room of the head of us all, and I had the right to be there, and we all had the right to the blessing of the good and kindly head of our family, who will

61

surely not refuse it to them that be of good will."[2] The passage summarizes Ford's attitude toward Catholicism: he embraced its inclusiveness and emphasized the importance of "good will" rather than a life of holiness, and he maintained a somewhat defensive insistence on his belonging. Rarely did Ford so unabashedly lay claim to any part of his identity.

Of course, Ford was also a grand liar, or at least a stylist of the truth. He believed a writer should not convey facts, plots, or morality to his reader but rather should reveal his "impression" of a moment, sentiment, belief, or relationship. If that portrayal required an exaggeration, a reordering of certain events or circumstances, or an addition or subtraction of seemingly vital information, then Ford advocated making the adjustment. He thought these amendments created a more accurate impression than the strict truth: "I have for facts a most profound contempt. I try to give you what I see to be the spirit of an age, of a town, of a movement. This cannot be done with facts."[3] Few would have difficulty with Ford's use of what he calls "impressionism" if he confined its use to his fiction, but he employed it in writing history, political tracts, biography, and memoir. Ford's penchant for misrepresentation has led most critics to dismiss his sporadic religious professions as imaginative visions of a self-portrait that likely came nowhere near reality.

Yet Ford's most recent biographer, Max Saunders, convincingly argues that dismissing Ford's claims because he misrepresents the truth in nonfictive mediums serves only to "belittle the writing, by seeing it ultimately as neurotic distortion rather than conscious elaboration and transformation of reality."[4] Allen Tate also has insisted famously that "Ford himself must be approached as a character in a novel, and that novel a novel by Ford."[5] In his own imagination, Ford's Catholic identity constituted an important part of his persona; therefore, any critical assessment of his work must consider his faith seriously, even if he practiced it only intermittently.

THE CRITICAL ATTITUDE AND *THE ENGLISH REVIEW*

A thorough understanding of how Ford envisioned his Catholic identity yields a great deal of insight into his critical view of En-

glish religion and culture, particularly as expressed in his most ac-
claimed novel, *The Good Soldier.* But to trace how that novel
became a depository for Ford's frustrations with the English and
their approach to religion, it is necessary to first recapture the circumstances that surrounded Ford's conversion and examine his
cultural writings concerning the English in the years before he
wrote *The Good Soldier.* Ford converted to the traditional Catholic faith of the Hueffer family while visiting his father's relatives
in Germany in 1892. Unlike nationalistic Catholics in Ireland or
Poland, German Catholics like Ford's family were closer to the
recusant English Catholics in that they attempted to keep their
faith separate from their domestic politics. Both Francis Hueffer,
Ford's father and one-time music critic of *The Times,* and his maternal grandfather, Ford Madox Brown, stressed the importance
of moving "above and beyond national rivalries" in religion, politics and art.[6]

This catholic attitude influenced Ford's formation of both the
English Review and *Transatlantic Review,* in which he desired to
create transcontinental journals that represented young European
writers. But it also explains a primary reason for his becoming
Catholic and his insistence on identifying himself as one throughout his life. Ford undoubtedly loved England, but the Anglican
faith was too nationalistic to complement his conception of the
Western world. In *England and the English* (1907), Ford outlines
this difficulty with England's Protestant faiths. "Speaking broadly,
we may say that the simple faith, the simple, earnest intolerance of
small or large knots of allied worshipers—the Protestant-Puritan
spirit, is precisely 'provincial.'"[7] Ford consistently resisted con-
centrated "alliances" in his own faith as well as in his work; for
him a valid religion, like a valid literature, must transcend provincialism.

Ford envisioned his faith as a tie to the past—inspired in part by
what he called the "Tory-Papist-Socialist-Anarchism" of his
grandfather, Madox Brown.[8] Although Ford never adopted the
Socialist-Anarchist aspect of the equation, he certainly embraced
the Tory-Papist label. The Catholic conception of an interconti-
nental community that transcends time also attracted Ford's sentimentality. The lives of the saints in fact often reflect Ford's
"impressionistic" model of constructing narratives: where no information is available, tales of great sacrifices, miracles, and vi-

sions often surface to convey holiness. A Continental Catholic would not be concerned with the historical veracity of hagiography, but would seek to be entertained and inspired (probably in that order) by the legend.

Ford also converted because of his sentimental belief that all men—including those born into the "provincial" Protestant faith—should uphold their inherited cultural and spiritual traditions. The nature of his Catholic conversion therefore suggests that Ford considered himself more culturally German than English, or as Ford himself explained, he was not "to the English manner born."[9] Although he was raised in England, the German identity of the Hueffer family dominated the culture of Ford's childhood environment. In an attempt to establish this belief, Ford went so far as halfheartedly to seek German citizenship shortly after his reception into the church to complete his conversion.[10] However, Ford quickly abandoned the idea of becoming a German citizen, professed his loyalty to the British Empire, and in 1915 wrote *When Blood Is Their Argument* in response to the brewing militarism in Germany before the Great War. Yet while at times he could be virulently nationalistic, Ford still never considered himself authentically English.

Because Ford was comfortable with paradox—even contradiction—he did not agonize over the conflict between his newly adopted Catholic faith and support for the British Empire. After his conversion, Ford openly confessed, "I consider that there are only two organisations that are nearly perfect for their disparate functions. They are the Church of Rome and His Brittanic Majesty's Army. I would cheerfully offer my life for either if it would do them any good and supposing them not arrayed the one against the other."[11] Not surprisingly, Ford does not explain which side he might favor in the event of the hypothetical conflict. This statement suggests that Ford's Catholicism was essentially an emotional and not a political faith. It is fair to say that Ford believed the foundations of a people's religious faith determine their emotional constitution. Even more consequentially, Ford argues in *England and the English* that, due to a religious and emotional error, the Englishman has become the standard of manners but "has sacrificed the arts—which are concerned with expressions of emotion—and his knowledge of life."[12] Accordingly, it was along emotional lines that Ford most virulently criticized and distanced himself from the English people. In *England and the English,* Ford unequivocally stated, "The defects of the Englishman's qualities are . . . simply that [he] feels very deeply and reasons very little."[13] This fault forces the English to value a composed exterior that conceals their true feelings and prevents them from ever making the changes in their lives and relationships that would be beneficial to them. They maintain this social grace "at the cost of sufferings that may be life-long."[14]

The only potentially redeeming quality of the English on an emotional level, especially with regard to religion, is their ability to simply "muddle through" moral conflicts. In *England and the English,* Ford maintains that, when faced with his own moral failure, a true Englishman "will protest, and it will be true: 'This is not the real I; this is not the nominal I; I am, really, a man of high standards. This is an accident that, set against my whole record, does not really count.'"[15] While Ford condoned such moral leniency in the English, he lamented their need for a firm resolution that answered all political and religious conflicts. The Englishman's insistence on "high standards"—which he of course will never reach—prevented him from embracing a spirit of religious tolerance and envisioning a politically and artistically diverse but unified Europe. These ideas were at the forefront of Ford's mind when he founded the *English Review,* in which he continued to develop his view that the Catholic faith predisposed men to a critical open-mindedness in art and literature; he eventually defined this concept as "the critical attitude."

Ford intended the *English Review* to promote the "catholicity" of European literature and embody "the critical attitude," a phrase he later used to title his collection of writings published in the journal during its short existence. He founded the journal under "a splendid, forlorn hope" that it might influence the English's ability to approach art critically; but he later admitted that this transformation was impossible and admitted with disappointment that "an *English Review* is a contradiction in terms."[16] Ford explicitly wanted the journal to reflect a Roman Catholic critical standpoint, an approach Ford defined in opposition to the critical practices of a typical Englishman who, because he is Protestant, looks at his faith and art in too principled terms and thereby opens the door for easy compromise. Ford observed that, from the Bible, the English derive "teachings from their birth" and by these general "standards measure good and evil," whereas "Roman Catholics and free-thinkers approach the Bible with an attitude much more critical, and find in it barbarisms, crudenesses, disproportions, and revelations of sickening cruelties."[17] The passage likewise stems from Ford's emotional critique of the English, who as good Protestants try to clean up the contradictions and ugliness not only in the Bible but in life and art, while Catholics embrace the uncertainty and even the violence of religion and life. Through the publications in the *Review,* Ford wanted to promote this more realistic, critical, and, to his mind, more Catholic view of the world.

In addition to its Catholic aims, Ford wanted the *English Review* to reflect his "progressive Tory" politics, partially because Ford's extremely conservative friend Arthur Marwood contributed a great deal to the journal's funding. Occasionally, Ford's editorials appear radically conservative. "We need a national army, simply because we stand in a different plane of civilisation from almost all our neighbors, and . . . we must be prepared, for the sake of humanity to be able . . . to maintain the integrity of the nations most allied to us in the love for peace and civilisation. That is . . . the duty of an Imperial race."[18] The language is not so different from Hopkins's rhetoric two and a half decades earlier, although Ford's national-imperial loyalties would temper with age.

At the same time, Ford denounced the Tory insistence on denying Ireland Home Rule. He argued that "the domestic government of Ireland—that little remote island of the Western Seas—is none of our business."[19] In this passage, Ford rather misleadingly gives the sense of Ireland's great distance from England, geographically and politically. But while Ford's views on imperialism and on Home Rule ultimately differ very little from Hopkins's, Ford did not believe that his views on the British Empire compromised his faith. Obviously, Ford was neither a member of a Catholic religious order nor working in Ireland as was Hopkins, so his inconsistencies did not cause much turmoil. It is nonetheless striking that, as a Catholic who generally supported Tory arguments to grant Ireland independence peacefully, he boldly argued that England would have to suppress any Catholic or Protestant uprising in Ireland before that moment for the simple fact that, as he unequivocally explained, "We can't have sectarian nonsense of that sort in an empire or even a bureaucracy today."[20] Ford did not identify with the form of Catholicism that primarily flourished within a provincial culture (the very principle on which he based his trust in nationalism), and he could easily disregard the political claims made by the Catholic Irish nationalists.

Ford's most vocal supporter was probably Ezra Pound, who consistently praised Ford for his commitment to the modernist aesthetic. The other writers whose careers were advanced by the journal—like Wyndham Lewis, who respected Ford but despised his politics, or D. H. Lawrence, whose "Odour of Chrysanthemums" was first printed in the *Review*—grew apart from Ford, but they were forced to acknowledge the journal's important contribution to the modernist movement. Ford and Pound also found common ground in their political and social views. Pound's essay "Provincialism the Enemy" argues against the dangers of provincialism in art and in politics. Although Pound believed religion was necessarily provincial and therefore dangerous, he insisted that only Catholicism had cultural value because of its traditions and inclusiveness.[21] In *Return to Yesterday,* Ford remembers thinking as early as 1914 with the production of *Blast* that he played an important role in the advancement of these young authors' careers. "*The English Review* seemed then profoundly to have done its work. Ezra and his gang of young lions raged through London."[22] And if some of those writers would later attack Ford's artistic and political views, they would also promote the transnational and experimental approach to art that Ford so desperately advocated, and *le maître* at least assisted in opening their cage.

Ford ran out of money for the review in May of 1909, and a devoted Liberal, David Soskice, purchased it. The journal ultimately failed to achieve Ford's grand objective of influencing the English's simplemindedness in terms of art and religion. He bitterly ascribed its failure in less than two years to the fact that "nothing will make the Englishman adopt a critical attitude," which Ford also believed was the reason the Englishman "has founded three hundred and forty-seven religions. And each of these religions is founded upon a compromise. That is what the Englishman does to, that is how he floors—the critical attitude."[23] The "compromise" is enacted each time a Protestant creates a new, more simplistic and allegedly pure form of the Christian faith because the previous creed still contains the "crudenesses" and "disproportions" of life—the very things that Ford believed made religion and art interesting and relevant. This statement also highlights Ford's notion that religion, with its cultural and emotional influence, plays the central formative role in a society's attitudes toward nearly all philosophy and art. Ford's explanation for the failure of the *English Review* reveals the extent to which he believed his artistic vision was dependent on religious conceptions and loyalties, even if most of his English audience was not conscious of its own prejudices and ignorance.

After the failure of the review, Ford knew that writing any direct apology of his Catholic outlook would be fruitless in a nation that cared less about religion than at any previous point in its history, and he was not concerned with the dogmatic beliefs of religion anyway. However, Ford still believed that Catholic culture was not only compatible with but a necessary component of his artistic and (less importantly) political vision. When *The English Review* failed to articulate that vision, Ford attempted a different strategy in writing *The Good Soldier*. The novel represents Ford's attempt to explore and lament what happens to a society that has no sense of C/catholicism and no grasp of "the critical attitude." Through-out *The Good Soldier*, Ford manifests his frustration with the Protestants in England who "floor the critical attitude," as well as the pretentious nonmodernist English Catholic converts of the twentieth century, particularly Hilaire Belloc; Ford also advocates a more lenient and culturally sensitive version of Catholicism in England. Ultimately, Ford uses the novel to delineate his notion of the proper way to practice Catholicism in the twentieth century and thereby implicitly justify his own approach to the faith.

THE GOOD SOLDIER

The Good Soldier is a model work of impressionism in which the American narrator, John Dowell, attempts to make sense of the numerous lies, affairs, and deaths that have marked almost a decade of interaction between him and his American wife, Florence Hurlbird, and a superficially model English couple, Edward and Leonora Ashburnham. From a critical standpoint, Dowell's impressions—and the novel as a whole—have frequently and accurately been read as a nostalgic apology for Toryism or even feudalism, a reflection on the complexity and destruction of sexuality in the modern world, or a harsh criticism of pragmatic and aesthetically deprived modern society; in fact, Dowell engages in some of this critical work himself. But Ford structures Dowell's narrative in a manner that connects each of these themes to Protestant and secular culture's triumph over Catholic culture and faith in Europe. As expected, this victory occurs not on a doctrinal plane, but on an emotional, aesthetic, and sexual one.

Ironically, the Tory-Papist hero of the novel is none other than Edward, who to all initial appearances is the classic Englishman, complete with severe emotional reserve and an impeccable sense of social duty. Because Dowell's narrative unfolds with a fragmented chronology in keeping with his desire to allow his memory to guide him as if he were speaking to a listener beside a fire, it is initially difficult to determine that it is to Edward and not Leonora that he will offer his sympathy and loyalty. In the opening pages, Dowell reveals his preoccupation with how the Ashburnham's Englishness has prevented him from making accurate judgments of the couple. He repeatedly clarifies, "Six months ago I had never been to England, and, certainly, I had never sounded the depths of the English heart" and notes that the Ashburnhams were "what in England it is the custom to call 'quite good people.'"[24] These observances initially sound innocuous, but Dowell eventually perceives that this superficial English composure has not only clouded his eyes from Edward's numerous affairs and Leonora's painstaking and ruthless attempts to control her husband, but it has prevented the Ashburnhams from discerning resolutions for their silent conflicts. As the fissures in the couple's relationship become evident to Dowell years later, he begins to make accusations against "the modern English habit of taking everyone for granted," a trait that clouds meaningful communication and the possibility of self-knowledge.[25]

The same problems exist between Dowell and his New England-born wife. Florence affects to have a heart problem to avoid sexual relations with her husband and intends to use Dowell to achieve her dream of settling on an English estate. She wants to return permanently to Fordingbridge in England, where the Hurlbird family was established until 1688. And although Dowell eventually comes to despise his wife for lying and cheating on him with a young attendant and then with Edward, thereby damaging the

Ashburnham's marriage beyond repair, he never consciously notes that she embodies all of the culturally English traits he finds most intolerable. Furthermore, Dowell has to keep the conversation off topics that involve "what the English call 'things'—off love, poverty, crime, religion, and the rest of it."[26] Like the English, Florence wants to avoid these unsettling topics and only pretends to care about religion to draw a line between her and Edward, who are both Protestants, and the Irish Catholic Leonora.

Many of Ford's criticisms of the English in *The Good Soldier* were drawn from personal experiences he recounted in his memoirs and social commentaries. For example, Florence's fear of "things" is derived from a passage in *England and the English* in which Ford recalls when an Englishwoman warned him against speaking to her daughter about "things." He explains, "I did not know just what 'things' were. . . . Nowadays I know very well what 'things' are; they include, in fact, religious topics, questions of the relations of the sexes; the conditions of poverty-stricken districts—every subject from which one can digress into anything moving."[27] Not coincidentally, these also are the three matters that most concern Edward Ashburnham. In addition to transforming into an emotional Catholic (a process I will describe later), Edward embarks on a never-ending search for the woman who will completely satisfy his need for emotional identification, he cares deeply for his tenants and all of the destitute, and he would ruin himself financially or publicly to assist those in need. Through Dowell, Ford implies that, if Edward were permitted to follow his desires in each of these matters, he might help create a tolerable world. Of course, this culture would have its "barbarisms, crudenesses, and disproportions," but those unavoidable problems contribute to a meaningful human experience. In trying to conceal them, the English only prolong the agony of sociocultural instability and inhibit the resolutions that might bring happiness.

The sense of social fragmentation is one of the most prevalent motifs throughout Dowell's narrative and points to the culturally shattering effect of a people who have no sense of the critical attitude. Like Ford after the failure of the *English Review*, Dowell has given up trying to fit the broken pieces back together, and he can only marvel that the cultural fabric with so much potential for beauty is rotting. Even in his prefatory frame for the story, Dowell ponders his confusion. "Permanence? Stability! I can't believe it's gone."[28] Despite his sense of desperation, Dowell does manage to identify the much-less self-conscious Edward as the embodiment of the values Dowell (and Ford) believes might preserve his ideal of a Papist-feudalistic society. In accordance with Ford's sense of irony, Edward is the unlikeliest of heroes, since in his manners and emotions he possesses "all the virtues that are usually accounted English" and his very face "in the wonderful English fashion, expressed nothing whatever."[29] Nevertheless, Edward's excessive sentimentality and his feudalistic historical-political views earn him Dowell's devotion. Unlike Dowell, Edward is a compassionate man with "a sentimental yearning" for "all children, puppies, and the feeble generally."[30] But what Dowell identifies behind this sentimentality is Edward's instinct to preserve, and preservation is precisely what Dowell seeks when confronted with the ubiquitous decay of English (or even Western) society. Dowell insists Edward was not "a promiscuous libertine" but simply a "sentimentalist" who serves as the "painstaking guardian" of society's weakest members, from drunkards to delinquent tenants. This role sometimes leads Edward to express too much affection, such as in the "Kilsyte case" when he kisses a crying young servant girl on a train because "he had desired to comfort her."[31] But Dowell judges these promiscuities as excusable aftereffects of Edward's generosity.

Dowell surmises that Florence and Leonora cannot comprehend the beauty and effectiveness of Edward's "own theory—the feudal theory of an over-lord doing his best by his dependents, the dependents meanwhile doing their best for the over-lord."[32] Dowell even imagines Edward explaining to La Dolciquita—another of his mistresses—that "salvation can only be found in true love and the feudal system."[33] The English feudal system, which significantly thrived in medieval Catholic Europe, would allow Edward to treat his tenants like they were part of his family and participants in a collaborative social and religious project. For Edward, therein lies salvation. Ford uses Edward to suggest that the modern economic system, which contains no religious foundation and in which the landowners view their tenants as mere cogs in a financial machine, underscores the lack of community and substantial communication that Edward despises but the English cultivate.

By creating a sentimental character with a strong sympathy for the feudal system, Ford could more seamlessly portray Edward as a figure increasingly drawn to the Catholic Church. This process can be inferred through Dowell's narration, but Dowell himself does not initially find it remarkably significant, especially in light of his later preoccupation with the harmful effect Catholicism has on Leonora. Edward's instinct for cultural preservation leads him to propose building a Catholic chapel for his Irish Catholic wife just after their marriage, a suggestion Leonora (thinking economically and not sentimentally) declines because she can easily drive to a nearby parish. Dowell also recalls that Edward was willing to allow any prospective female children in the family to be Catholic like their mother. However, in a decision that reflects Ford's own religious opinions, the boys must remain Anglican to preserve the family's spiritual tradition.

In a fascinating twist, however, Edward himself "was perfectly ready to become a Romanist" and rather regrets that Leonora's relatives did not try to convert him.[34] Even Dowell, although uncomfortable with religious topics, confesses that Edward "was quite ready to become an emotional Catholic."[35] Edward's identification with Catholicism grows stronger after he falls in love with the young Catholic, Nancy. Nancy has lived with the Ashburnham's since her childhood, and her friendship with Edward develops into an intimate affair that is never sexually consummated. Edward's emotional devotion to Nancy inspires his sentimental attachment to Catholicism. After one particularly happy night together that ends without physical intimacy, Edward's yearning for Nancy causes him to weep "convulsively" while holding "out before him a little image of the blessed virgin."[36] The statue represents the beauty and joy he might possess if he did not have to preserve his public image and pretend to love his wife; it signifies the freedom of being a Papist and not an English gentleman.

Ford depicts Edward as an emotional Papist trapped inside the skin of a calculating, reserved Englishman—and it is not presumptuous to suggest that Ford felt something of the same about his own life after the failure of the *English Review* and the implicit rejection of his religious and cultural views. Edward is a soldier committed to the empire's expansion, and he therefore defends the two organizations Ford found most worthy of self-sacrifice, "the Church of Rome and His Brittanic Majesty's Army." Of course, Edward must, like Ford, renounce or ignore the legalistic side of the church and the aggressively imperial nature of the British army, but those were not the elements of faith and nation that inspired Ford's devotion. Unfortunately, the social parameters of English society, fiercely guarded by Leonora, inhibit Edward's Papist development. This torturous experience leads to Edward's suicide.

While Dowell's professed loyalty to Edward increases dramatically as he reconstructs the narrative, his opinion of Leonora declines rapidly. It is easy to forget at the conclusion of Dowell's narration that one of his first comments about Leonora professes a deep commitment. "I loved Leonora always and, to-day, I would very cheerfully lay down my life, what is left of it, in her service."[37] But as he makes sense of Leonora's destructiveness, Dowell pegs her as a "woman of a strong, cold conscience, like all English Catholics" who no longer loves her unfaithful husband but remains with him to win "a victory for all wives and a victory for her Church."[38] The passage follows the (moderately consistent) distinction Ford began to make after his conversion between open-minded "Papists" and ruthless "Roman Catholics." He predictably applied the difference between these approaches to the same religion to his art. For example, in Ford's 1911 essay "On Impressionism," he explained that an artist must "adopt a frame of mind, less Catholic possibly, but certainly more Papist" when seeking to earn sympathy with his audience.[39] A "Papist" for Ford was a cultural Catholic who still professed the faith and believed in its potency as a transcendental answer to the problems of modernity, but did not judge others according to their religious orthodoxy or ability to attain personal sanctification.[40] The "Roman Catholics" were legalists like so many English Catholics who treated their faith as if it was simply another sect in the innumerable, culturally vacant forms of English Christianity or who viewed the Roman religion as an elitist club open only to those able to follow its strict dogmatic tenets.

Ford singled out Hilaire Belloc as a typical "Roman Catholic," whose pretentious faith bothered Ford immensely (a dislike also recounted by Ernest Hemingway in *A Moveable Feast*, which also contains Hemingway's notorious portrayal of Ford). Ford remembers meeting Belloc and G. K. Chesterton at a political dinner and finding the former "filled with the woes of all the world."[41] Belloc supposedly chastised a member of the party, crying, "Our Lord! What do you know about Our Lord? Our Lord was a gentleman."[42] Such a comment would instantly make Ford defensive, even if not directed at him. Ford expresses his distaste for Belloc's judgmental attitude by ironically asserting, "Heaven forbid that I should set myself down as good a Papist as Mr. Belloc, but I dislike to think of myself as a worse."[43] For a man whose attraction to Catholicism centered on its inclusiveness, Ford revolted against Belloc's demanding style of faith and rhetoric of exclusiveness.[44]

As *The Good Soldier* unfolds, Leonora becomes a female manifestation of what Ford condemned in pious Catholics like Belloc. Leonora has no sense of her religion's emotional and artistic wealth; therefore, she cannot appreciate private chapels or tacky windowsill Virgin Mary statues. Whether Ford intended Dowell to mistakenly call Leonora English Catholic when she is in fact Irish Catholic or if Ford was deliberately comparing the Irish Leonora to legalistic English Catholics, Ford expresses his disillusion with the somber faith of English Catholics who did not accept the relaxed, Continental style of his own faith. Even Dowell comments on the Protestant-like behavior of English Catholics. "I suppose that Papists in England are even technically Nonconformists. Continental Papists are a dirty, jovial and unscrupulous crew."[45] Of course, Irish Catholics could be moralistic also, but at least the faith of most lay Irish Catholics was romantically tied to the desire for Irish independence.

Leonora is too concerned with maximizing the profitability of Edward's estates and desperately trying to protect the couple's public image after each of his affairs to be concerned with a matter as romantic as Irish nationalism or religious persecution. However, Ford subtly and misleadingly suggests otherwise in the crucial scene in which Florence brings the two couples to Marburg to see a Protestant document outlining their common anti-Catholic principles signed by Luther, Zwingly, and other central figures of the Reformation. Leonora insists that this document is the source of all modern ills and runs from the room, exclaiming to Dowell, "Don't you see that that's the cause of the whole miserable affair; of the whole sorrow of the world? And of the eternal damnation of you and me and them."[46] Her passionate response might imply Ford's sentimental sympathy, but the truth is that Leonora is not taking an emotional public stance for her religion but responding to Florence's flaunting of her affair with Edward.

Although the melodrama of the scene focuses on Leonora, Flor-

ence initiates all actions until that final moment. There is no previous evidence that Florence lives her Protestant faith with any
seriousness, but she compels her uninterested friends to acquiesce
in joining her on this Protestant pilgrimage nonetheless. Through
the apparently harmless visit, the manipulative Florence intends
to dismantle Leonora's Catholic conscience. Florence even reads
anti-Catholic books such as "Ranke's *History of the Popes* . . . and
Luther's *Table Talk*" to prepare for her assault on Leonora. Florence's primary objective, which Dowell never explicitly articulates, is not to make a Protestant apologetic attack on Leonora's
theology, but theatrically to lay claim to Edward along religious
lines.[47] Florence looks into Edward's eyes and cruelly explains, "If
it weren't for that piece of paper you'd be like the Irish or the Ital-
ians, but particularly the Irish."[48] The Anglophile Florence uses
the last phrase to emphasize Edward's national and religious difference from Leonora, and Florence then deviously places "one
finger upon Captain Ashburnham's wrist."[49] This final act pro-
vokes Leonora's outburst; however, in accordance with the English manners she emulates so well, she recomposes herself before
the ignorant Dowell, who has no notion of his wife's affair with
Edward and only admits to having been aware of "something evil
in the day," and with a "clear hard voice" clarifies her reaction,
"Don't you know . . . don't you know that I'm an Irish Catholic?"[50]
Like Florence, Leonora uses religion to mask her intended meaning. She knows that the imperceptive Dowell will conclude she is
offended because of Florence's assault on her faith or national
identity. That explanation makes little sense, however, because if
she was so sensitive to those issues she would have prevented the
pilgrimage before it commenced. Nevertheless, there is a sense in
which her explanation to Dowell is honest: as an Irish Catholic
she does not condone extramarital affairs, and in a tone of private
bitter irony she reveals that she is particularly concerned with one
that involves her husband and Dowell's wife.

Leonora's lament that the Protest document is "the cause of the
whole miserable affair; of the whole sorrow of the world," represents more than a veiled reference to Florence's adulterous performance; in keeping with Ford's socioreligious themes in the
novel, the document does in fact form part of the Protestant foundation that Ford believed "floors the critical attitude." John A.
Meixner argues that "Ford is saying that the rise of Protestantism,

which symbolizes the entire modern, sceptical, fragmenting impulse, is the source of the destruction of the old consoling religious framework and the whole present sorrow of the world."[51] Ford intends the reader to look beyond Leonora's private torture and witness the religious activity that destroys the traditional, inclusive, Papist worldview and culture.

In retrospect, Dowell believes that this terrible scene presented Leonora with a chance to adopt a Papist mentality by emotionally and publicly defending her faith and confronting her husband. When Dowell thinks, "If there was a fine point about Leonora it was that she was proud and that she was silent. But that pride and that silence broke when she made that extraordinary outburst, in the shadowy room that contained the Protest," he actually believes that Leonora's fit might have proved a fruitful opportunity for the Ashburnhams to confront their problems.[52] A painful and un-English discussion might have ended the relationship or saved it, but at least it would have resulted in some resolution. Despite knowing of his previous affairs, Leonora had at that point not given up on her marriage and even slapped the young Maisie Maiden before she ever had a physical affair with Edward—an act Dowell approves of because it led to a growing intimacy between Leonora and Edward. Unfortunately, Dowell realizes that this momentum "went to pieces at the moment when Florence laid her hand upon Edward's wrist."[53] Leonora's breakdown only causes her more conscientiously to repress her frustrations. She begins to monitor Edward's finances meticulously and limits his allowances so as to prevent affairs and blackmail payments to his lovers. When Edward's intimacy with Nancy grows, Dowell believes Leonora wants to torture them by allowing them time together but preventing a meaningful relationship.

Leonora becomes, in the Fordian sense, much more of a judgmental Roman Catholic concerned with moral strictness than an emotionally and culturally sensitive Papist. But Dowell cannot decide whether to blame Leonora's Catholicism or her subsequent lack of faith. At one point he reflects, "Having been cut off from the restraints of her religion . . . she acted along the lines of her instinctive desires," which suggests that her loss of faith has led to a loss of her humanity.[54] But he also implies, in accordance with Ford's theory, that her specific type of Catholicism is to blame for her behavior. After Edward has committed suicide and Leonora remarries a classic English gentleman, Dowell's final thoughts evoke his disgust with the superficial, "perfectly normal type" like Leonora who secretly embodies the "not very straight methods that Roman Catholics seem to adopt in dealing with matters of this world."[55] In this passage, Dowell uses "Roman Catholics" in the Fordian sense to define the type of Catholic he despised; however, Dowell's inconsistent view of religion as both a check on Leonora and an instigator of her behavior only underscores his ignorance of religion.

Through Dowell's judgments, Ford does not portray any woman positively in *The Good Soldier*. In addition to condemning Leonora's tactics, Dowell reviles his devious wife Florence—not because of her affairs, but because of her duplicity and English concern with her reputation. She does not love her husband, but when Florence mistakenly believes that Dowell has learned of her affair with Jimmy, a lower-class deckhand on the ship that brought them to Europe after the marriage, she drinks prussic acid. Florence commits suicide simply because she cannot live with the shame of anyone knowing she slept with such an unworthy figure. Dowell also faults Nancy for participating with Leonora in torturing Edward. When Nancy offers herself to Edward, she adopts Leonora's tone and says cooly, "I will belong to you to save your life. But I can never love you."[56] This comment reveals as much about Leonora as it does about Nancy: it proves that neither figure understands that Edward's promiscuity is rooted not in an insatiable sexual desire but in his overpowering sentimental attachment. Only Dowell understands this aspect of Edward's character. Consequently, only Dowell can claim to know Edward on emotional and religious grounds, although his knowledge seems impotent.

Ford's portrayal of the women in *The Good Soldier* likely has its roots in his belief that women were the key to maintaining authentic Catholic culture when confronted with the values of legalistic Catholics, Protestants, or secularists. As he explains in *England and the English*, "Catholicism—with its female saints, with its female religious, with its feminine element in the Divine Concord—has its chief safeguard in women."[57] Such was the faith of Leonora's and Nancy's youth, and it was the faith that Edward admired. Therefore, Nancy initially had great camaraderie with the more truly Papist Edward. Nevertheless, Nancy's faith in what Ford constitutes as traditional Catholicism—a comprehensive moral, emotional, and cultural system—proves naïve and inadequate when confronted with modernity. Dowell believes that if she had not been corrupted by Leonora, Nancy might have provided Edward what he needed because Edward has groomed Nancy to cultivate his Papist approach to the world. Still, Leonora's victory over Nancy is not complete; Nancy's madness suggests that she was incapable of modeling Leonora's emotionless Catholic rationalism.

Through Ford's depiction of Edward's suicide and Nancy's madness, he evinces his own alienation in England as he tried to preserve his obsolete form of faith, economics, and emotional sensibility. *The Good Soldier* echoes Ford's argument in *England and the English* that modern societies, and the English in particular, have embraced reason and principles and sacrificed "a great deal of [religion's] theological traditions and of its popular comprehensibility."[58] As an impressionistic work, Ford's novel does little to regain a social "comprehensibility" that no longer exists, but *The Good Soldier* at least serves as a remnant of the dying but not quite extinct feudal-Papist values. In bidding adieu to that world, however, Ford took recourse in a very modern form of the novel: complete with a disjointed narrative, ironic tone, and unconsummated resolutions. The Great War would speed the death of Ford's ideal culture and likewise accelerate the modernist style of literature that *The Good Soldier* models.

FORD AND THE GREAT WAR

It is tempting to base a study of the emotional effects of the Great War on Ford on the semiautobiographical character Christopher Tietjens in Ford's war tetralogy *Parade's End*. Yet Ford did not begin writing those novels until more than five years after his own tour in France, a distance of time that allowed him to recover from the initial psychological toll of his experience of war and make his own judgments of its effect on his and his nation's psyche. Ford insisted on joining the English military in 1915, although he was hardly compelled to do so. His sentimental imagination possibly inspired him. Yet, even in making this great act of sacrifice, Ford still articulated his commitment in terms that called in to question his identity as a native Englishman. A letter to his mother shortly after enlisting reveals Ford's patriotic inspirations: "You ask me why I have gone into the army: simply because I can- not imagine taking any other course. If one has enjoyed the privi- leges of the ruling classes of a country all one's life, there seems to be no alternative to fighting for that country if necessary. And in- deed I have never felt such an entire peace of mind as I have felt since I wore the King's uniform."[59] Ford significantly calls England "a" country not "his" country; and, unlike an eager patriotic com- batant, Ford suggests that he must fight to assuage his personal sense of duty to assist the country that has contributed to his de- velopment as an artist.

Ford also drew on his Catholic faith for support when involved in the conflict. In July of 1916, just before the extraordinarily costly Battle of the Somme where Ford served on the transport lines, he wrote to his Catholic children, "You know I have loved you both very, very dearly. . . . I took the Communion this morn- ing & prayed for you both. Pray for me."[60] Ford's turn to faith for comfort reflected a typical pattern for a soldier on the front. In Richard Schweitzer's study of the role of faith in the Great War, *The Cross and the Trench,* he contends that new soldiers at the front and all men preparing for an intense offensive were the most likely to grasp at faith for solace and strength.[61] But as Schweitzer, Paul Fussell, and other historians have noted, the length and atrocities of the war ultimately had a negative effect on the state of Christianity in England, and particularly on the reputation of the Anglican Church. Poets and writers such as Siegfried Sassoon and Robert Graves increasingly saw the war as an economic en- deavor that could have been ended much earlier but was contin- ued under the pretense of defending the nation from German invasion—an event that seemed unlikely after the United States entered the war early in the summer of 1917. English soldiers re- peatedly blamed political leaders and the Anglican Church hierar- chy, who almost unanimously supported them, for the lack of a resolution.[62]

Clergymen who did impress the British soldiers were the Catho- lic priests at the front, which in part explains why Ford retained his Catholic faith after the horrible experiences of the war. Accord- ing to historian Duff Crerar, "Anglican chaplains were afraid to share the dangers of the trenches with the troops, while Roman Catholic padres were continually found in the front line, visiting with and offering prayers for their men."[63] Not having families to consider may have helped the celibate clergy gather courage in battle. In *Good-bye to All That*, Graves claims one of his command officers got rid of four Anglican chaplains in exchange for one Catholic priest, "alleging a change of faith in the men under his command. For the Roman Catholic chaplains were not only permitted to visit posts of danger, but definitely enjoined to be wherever the fighting was. . . . And we had never heard of one who failed to do all that was expected of him and more."[64] Although readers must guard against Graves's penchant for ironic exaggeration, even an ironic reading can only derive from the actual positive reputation of Catholic priests on the front.[65]

Because Pope Benedict XV repeatedly condemned the war while refusing to publicly support either effort, Catholic clergy were better able to tend to individual men without seeking some hollow justification for the fighting.[66] Ultimately, this type of spiritual and moral care proved valuable to the soldiers confronted with the ubiquitous horror of human suffering in the trenches. Unfortunately, Ford wrote very little about the state of his faith during the actual conflict—even after being knocked unconscious by a shell during the battle of the Somme—but his experience seemed to solidify his Catholic identity, as is evident in his *Transatlantic Review* editorials. It is especially peculiar that in his postwar novels Ford did not capitalize on the successful mix of despair and irony that proves so effective in *The Good Soldier*. The central characteristic of postwar literature is its ironic tone—aimed at state, church, and culture—because the very real melodrama of the war made irony a typical response to its atrocities. Yet Ford's works concerning the war reflect a prewar concern with chivalric conduct and cultural preservation. Ford's military experience ended in March of 1917, when he was judged unfit for service due to his deteriorating mental condition, although it took him many more years to fully recover. Possibly the war was too sublimely frightening for him to write about it in the tragic but disparaging manner with which he depicted the moral degradation of culture in earlier works; he might portray divorce and social disintegration ironically, but not war.

The war clearly threatened the culture that Ford so desperately wanted to preserve and explains why his tour secured him in his dedication to faith and nation, when it had the reverse effect on many veterans. A decade after the Armistice, Ford even criticized the unapologetic realism of the war poets. "I must confess to a deep depression . . . when I read [this generation's] poems about this war. It is all about mad dogs, and throttling fists, and trampling heels."[67] His first work after the war, *Thus to Revisit,* strives for cultural repossession in a manner that is sentimentally impressionistic (almost to the point of delusion). The war may have made England more "modern" and cynical, but it seems to have made Ford in some respects more archaic and also increasingly dedicated to a unified Europe. In 1926, he wrote in the *New York Herald Tribune* concerning the Armistice, "For we are all one people—we races who dwell on the shores of the north Atlantic Ocean. If November the Eleventh did nothing else for us it made us all one people—we English, French and Americans. That is an accomplished fact."[68] In the same essay, Ford attempted to include Germany in his hegemonic notion of the West (recall that he was of German descent); he claimed that any new dictator in Germany "would find no followers. . . . And we, who are one people, achieved that by dying together."[69] How terribly inaccurate Ford's prophecy would prove.

Yet Ford's comments are motivated by the same desire for transnational unity that led him to embrace and retain his Catholic faith, and he likely recognized the idealistic quality of his rhetoric, as he similarly viewed his oaths to religion. Ultimately, Ford argued that true unity and peace would occur through art. "[M]ilitarism is the antithesis of Thought and the Arts, and it is by Thought and the Arts alone that the world can be saved."[70] In the two greatest endeavors of Ford's postwar career, he would strive for an understanding of the Great War and its effect on his own faith and nationalism in *Parade's End* and simultaneously found another journal that promoted his international notions of art and culture, the *Transatlantic Review,* begun in Paris in 1923.

PARADE'S END

Many of the themes prevalent in *The Good Soldier* return in *Parade's End,* such as the rampant decay of culture, the corruptibility of modern women, and the need for religious and political preservation. But the difference in tone can be observed in the presentation of the two male characters who embody Ford's values. While Edward Ashburnham is a comic figure undermined by his ridiculous sentimentality as much as the deceit of his wife and others, Christopher Tietjens maintains an honorable yet ultimately unappreciated fortitude in the face of the insanity of the war and the malice of his wife and supposed friends. Tietjens, like Ashburnham, must contend with a vengeful wife, but in *Parade's End*, Sylvia initiates the infidelities and is portrayed as a more unequivocally guilty (albeit more complex) character than Leonora. Like Leonora, she is Catholic, but the male figure assumes the position that Ford would consider more acceptably "Papist."

Tietjens belongs by birth to the conservative aristocracy, but he will not engage in the political nepotism and dubious economic morality of that class. He desires all men to have a living wage but rejects socialism—and even nineteenth-century liberalism—which he finds ineffective and unable to keep intact the elements of social structure that he consistently defends. Ford claimed that Tietjens's character was based on his conservative friend Arthur Marwood, who was likewise a soft-spoken High Tory and a brilliant mathematician. But Ford's insistent denial that Tietjens's character had any autobiographical basis is misleading for an assortment of reasons, especially when considering the experience in war and resultant madness that Ford shares with this character. There are also religious similarities between Ford and Tietjens, who desires "to be a saint of the Anglican variety," which consists of a Catholic morality "without convent, ritual, vows, or miracles to be performed by . . . relics!"[71] With this simple aesthetic sensibility and reticent evangelism, Tietjens faith seems to model the recusant Catholic tradition in England, even though he remains Anglican to protect his family tradition. Ford himself was at this time guarded about pompous external Catholic expressions after his eldest daughter Christina entered a Catholic convent against his unsolicited resistance. Not surprisingly, one of Tietjens's conflicts with his wife centers on their child's faith.[72]

Tietjens's interest in Catholicism is intellectual and political, and not sentimental, as was Ashburnham's in *The Good Soldier*. Awaiting the fight on the front, Tietjens eruditely explains to his company the particular metaphysical differences between Eucharistic consubstantiation (the Anglican belief) and transubstantiation (the Catholic belief); and he also issues formidable objections to one English subaltern's theory that Roman Catholicism is the driving force of the Central Powers, and the best way to "save civilization" would be to form a union between the Church of England and the Greek Orthodox Church.[73] Presumably, this proposal would unite liturgical Christians of the East and West in a way the Catholic Church had not since the Orthodox Church broke with Rome. Of course, the notion is logistically absurd. Through Tietjens's measured defense of Catholic tenets, Ford creates an Anglican hero who still at least understands and respects the English Catholic faith.

While soldiers and citizens alike criticized the Anglican communion for its attempt to give political justifications for the war, Ford presents the Catholic stance on the war through Tietjens, who focuses on personal behavior and sanity without seeking vindication for the widespread human destruction. One seemingly offhand statement is rather vital in identifying Tietjens's belief that the war, ultimately, cannot be justified politically: while watching ducks darting across a lake, Tietjens reflects, "If they had been hens there would have been something the matter—a dog chasing them. Ducks did not signify. They went mad, contagiously. Like nations or all the cattle of a country."[74] But although he recognizes that the war pushes individual men "towards places . . . they desperately don't want to go," Tietjens insists each individual's redemption lies not in his or his nation's success or failure, but in one's ability "to stick to the integrity of your character, whatever earthquake sets the house tumbling over your head."[75] Consequently, the greatest comfort for a soldier consists in whatever actions preserve human dignity. Therefore, Tietjens applauds the work of a Catholic priest who preaches on the "difficult points in the doctrine of the Immaculate Conception" during a ferocious shell raid because the soldiers wanted "their minds taken off" the threat before reengaging the enemy.[76] Reflecting on religious issues helps distract soldiers and guides them to see their fate in a broader context than that provided by the material hell of the front.

Tietjens uses his faith to keep self-composure on the front and in the morally destructive modern world, which proves valuable when his Catholic wife Sylvia cheats on and slanders him. His frustration causes him to ponder whether all the world's ills stem from "the whole problem of the relations of the sexes," but Ford expects the reader to doubt that easy explanation.[77] The notion, of course, is a central theme in *The Good Soldier*, but it does not adequately describe the source of the tragedies of the war and the cultural disintegration depicted in *Parade's End*. The idea that sex causes all social conflict is professed by duplicitous characters such as General Campion, who has an affair with Sylvia and, like David sending Uriah into battle, pushes Tietjens's company to the front to get him killed. Campion asserts that "modernism" can be defined by a subaltern demanding leave so that he may have a threesome with his wife and another man.[78] But a composed Tietjens quietly objects to this automatic assignment of blame on sexual immorality and continually demonstrates that greed, disregard for cultural traditions and authority, and an amalgamation of political problems are more harmful than Campion's simplified theory of what primarily degrades modern man.

In a 1922 article in the *Yale Review*, Ford reacted against the saturation of sexual themes in literature and their predominance in the public consciousness. "The fact is that sex discussion occupies . . . far too great a part in the public mind of the lands that border the Atlantic. It becomes an obsession; it ends as a nuisance."[79] This notion appears to have carried over as one of Ford's central and widely overlooked themes in *Parade's End*, in which sex is a nuisance, not an obsession as in *The Good Soldier*. It is also worth noting that high liturgical forms of Christianity like Catholicism and High Anglicanism stress that sexual sins are secondary to spiritual sins such as avarice and jealousy, whereas the Protestant or secular moral code embraced by the modern men of Tietjens's world tend to overemphasize the frequency and moral harm of sexual sins and physical violence because of their greater visibility.

While Tietjens rigorously defines his political and religious beliefs, Sylvia seems trapped between the morality of the modern world and that of her Catholic upbringing. Her conflict makes her a more complex figure than Leonora in *The Good Soldier*, whose anger at and revenge against her husband are largely motivated by public image. Unlike Leonora, Sylvia initiates the infidelities even before her marriage to Tietjens, and thus she provides grounds for questioning the identity of the child's true father. Yet although Sylvia initially expresses her frustration through sexual revenge, her discontent arises from a much deeper personal and social problem:

her husband's refusal to conform to the modern world's ideologies, a decision Sylvia finds intolerable.

Ultimately, Sylvia's attempt to use sexuality as a weapon is rendered ineffective because it represents only one small element of the conflict between modernity and her husband's personal and political moral beliefs. Sylvia's difficulty is revealed early in the novel when she tries to shock Fr. Consett, her confessor, by describing her desires to commit innumerable sexual sins. The priest discounts her threat, insisting she will merely get bored (which she does). His response leads her to a more genuine confession. "You want to know why I hate my husband. I'll tell you; it's because of his simple, sheer immorality. I don't mean his actions; his views! Every speech he utters about everything makes me—I swear it makes me—in spite of myself, want to stick a knife in him, and I can't prove he's wrong, not ever, about the simplest thing. But I can pain him."[80] "His views," as Tietjens himself continually insists, are markedly unmodern, so much so that he can claim, "What I stand for isn't any more in this world."[81] Like Edward Ashburnham, Tietjens wishes to preserve an extinct cultural code, but unlike Edward, Tietjens can actually embody the ideals he professes.

Tietjens does not believe the modern world contains no system of morality but that, on the heels of Victorianism, sexual morality seems to be the only matter that inspires widespread public condemnation. This social reflex is too simplistic for Tietjens. Sylvia wishes her husband would react to her infidelity and once laments to him, "If . . . you had once in our lives said to me 'You whore! You bitch!' . . . If you'd only once said something like it . . . about the child! About Perowne! . . . you might have done something to bring us together."[82] But ultimately Sylvia's sexual endeavors disappoint but do not enrage Tietjens, who holds a more comprehensive notion of marital fidelity based on protection of the family name and preservation of its traditions. Therefore, Sylvia's cutting down the majestic, symbolic tree that stands at the center of his Groby Estate and represents a remnant of Tietjens's family history proves much more effective in driving her husband to despair than her infidelity.

Besides her difficulty finding adequate means of revenge against her husband, Sylvia's Catholic faith prevents her from fully embracing the modern world she wishes her husband would join. For example, she will not consider divorcing him and can only symbolically discard a medallion of St. Michael, "the R. C. patron of soldiers in action that she had worn between her breasts"—a symbolic scene that Tietjens interprets as "the final act of parting."[83] Sylvia's acts of defiance are bound up with elements of the complex moral system she wants to abandon.

Sylvia's final tactical error in her assault on Tietjens is her mistaken belief that he hates her faith, a presumption that motivates her insistence on raising their child Catholic. But Tietjens gives his consent and insists, "I have no objection to Papists," whom he respects and admires.[84] His later lament, "His heir was to be brought up as a Papist—the mother's religion!" suggests that the offense arises not from Catholicism itself but from the social violation of his son not inheriting his own faith but that of the child's maternal descendents.[85] Similarly, Ashburnham permitted his daughters to be Catholics but wanted his sons to remain Anglican; that way, Ashburnham's family name and property would stay in Anglican hands. The narrator in *Parade's End* reveals that Tietjens "hated converts," and this sentiment may actually have reflected Ford's own opinion. Although technically a convert himself, Ford viewed his own conversion as a corrective act to his parents' decision to leave the Catholic faith on moving to England.[86] He simply returned the Ford family to its proper spiritual tradition. By 1932, Ford changed his tone slightly in claiming, "I should advocate all children being brought up as implicit Roman Catholics," because Catholics either completely believe or disbelieve in their faith, while "Protestantism is a continual and gradual refining away of beliefs."[87] Ford gained admiration for the resiliency of the recusant Catholics in England as he became more familiar with them. Furthermore, after World War I, Ford had witnessed England's widespread disregard for the authority of the Anglican Church, and he was more comfortable with society consciously rejecting traditional social structures rather than allowing them to corrode from cultural neglect.

Like *The Good Soldier,* the conclusion of *Parade's End* in the final novel, *The Last Stand,* depicts the inevitable victory of modernity over its protagonist's (and Ford's) worldview, even if it might take a few years to completely take effect. The war leaves Tietjens, as it left Ford, with impaired reasoning abilities—although Tietjens, unlike Ford, never fully recovers. The only way

Tietjens can function is by living with Valentine Wannop, the woman he loved before the war but refused to live with to preserve his marital fidelity. Even his extraordinary knowledge of antique furniture can only be employed by engaging in a very modern form of trade with rich and ignorant Americans who "come flying in the beastly machines" to rampage Europe, "stripping the unfortunate land of France of her choicest art treasures."[88] The Americans embody a composite of modernity's sociocultural depravity: they covet wealth for its own sake, have few cultural or spiritual traditions to uphold, deface those that exist, and treat art as a commodity to be traded for profit.

The Last Stand ultimately excuses Tietjens's participation in the modern world. Ford frames Tietjens's fate in a manner that demonstrates the hopelessness of protecting spiritual, moral, or cultural traditions, and his survival at least stands in contrast to Ashburnham's suicide. However, this depiction is awkward and offers nothing new to the central themes *Parade's End;* if anything, it distracts the reader from the power of the other three works that do not try to find a secure place in the modern world for the anachronistic Tietjens. Yet *Parade's End* as a whole is an underappreciated twentieth-century work, and it is almost certainly one of the best World War I novels in English.

THE *TRANSATLANTIC REVIEW*

The Good Soldier, Parade's End, and memoirs such as *Thus to Revisit* (1921) all demonstrate Ford's emphasis on the importance and difficulty of Europeans preserving their distinct spiritual and cultural traditions, but Ford paradoxically also wanted Europeans to find artistic unity and at least political consensus, as his postwar rhetoric makes clear. This desire for unity motivated Ford to found another journal, the *Transatlantic Review,* which sought to bring together modernists in art, painting, and literature. He chose to publish from Paris probably because Pound lived there and had many connections, but ostensibly because, as Ford later related, "Paris gyrated, seethed, clamoured, roared with the Arts. Painters, novelists, poets, composers, sculptors . . . came from Tokyo, they came from Petrograd; they poured in from Berlin, from Constantinople . . . they flew in locust hordes from Spokane, from Seattle, from Santa Fé, from all the states and Oklahoma."[89] It was to be a truly "catholic" journal of the arts, even more so than its precursor, the *English Review*. Unfortunately for Ford, the dream of such a transnational journal quickly withered into one that published primarily and inevitably works by the English and Americans, with an occasional piece from France.

It was the ubiquitous presence of the Americans on the literary scene that initially excited and eventually exasperated Ford. Although he tried to convince himself when announcing the publication of the new journal that "there is no British Literature, there is no American Literature: there is English Literature which embraces alike Mark Twain and Thomas Hardy," he clearly felt the distinction when editing the review and especially when it failed.[90] The *Transatlantic Review* would successfully publish promising young Americans such as William Carlos Williams, Gertrude Stein, E. E. Cummings, and Ernest Hemingway, who only later professed his dislike for Ford's politics, artistic theories, and personality. In one of Ford's final editorials in the by then dying review, he commended the Americans for their greater willingness to engage in experimental literary forms, but he also claimed "the young English writer is the less arrogant and in consequence the more sincere."[91] It is hard not to view this comment as an oblique shot at Hemingway. The swarming Americans who infiltrate Europe for their furniture at the end of *Parade's End* may be derived from Ford's trying experiences with Americans as an editor.

Besides the influx of Americans, Ford's failure to attract some of the popular artists of the time prevented him from realizing the international publication he envisioned. He begged James Joyce frequently for a contribution in order to include the Irish in the international menu, but when Joyce finally relented, he issued only a sparing few excerpts from *Finnegans Wake* entitled "A Work in Progress." T. S. Eliot declined to submit any poetry but wrote Ford a letter of encouragement that began, "I welcome with extreme curiosity the appearance of the *Transatlantic Review*."[92] "Curiosity," even of the "extreme" variety, does not betray a great deal of confidence, but Ford nevertheless printed Eliot's letter (against Eliot's expressed intentions) to at least include his words in the first installment.

While Ford championed modernism and internationalism in the arts, he also used the journal as a medium to broadcast his conservative political views. In the announcement of the journal's intended formation, Ford declared, "The politics will be those of its editor who has no party leanings save toward those of a Tory kind so fantastically old fashioned as to see no salvation save in the feudal system."[93] The words come straight out of the mouths of Ashburnham and Tietjens and hardly differ from Ford's explicitly "Catholic" viewpoint in the *English Review*. Ford despised liberalism because, as he stated in a *Transatlantic Review* editorial, its proponents "ignore not only the historical sense but the historical sentiments of nations"—and to disregard history is to assault the cultural and spiritual traditions Ford wanted to preserve.[94] Later editorials even joined in blaming the Liberals in particular for prolonging the Great War. Ford's only continuing dispute with the modern Tories was their refusal to grant Ireland independence, a denial he thought did not improve the culture or faith of either country and therefore was a waste of time and money.

While Ford was in Paris working on the review and writing *Parade's End,* he continued to embrace his identity as a Catholic. He had by this time separated from Violet Hunt and began his relationship with Stella Bowen. When Stella visited him in Paris, she enjoyed France but complained, "Your darn'd religion is a queer thing"; Ford sympathized, responding, "I feel just as *frightened* when I go into a Protestant place of worship!"[95] And yet, despite his rejection of the national church, his desire for international art that looked beyond nationalities, and even his wish for the people of Europe to find a common political objective, he remained loyal to the English. In the final *Transatlantic Review,* he defended his inclusive view of art, insisting, "We [English] will champion His Majesty's 41st–69th Regiment of Foot any day against any military unit the world has ever known; any day we would champion the game of cricket against the game of baseball . . . the buttercup against the gaudy melon flower. . . . But when it comes to the novel . . ."[96] Art might be the only area where Ford encouraged the rise of modernity, possibly because, within modernism, art's traditions can still be preserved and developed.

The *Transatlantic Review* failed quickly because of finances and was, like the *English Review*, ironically sold to a group of Liberal purchasers. The ironies continued when Ford spent a great deal of time in America during his final decade and a half. He even embarked on a lecture tour in the United States and took a teaching position at Olivet College in Michigan. But a man of German blood who fights against them in a war and a devout Englishman who abandons the Anglican Church to convert to the Catholic faith of his German ancestors learns to tolerate an amount of irony. Like Tietjens, Ford adapted to the present reality to survive, while at least rhetorically defending his faith and nation.

Pound's 1939 obituary judges Ford in a very fair light: it commends Ford for his unacknowledged work as a critic and as a crucial actor in the formation of literary modernism, but it also recognizes his penchant for misrepresentation and untrustworthiness as a friend, faults for which he suffered dearly. Yet Ford's is not the "saddest story" it is sometimes made out to be, with the most tangible regret for his readers being that, as Pound explained, "His own best prose was probably lost" in the sheer volume of his work.[97] But for a man who considered it his vocation to preserve and defend the cultural and spiritual traditions of a continent, a great deal had to be written.

3

T. S. Eliot: Anglo-Catholic
Visions and Revisions

*Eliot began to love his doom, and regretfully resigned to set
about perpetuating the causes of it—kings, religion, and for-
malism.*

—Basil Bunting

IN A 1911 *ENGLISH REVIEW* EDITORIAL, FORD MADOX FORD SURMISED,
"It is possibly true that, at the very present moment, we have
among us no figure that is very monumental. We write this with
some diffidence, for at any moment a giant may loom on the hori-
zon."[1] That T. S. Eliot, born and raised in St. Louis and educated
at Harvard, was to come closest to embodying the figure foretold
by Ford may have shocked Ford in 1911, but not after the war
when Ford began to accept the infiltration of Americans into England's literary world. In many ways, Eliot fulfilled Ford's vision
of the quintessential modernist: he engaged in experimental verse
but cherished literary traditions; he upheld the religious traditions
of England (and like Ford did so by returning to the faith of his
ancestors); and he maintained a proempire political stance that rejected the ideals of Liberalism. Yet Ford said very little about Eliot
specifically, an omission that suggests Eliot's distance from the literary establishment in London, even while he associated with the
Woolfs, befriended Ezra Pound, and edited *The Criterion*. His distance was a cultural one: no matter how diligently Eliot attempted
to transform himself into a political, spiritual, and social Englishman, he remained foreign, an American. Speaking as a fellow
American expatriate, Pound insisted, "It can't be said that an al-
teration on Mr. Eliot's passport has altered the essential America-
ness of his work."[2]

In addition to an inauthentic Englishness, Eliot's contemporar-

91

ies charged him with not being truly Catholic (for regardless of his own terminology, he was raised Unitarian and converted to and never left the Anglican Church), nor truly modernist, especially later in his career. Arthur Mizener even questions Eliot's claims to grasp the English literary tradition. "Mr. Eliot's possession of his tradition . . . has been acquired, as fully acquired as a fine intelligence and a powerful will can make it. But it is acquired, and it never becomes entirely habitual."[3] In spite of these accusations, Eliot undoubtedly did more to preserve the English literary tradition, to propel and legitimize the modernist movement in England, and to articulate an apologetics for the existence of Catholic literature than any poet in the twentieth century. Like Ford, but with more gravity, Eliot aimed to preserve European faith and culture through modernist art, driven in awe and fear of what Wyndham Lewis called "the spectacle of Europe committing suicide."[4] Eliot therefore not only belongs in this study of Catholic modernists, but is in fact central to it.

ELIOT'S EARLY POETRY

Eliot's announcement in the preface to a 1928 essay collection *For Lancelot Andrewes* that he was "a classicist in literature, a royalist in politics, and an anglo-catholic in religion" provoked many of his contemporaries to react with a sense of betrayal and disappointment, while Eliot insisted his conversion merely reflected an "expansion or development of interests."[5] His decision to join the Anglican Church also incited an interpretive war over his preconversion poetry that still sporadically ignites critical debate. Recent studies such as Lawrence Rainey's *Revisiting the Waste Land* and Susan Blalock's compilation *Guide to the Secular Poetry of T. S. Eliot* attempt to mark a definitive boundary between Eliot's pre- and postconversion poetry and critical thought. This scholarship promotes a "secular" reading of Eliot's preconversion poetry, intending to reclaim Eliot's early work and critical thought as artifacts of the avant-garde movement that, allegedly, the New Critics and even Eliot himself cunningly but deliberately misread into works of conservative spiritual expression, thereby distorting subsequent interpretations.[6]

There is a level of artificiality in marking a fixed secular-religious boundary even in Eliot's preconversion work. A glance at Eliot's earliest poetry reveals that he was never completely secular: his allusions, language, tone, and subject consistently reflect a more or less religious mind. Meanwhile, his later "religious" poems reflect spiritual tension and exploration and are not generally laden with praise or apologetics. While still at Harvard, Eliot considered converting to a more liturgical and traditional form of Christianity than the Unitarian beliefs of his youth from which he had strayed. He diligently studied mystical movements and focused his attention on Evelyn Underhill's text on contemplative spirituality, *Mysticism*. Eliot's most recent biographer, Lyndall Gordon, explains that Eliot's "copious notes" on Underhill focus on "the traditional pattern of progress towards sainthood through phases of awakening, unworthiness, mortification of the senses, and illumination," stages that Eliot consciously would explore in his later mystic poetry.[7] Four unpublished religious poems from Eliot's Harvard years, including "I Am the Resurrection" and "The Burnt Dancer," contemplate serious commitment to the Christian faith specifically and express a mystical desire for purification and self-sacrifice. Gordon claims, "The implicit question, throughout this group [of poems], is how to behave in relation to the unknown. . . . The 1914 poems suggest that, for a time in his youth, Eliot's imagination toyed with the saint's ambitious task."[8] Although he postponed conversion, his interest in mysticism immediately influenced his poetry.

Even "The Love Song of J. Alfred Prufrock" represents an extension of his desire to answer the question of the unknown from a religious perspective rather than a refusal to contemplate it. Born partly from the mind of Eliot the philosopher and potential religious convert, Prufrock primarily serves as an inquirer. His first question—"What is it?"—refers to "the overwhelming question," but it also echoes Pilate's "What is truth?" (11).[9] Although Prufrock, like Pilate, understands the futility of existential inquiry, he willingly embarks on an examination of himself and the world for answers and rhetorically invites his audience to join him. The need for such an exploration resonates with Eliot's religious and philosophical explorations. Each of Prufrock's most vital questions—"Do I dare / Disturb the universe?" (45–46); "And how should I presume?" (61); "Should I . . . / Have the strength to force the moment to its crisis?" (80); and "Would it have been worthwhile?" (100) can be read as derivatives of the overwhelming question. These questions suggest that Prufrock functions as Eliot's vehicle of self-interrogation, and he thereby challenges himself to see if he contains the moral will to actually adopt philosophical conclusions or make spiritual commitments.

With Europe mired in the Great War when "Prufrock" was finally published in 1917, Eliot waited out the war in London and suspended his contemplation of conversion while he attempted to integrate himself into the city's social and literary world. Through Pound he met many key literary figures and longtime friends, but it was his ill-fated marriage to Vivien Haigh-Wood in August of 1915 that would determine the course of his life in the following years. Her mental health proved unstable shortly after their marriage, and Eliot worked long hours at Lloyd's Bank to afford her medical bills. This stress, along with Eliot's Fordian sense of the decay of European culture well before the war, is reflected in the despairing tone of *Poems*, his 1920 verse collection.

During the war years in which the poems were written, Eliot tried to assimilate himself into British culture and adopt the sentiments of English nationalism, although he frequently wrote to friends in Boston and St. Louis that he felt self-consciously American among his literary colleagues. He had not yet developed his English identity and even confessed that his sympathy for German literature and culture "has made it impossible . . . to adopt a wholly partisan attitude . . . though I should certainly fight against the Germans if at all."[10] Eliot confirmed the sincerity of this vow in August of 1918 when he tried to enlist in the American armed services. He was denied, but those like Eliot who did not fight still had to contend with the national tragedy of a war that took so many men of their own generation. Vivien explained to Eliot's sister Charlotte concerning the war's psychological damage to soldiers and citizens, "You, over there, do not realize the bad and dreadful effect war has on the characters of young men. . . . A sort of desperation, and demoralisation of their minds, brains and character."[11]

Eliot's 1920 collection reflects this postwar sense of alienation and guilt. In "Gerontion," a poem in which a dying old man embodies the soul of European culture (first intended as a prelude to *The Waste Land*), Eliot imagines the long-term psychological effect of not fighting. The speaker confesses:

> I was neither at the hot gates
> Nor fought in the warm rain
> Nor knee deep in the salt marsh, heaving a cutlass,
> Bitten by flies, fought.
> My house is a decayed house.

(3–7)

His "house" represents all of European culture, which has crumbled economically, socially, and spiritually. After the Great War, Europe faced an imposing process of emotional regeneration with which any survivor had to contend, and some like Eliot took refuge in the past. In "Whispers of Immortality," Eliot respectfully but somewhat ironically looks back to the past fixtures of England's literary tradition through images of death. "Webster was much possessed by death / And saw the skull beneath the skin; / . . . He knew that thought clings round dead limbs" (1–2, 7) or "Donne, I suppose, was such another / . . . He knew the anguish of the marrow / The ague of the skeleton" (9, 13–14). The spirit and struggle of Webster and Donne survive, paradoxically, because they knew the fleeting nature of human existence but were nonetheless sensitive to its inherent value. They were unlike modern men and artists who, Eliot implies, live and write as if no tradition came before them. G. K. Chesterton once called this attitude "the oligarchy" of those "who merely happen to be walking around."[12]

If the controversial poem "The Hippopotamus" is any indication, Eliot continued to struggle with the notion of conversion to a high liturgical form of Christianity during this postwar period. The poem, which Eliot would later discount as a remnant of juvenilia, attacks "the True Church" that "can never fail / For it is based upon a rock," but nonetheless never ceases "To gather in its dividends" with its days "passed in sleep" (7–8, 12, 20). This caustic attack comes from a man wrestling with the incompatibility between the claims and realities of a universal church, difficulties Eliot would soon overcome. The 1920 poems also mark Eliot's return to more standard metrical structures and a singular narrative voice, an aesthetic practice less modernist than the rambling yet rhythmic verse of "Prufrock" that inspired Pound to rejoice in having discovered a poet who "has actually trained himself *and* modernized himself *on his own.*"[13] After reading "Prufrock"

Pound exclaimed, "PRAY GOD IT BE NOT A SINGLE AND UNIQUE SUCCESS!"[14] His petition was answered when Eliot sent Pound the first manuscripts of *The Waste Land* in 1921.

THE WASTE LAND

The eventual epigraph for *The Waste Land*, in which the immortal but decaying Sibyl expresses her wish to die, echoes the theme of Europe's degeneration emphasized in "Gerontion." (Pound slashed the longer original one that ended with Kurtz's ghastly utterance "the horror, the horror" from Joseph Conrad's *Heart of Darkness*.) Yet this epigraph also points toward one of the central themes of *The Waste Land:* the redemptive need for death. Eliot emphasized the "life-in-death" motif through his deliberate use of Jessie L. Weston's synopsis of the grail Legend in *From Ritual to Romance*. This theme also lies at the center of the "religious-secular" interpretive debate that continues over the poem's meaning, rooted in a decades-old conflict between Cleanth Brooks, who saw the narrator as a mobile figure on a methodical "death-to-life" path, and F. R. Leavis, who argued that the narrative voice in the poem "exhibits no progression" and experiences "no resurrection or renewal."[15]

In his recent study, Rainey invokes Leavis's argument for support and worries that readings of the text that impose structural unity or a narrative progression of faith ruin the poem's dramatic aesthetic effect. Rainey argues that the initial critical reaction to *The Waste Land* is best reflected in the response of a contemporary of Eliot's, poet John Bishop Peale. "It is IMMENSE. MAGNIFICENT. TERRIBLE."[16] According to Rainey, any critical attempt at salvaging unity in the 1922 text cut and edited by Pound obscures the poem's influence on modernism. However, I believe that piecing together some semblance of narrative progression and unity in the poem does not negate its depiction of a disordered, crumbling world. To substantiate this claim, I will trace the narrative development in the poem to parallel the narrator's experiences with Underhill's first stage of mystical development, the "Awakening of the Self." Underhill describes this step as "a disturbance of the equilibrium of the self, which results in the shifting of the field of consciousness from lower to higher levels. . . . the necessary beginning of any process of transcendence."[17] Even when the potential mystic achieves this transcendence, the temporal world is not instantly repaired or redeemed but can be seen and judged through the mystical perspective.

The narrative voice of the poem, expressed through numerous mediums, echoes "Prufrock" by seeking eternal answers, although in more comprehensive cultural and spiritual contexts. It examines the vestiges of literary and spiritual tradition that retain meaning and a redemptive quality and thereby echoes Weston's discussion of the hero's practice of a tradition or ritual. According to Weston, this great tradition "at one time of universal observance has, even in its decay, shown itself possessed of elements of the most persistent vitality."[18] Throughout the poem, the narrator sifts through the remnants of tradition in search of traces of meaning that might give him direction. The first question of *The Waste Land* (as in "Prufrock") outlines the central exploratory theme that guides the direction of the poem. "What are the roots that clutch, what branches grow / Out of this stony rubbish?" (19–20). The narrator searches for an ideological or spiritual answer that can preserve order and meaning when all other systems fail men in the moral desert. But even the existence of such an answer initially seems questionable.

Weston notes that in ancient Grail traditions, "The hero sets out with no clear idea of the task before him."[19] However, she also explains that the first essential "task of the hero consists in asking concerning the Grail."[20] Therefore, this first question, reflecting the narrator's desire for truth, must be contemplated if he is to progress beyond the waste land. Eliot emphasizes the biblical aspects of the question in responding to it with allusions to Ezekiel and Ecclesiastes. "Son of man / You cannot say, or guess, for you know only a heap of broken images, where the sun beats / And the dead tree gives no shelter" (20–22). Both verses refer to Israel's need to repent before God unleashes his wrath and therefore imbue the narrator's mission with a sense of urgency.[21] Somewhat ironically, the biblical counsel is wisely ignored, for the narrator uses a "heap of broken images"—the living remnants of Europe's spiritual, literary, and mythical traditions—to supply the necessary material to continue to revive some sense of tradition. Ultimately, the narrator defiantly insists, "These fragments I have shored against my ruins" (431), but he first must assume the eye of a cultural anthropologist in traversing the modern waste land of Europe to determine what is worth saving.

"The Burial of the Dead" serves to identify the Grail legend as the central organizing myth in the poem. Eliot rather self-servingly describes the effectiveness of this aesthetic strategy in *"Ulysses, Order, and Myth,"* a response to Richard Aldington's insistence that Joyce's novel is a "libel on humanity" that misleads less erudite artists and readers alike.[22] Dismissing Aldington's "pathetic solicitude for the half-witted," Eliot instead argues that *Ulysses* demonstrates how myth provides an adequate "way of controlling, of ordering, of giving a shape and a significance to the immense panorama of futility and anarchy which is contemporary history."[23] Eliot's comment on *Ulysses* certainly describes his own use of myth in *The Waste Land;* furthermore, it betrays his desire to make moral sense of the futility and anarchy of postwar Europe, which eventually would lead Eliot into the arms of the Anglican Church.

The Waste Land, however, maintains its cynical stance toward the difficulties of the modern world. Instead of finding truth through a legitimate source of European tradition, the narrator encounters Madame Sosostris, a pathetic gypsy with a pack of tarot cards, who attempts to use her own concocted myth tradition to guide the narrator to redemption. Her counsel significantly ties the narrator's identity (and fate) with the drowned/baptized Phlebas of "Death By Water":

> Here, said she,
> Is your card, the drowned Phoenician Sailor
>
> . . . .
>
> Here is the man with three staves, and here the Wheel,
> And here is the one-eyed merchant, and this card,
> Which is blank, is something he carries on his back,
> Which I am forbidden to see. I do not find
> The Hanged Man. Fear death by water.
>
> (46–47, 51–55)

Throughout *The Waste Land,* the profane—here the "clairvoyante" and her cards—provides a medium of access to the sacred, often reflected in baptismal and crucifixion imagery. Eliot solidifies the Hanged Man-Christ association in his notes to these lines when he explains, "The Hanged Man . . . is associated in my mind with the Hanged God of Frazer, and . . . with the hooded figure in the passage of the disciples to Emmaus in Part V."[24] It is significant that Madame Sosostris insists "I am forbidden to see" what the Hanged Man "carries on his back"; in fact, she admits she does "not find" the Hanged Man. Her difficulty seems to fulfill Isaiah's prophecy, invoked by Christ and Paul, that idolaters will be blinded to revelation, "God hath given them the spirit of insensibility; eyes that they should not see; and ears that they should not hear, until this present day."[25] Furthermore, the clairvoyant's advice to "fear death by water" reveals her lack of understanding and mistrust of baptism on the route to awakening. In the waste land, the profane can neither comprehend nor contaminate the sacred and will not be able to discern its persistent message in the chaos of modernity.

The narrator likewise must contend with economic injustice and the abasement of carnal love, which are part of Weston's lower levels of consciousness that the narrator will transcend. In a scene modeled on Dante's vision of souls filing into hell in the *Inferno,* the narrator observes London businessmen damned to a futile existence. "A crowd flowed over London Bridge, so many, / I had not thought death had undone so many. / Sighs, short and infrequent, were exhaled" (62–64). As an employee at Lloyd's Bank, Eliot keenly understood the emptiness of toiling in modern economic systems, and he envisions the private hell of these businessmen with an intimate understanding. Eliot subsequently identifies the Great War as the by-product of rampant dubious economic activity. The narrator accosts "Stetson," a stock business figure, and questions him. "You who were with me in the ships at Mylae! / That corpse you planted last year in your garden, / Has it begun to sprout? Will it bloom this year?" (70–72). The passage reiterates the complaints of Siegfried Sassoon and other war poets who criticized the British government's failure to bring the fighting to an end because its continuation stimulated economic growth. This criticism is underscored by the reference to the Punic War at Mylae, an ancient war fought primarily for economic motivations. The corpses of the young soldiers become literal investments that will "sprout" and bring about the sought-after financial reward. Of course, it is easy to criticize a government's activity while enjoying the fruits of its corrupt policies, and as a bank clerk Eliot willingly indicted himself and any survivor applauding his criticism in quoting Baudelaire's censuring line, "You! hypocrite lecteur!—mon semblable,—mon frère!" (76). This accusation at the end of the first section indicates that those who would pass through the waste land must accept a share of the blame for participating in Europe's decay.

The second section, "A Game of Chess," implicates those who may have avoided association with economic and political injustice, but who are tainted by the corruption of carnal love. References to Cleopatra, whose fickle love disoriented Antony and disrupted the course of ancient Rome, and to the rape of Philomel depict lust devoid of love and sacrifice in antiquity, and the speaker suggests that this hollow love is typical in the modern world. The poem replaces the eloquence of literary lovers with the stultified communication between modern lovers: "My nerves are bad to-night. Yes, bad. Stay with me. / Speak to me. Why do you never speak?" (111–12). The attempts of using cheap entertainment to relieve tension—reflected in the popular chorus of the "Shakespeherian Rag"—prove ineffectual and provoke additional frantic questions. "What shall I do now? What shall I do? / . . . What shall we ever do?" (131, 134). Eliot portrays modern relationships that produce directionless boredom, which is alleviated only temporarily by vain and superficial distractions. He underscores this loveless condition and its life-killing qualities in the final scene in the section in which a cockney woman discusses her multiple abortions with a friend at a London pub. "The chemist said it would be all right, but I've never been the same" (161). These lines suggest that even when love produces life, those who adopt the principles of the modern world repeatedly thwart it, and in turn mindlessly do themselves harm.

In the first two sections of the poem, the narrator wanders through the disorganized remnants of tradition and identifies what is worth preserving (classical and national literature, Christian and contemplative tropes) and what can be burned into annihilation (false myth systems, economic injustice, the degradation of carnal love). The actual purifying process begins in the third section, "The Fire Sermon," which initiates the narrator's first deliberate steps out of the modern waste land. Eliot combines Buddhist and Catholic notions of purification in depicting the mystic's experience of the purgatorial fire that destroys the sins of the modern social landscape. First "the wind," the biblical signifier of the Holy

Spirit's presence (and also a harbinger of death), *"crosses* the brown land, unheard," presumably with the message of Christ's redemptive act (174–175, my italics). Eliot mixes biblical traditions—"Upon the rivers of Babylon, there we sat and wept" (Psalm 137)—with England's literary traditions in echoing Edmund Spenser's Prothalamion, as well as Andrew Marvell's "To His Coy Mistress":

> By the waters of Leman I sat down and wept . . .
> Sweet Thames, run softly till I end my song,
> Sweet Thames, run softly, for I speak not loud or long.
> But at my back in a cold blast I hear
> The rattle of the bones, and chuckle spread from ear to ear.
>
> (182–86, Eliot's ellipsis)

While Spenser's song celebrates love's union and London's beauty, Eliot depicts these once pleasing images ironically and describes a polluted and repulsive Thames River in the 1920s, crossed by an ominous "cold blast" that seems void of the Spirit. The Marvell reference complements the focus on the inevitability of death, with "time's winged chariot" driven by a laughing skeleton, an image that recalls the snickering "Eternal Footman" in "Prufrock." Although each of these lines seems to support Leavis's contention that the poem "ends where it began," there is also a sense of the need for return from exile.[26] Just as the Israelites cried from foreign shores for a return to the Promised Land, Eliot writes from Lake Leman near Lausanne, Switzerland, not from London, and apparently awaits his own triumphant, redemptive homecoming.[27]

The narrator's journey to illumination, however, is not linear. Eliot's allusions to Buddha and Augustine interrupt the progression homeward. "To Carthage then I came / Burning burning burning burning / O Lord Thou pluckest me out" (308–310). The appeal of lust and power the narrator encounters in the first two sections of the poem must first be purged and the disciple freed from the flames. In Buddha's original "Fire Sermon," the sage describes the flames that burn from "passion" and "hatred" until the soul develops "an aversion for things tangible" and "all consciousness . . . by the absence of passion becomes free."[28] Eliot's fire also more broadly points to God's redemptive fire predicted by St.

Paul: they are flames of hell for the damned, but flames of purgation from which God eventually "plucks" the repentant.[29] In his notes to the final lines of "The Fire Sermon," Eliot cryptically cites the importance of these religious allusions: "The collocation of these two representatives of eastern and western asceticism, as the culmination of this part of the poem, is not an accident."[30] Eliot subsequently leaves no explanatory notes for the most distinctive and structurally vital section, "Death By Water," where the water imagery contrasts with the ubiquitous fire of the previous section, dousing the burning of desire and damnation.

Phlebas's drowning connects Weston's description of the drowned and revived god with Paul's profession of baptism, in which the convert is buried in water only to rise again reborn.[31] Furthermore, the baptismal imagery in "Death By Water" suggests the narrator's deliberate progression rather than the incoherent wandering Leavis identifies in the poem. The drowned "Phlebas the Phoenician" forgets "the profit and loss" and thereby erases the memory of sordid economic activity referred to in the first section (314). Death still seems undesirable, but the language evokes a sense of relief in Phlebas's drowning. If this were the final section of the poem, the peace pervading the stanza could be interpreted as a type of triumphant Buddhistic elimination of consciousness and desire. However, the explicit Christian imagery in the final section, "What the Thunder Said," points to a regenerated life for the narrator. The image in which the sea "picked his bones in whispers" likewise suggests revival because it is reminiscent of Ezekiel's desert vision of dry bones that God reassembles and raises into life.[32] But Phlebas's drowning/baptism only serves as the precursor to true conversion. For Eliot, baptism functions in the traditional sense as an ending, bringing closure to the decay of the self, but also as a beginning in which the reborn or awakened must develop in a still unredeemed world—a mystical paradox he returns to, on one level, in the first line of East Coker: "In my end is my beginning."

Through the death of baptism, Eliot's narrator has attained a spiritual awakening and, in accordance with Underhill's second stage for the mystic, will undergo "The Purification of the Self," a process equally daunting as the cleansing of social sins in "The Fire Sermon." In his note for the title of "What the Thunder Said," Eliot refers the reader to the Upanishad for an explanation of the "fable of the meaning of the Thunder."[33] But the title also likely alludes to the Book of Revelation, in which God silences John before he can write down the thunder's message. "And when the seven thunders had uttered their voices, I was about to write: and I heard a voice from heaven saying to me, 'Seal up the things which the seven thunders have spoken; and write them not.'"[34] However, just as he does earlier in the poem, the narrator wisely marches beyond divine parameters in his search for truth. He confronts the cost of discipleship through images of Gethsemane with Christ's betrayers' "frosty silence in the gardens" and his own "agony in stony places" (323–24). Christ's death fits the pattern of Weston's Dying God: "He who was living is now dead / We who were living are now dying" (328–29). But the mystic's path does not conclude with death. He must endure a desert period before the Dying God's resurrection, a process invoked in Eliot's reference to the Antarctic explorers who felt the presence of an additional voyager in the frozen wilderness. "Who is the third who walks always beside you? / When I count, there are only you and I together," yet "There is always another one walking beside you" (359–62). The scene alludes to Christ's initial unrecognizability to his disciples after his resurrection. Furthermore, these lines highlight Christ's trinitarian nature—he is the "third" person completing the Christian Godhead—and imply that Christ has been a constant presence with the narrator in the waste land.

The allusions to exploration and guidance underscore the notion that the narrator has always had or at least has attained a sense of purpose and direction in the poem. But withstanding the desert of self-purification, described as "only the wind's home," again signifying the Holy Spirit's presence, is a trying endeavor. In her study, Weston significantly points out that the Perilous Chapel at the end of the Grail legend establishes the protagonist's journey as a "story of an initiation."[35] Weston also explains that "the *rôle* of the god" is primarily found in "his responsibility for providing the requisite rain upon which the fertility of the land, and the life of the folk, depended."[36] In *The Waste Land,* when the thunder finally responds, in "a damp gust / Bringing rain" (393–394), the narrator suddenly returns to a language and tone grafted right out of "Prufrock," describing "The awful daring of a moment's surrender / Which an age of prudence can never retract" (403–4).[37] However, the narrator here has the strength to surrender, a salvific act "not to be found in our obituaries" (405). Eliot's allusion to Peter's brief walk to Christ on the water—"The sea was calm, your heart would have responded / Gaily, when invited, beating obedient / To controlling hands" (421–23)—underscores the motif of surrender. The narrator's rebirth, however, does not suddenly mend the fragmented world, because London bridge still falls; but it does provide "Shantih" (434), "the Peace which passeth understanding" and strengthens him to confront the challenges of modernity. The narrator has not destroyed but passed through the waste land and thereby prepared himself for the mystical process of transcending the world and himself. As Underhill clarifies, the mystic's awakening "must not . . . be confused or identified with religious conversion" although the "mechanical processes may be much the same."[38]

The "mechanical processes" of conversion alluded to in Eliot's next publication, *The Hollow Men* (1925), which grew out of extracted sections from *The Waste Land,* more closely imply conversion. The apocalyptic themes of the poem and the *"For Thine is the Kingdom"* refrain point to Eliot's decision to convert to Anglicanism. The public uproar surrounding Eliot's official conversion suggests that few understood the magnitude of the mystical-Christian elements in these preconversion works, and it also indicates that modernism was already conceived of as a much more cohesive movement than was actually the case. Even in November of 1922, Eliot privately wrote to Richard Aldington concerning his aesthetic objectives. "As for *The Waste Land,* that is a thing of the past so far as I am concerned and I am now feeling toward a new form and style."[39] This "new style" highlights Eliot's interest in mysticism in *Ash Wednesday* and *Four Quartets.* In 1928, Eliot unequivocally denied that he ever supported the avant-garde or *vers libre* movements in literature. "There was no movement, no revolution," except "that Ezra Pound was born with a fine ear for verse."[40] Even these comments do not mark a drastic change in Eliot's aesthetic approach, because his 1917 essay "Reflections on *Vers Libre*" claimed in his characteristic style that *vers libre* "is a battle-cry of freedom, and there is no freedom in art."[41] Attempts to portray the early Eliot as a renegade artist turned conservative conceals the complex but still measured form and subjects of his pre-conversion works and the logic behind his conversion.

ELIOT'S "ANGLO-CATHOLICISM"

Pound responded with neither surprise nor support to news of Eliot's conversion. He exclaimed in a 1930 editorial concerning Eliot, "I believe that postwar 'returns to christianity' (and its various subdivisions) have been merely . . . signs of fatigue."[42] More provocatively, in 1942 Pound surmised, "It is amusing, after so many years, to find that my disagreement with Eliot is a religious disagreement, each of us accusing the other of Protestantism."[43] Certainly no liturgical Christian himself, Pound thought the problem with any religion was that it led humankind away from a universal, renaissance-driven revolution and inspired nationalism and various other forms of "provincialism," a problem he condemned as one of the primary ills of the twentieth century.[44] Pound particularly abhorred Eliot's identification with the Anglican Church: if a man must be a Christian he should at least have the foresight to be a Roman Catholic and not join the Protestant-Semitic movement Pound believed controlled the financial globe, ruined Western art and spirituality, and led to the Great War. He angrily asked in 1942, "Who destroyed the unity of the Catholic Church with this mud-wallow that serves the Protestants in the place of contemplation? Who decided to destroy the mysteries within the Church so as to be able to destroy the Church itself by schism?"[45] It is intriguing that many of Pound's views closely align with those of Eliot, who likewise felt in the 1920s and 1930s that Semites were bankrupting Europe, that Protestantism was too provincial, and that only Catholic Christianity could adequately defend traditional European culture from destruction. But Eliot determined that the Anglican Church, and not the Roman Catholic Church, better expressed historical Catholicism in England.

Although the Anglo-Catholic movement gained widespread publicity during the Oxford Movement in the mid-nineteenth century, its nascent stages can be traced to Richard Hooker's sixteenth-century treatise *The Laws of Ecclesiastical Polity*, which argued that Anglican theology should represent a sound compromise or "via media" between sixteenth-century Puritanism and Roman Catholicism.[46] The term via media has always sounded too Romanist to Protestants and unnecessarily contrived to English Catholics. Yet while Catholics came to view the notion at least as a step toward Rome, most English Protestants distrusted anyone employing the term as a definition of their faith.

Like many Anglicans who at one time or another used the term *via media* to describe their theological beliefs (including C. S. Lewis and even John Henry Newman before his conversion), Eliot identified Elizabeth, not the scandal-ridden Henry VIII, as the founder of his faith. This decision is peculiar from a strictly doctrinal point of view, for it was under Elizabeth's reign that sacramental confession, transubstantiation of the Eucharist, and various other Roman Catholic teachings were abandoned by the Anglican Church. Although Eliot believed in the importance of the doctrines discarded by the Anglican communion under Elizabeth, he still explicitly distanced himself from Henry VIII, despite the fact that the king wanted to be the supreme head of an English church that mirrored Catholic teaching on faith and morals. In Eliot's 1928 essay "For Lancelot Andrewes," his rhetoric closely resembles Newman's at the commencement of the Oxford Movement in claiming an Elizabethan foundation for his Anglo-Catholic faith. "The Church of England is the creation not of the reign of Henry VIII or of the reign of Edward VI, but of the reign of Elizabeth. The via media which is the spirit of Anglicanism was the spirit of Elizabeth in all things."[47] While embracing Newman's pre-conversion views, Eliot said conspicuously little about Newman as a spiritual thinker or influence. Eliot's reticence may be due to the fact that Newman ultimately determined that to be Anglican was to be Protestant, while Eliot persevered in honoring what he considered the Anglican "persistence in finding a mean between the Papacy and Presbytery."[48] Since the Reformation, this distinction has been employed by numerous liturgically conservative Protestants, but Eliot functionally pushed his understanding of a via media faith toward English Catholicism rather than toward Presbyterianism.

High Church and Anglo-Catholic movements had been active intermittently in England since Newman's controversial and well-publicized conversion in 1843. In the 1920s when Eliot was formulating his spiritual and political English identity, High Church movements throughout England again had been gaining popularity, in part because of the Anglican Church's loss of power after World War I. Anglo-Catholics also typically gained steam after changes in Vatican policy toward England. For instance, the Vatican's decision in 1850 to reinstitute Catholic bishops in England inspired anti-Catholic sentiments around England and caused Anglo-Catholics to reexamine their own theological and political position. Similarly, Pope Leo XIII's papal bull *Apostolicae Curae,* or "On the Nullity of Anglican Orders," issued on September 15, 1896, ignited anti-Catholic sentiments that were still brewing in England. Leo XIII unequivocally declared "null and void anything which, in these matters, may happen to be contrariwise attempted, whether wittingly or unwittingly, by any person whatsoever, by whatsoever authority or pretext, all things to the contrary notwithstanding."[49] Thus, the Vatican comprehensively denied the status it had given the Eastern Eastern Orthodox churches, whose clergy were considered apostolic and all sacraments determined efficacious.

In reaction to the papal decree, Reverend Vernon Staley's 1893 classic *The Catholic Religion: A Manual for Instruction for Members of the Anglican Church* was reissued. Staley argues that the Anglican Church willfully relinquished its authority to the Roman Catholic Church when Augustine of Canterbury attended King Oswy's conference held at the Abbey of Whitby in 664. His contention that "the English Church came to accept the Church of Rome" may reveal something of Eliot's own logic in determining the historical foundation of his Anglo-Catholicism.[50] Staley continues, "It naturally followed that Rome should be looked to as the arbiter of all differences, and the referee in questions which afterwards might arise. It is however to be observed, that important as the decision at Whitby was, it was but a voluntary act on the part of the English Church acting under royal authority."[51] Staley's account suggests that, during the nine centuries the Vatican guided the church in England, it was not responsible for defining dogma, instituting the hierarchy in England, or maintaining liturgical and doctrinal unity with the greater Catholic Church. According to Staley's version of church history, the Vatican merely served as a doctrinal or liturgical troubleshooter when matters of dispute surfaced in the national church of England.

One consequence of this dubious reading of the history of Catholicism in England is that the term *Reformation* loses its schismatic connotations. Staley seizes this opportunity to redefine the term by arguing that the "Reformation is not the destruction of an old thing, and the making of a new thing to take its place, but the improving of the old, so that it still lives on under restored conditions."[52] Ultimately, what is at stake in Staley's text and in much of Anglo-Catholic rhetoric in the late nineteenth and early twentieth centuries is the validity of the Anglican orders. If the Anglican orders are historically invalid and the clergy unable to efficaciously perform certain sacraments, then the church is unequivocally Protestant. The Vatican recognized the validity of baptism and marriage in the Anglican Church, but nearly every other Protestant church, no matter how untraditional the liturgy or doctrines, held that distinction.

Staley's treatise influenced the direction of the Anglo-Catholic movement that Eliot associated with in the first half of the twentieth century. In addition to the annual High Anglican Church Lambeth Conference formed in 1867, various other High Church and Anglo-Catholic assemblies flourished just after the Great War in the early 1920s. In 1923, Bishop Frank Weston gave an influential speech entitled "Our Present Duty" to a prominent group, the Anglo-Catholic Congress. Weston's address is still highly regarded by members of Anglo-Catholic movements. In the occasionally profound, sometimes confounding speech, Weston explains that Anglo-Catholics must reform the Anglican Church from its doctrinal roots. However, he warns his brethren that in becoming more Catholic, they must not become less English. "You cannot simply sweep away the social customs in which we have been born and bred, and God forbid that we should try. You cannot pretend to an equality of culture and an equality of taste and temperament which does not actually exist."[53] Such rhetoric echoes Eliot's sense of English superiority, a central reason many Anglo-Catholics did not become Roman Catholic.

Anglo-Catholics like Bishop Weston and Eliot insisted that most Anglicans were lax followers of unhistorical Protestant liturgies. In "Thoughts After Lambeth," Eliot avoids serious discussion of disestablishment of the Anglican Church but acknowledges the Anglican Church's ever loosening grip on the English people. He somewhat wistfully alludes to the Anglican Church's increased emphasis on the preservation of sound theology and liturgy rather than on the clergy's political and cultural reputation. "The orthodox faith of England is at last relieved from its burden of respectability. A new respectability has arisen to assume the burden; and those who would once have been considered intellectual vagrants are now pious pilgrims."[54] Eliot often described his hopeful visions in a manner that made it seem as if they had already begun to materialize, and he here expresses his desire that the postwar Anglican Church would promote conservative intellectuals like himself who practiced a traditional, highly liturgical form of the faith. Eventually, Eliot's dramatic and mystical expression of Anglican spirituality necessitated he draw on Roman Catholic traditions in monasticism and mysticism. But actual conversion to Rome remained socially and culturally untenable for him.

Eliot wanted to establish and claim membership in a "pure" English literary and spiritual tradition. Thus, in 1921, he argues that "Mr. Yeats is an Irishman" and is therefore "outside of the tradition altogether."[55] Given that Yeats lived and wrote for a substantial amount of time in London, such a limited view of England's literary tradition should also disqualify the American Eliot himself. Eliot had not yet accepted in his criticism, as he had already in his art, that England's literary tradition was and continues to be influenced by diverse cultural and historical movements. This problem is directly related to Eliot's difficulty making sense of England's spiritual tradition. One transparent objective of Eliot's "Lancelot Andrewes" essay is to link the seventeenth-century preacher with the less-obscure Jeremy Taylor and Richard Hooker as "fathers of a national church," whose written works evidence a "determination to stick to essentials" and "desire for clarity and precision on matters of importance" that preserved "the general policy of Elizabeth."[56] Conceding that the Anglican Church had no Thomas Aquinas or Augustine of Hippo, Eliot nonetheless argues that "a church is to be judged by its intellectual fruits" and makes it his business to nominate historical intellectual fathers.[57] The best poet he could elect was George Herbert.

Eliot promoted Andrewes primarily because his preaching articulated a foundational Anglican theology that Eliot wanted to identify as the legitimate ancestor of twentieth-century Anglo-Catholicism. Eliot's intentions are rather explicit in his apology for Andrewes. "Latimer, the preacher of Henry VIII and Edward VI, is merely a Protestant; but the voice of Andrewes is the voice of a man who has a formed visible Church behind him, who speaks with the old authority and the new culture: Andrewes is the first great preacher of the English Catholic Church."[58] Eliot's reference to the "English Catholic Church" (which should not be confused with the actual Roman Catholic Church in England) is especially significant because it is written before his actual conversion, which suggests that Eliot always considered Anglo-Catholicism the only form of Christianity to which he could conceive yielding his allegiance. But this argument conflicts with Eliot's original support for a via media and interferes with Eliot's attempt to define and defend a hegemonic English spiritual tradition.

Not surprisingly, Eliot failed to uphold this strict notion of a pure Anglican spiritual tradition. In "Thoughts After Lambeth," Eliot nonchalantly invokes his church's "intellectual ability" as a way to attract the English youth because "two thousand years has gone into its formation."[59] Even when taking into account Staley's conception of the Anglican Church's formation, Eliot's statement is historically ambiguous. The central problem with Eliot's Anglo-Catholicism lies in the simple fact that England's history possesses both a Catholic and diverse Protestant tradition, and for Eliot to ignore one at the expense of the other would undercut the historical premise on which he based many of his spiritual beliefs. It is not coincidental that Eliot gained British citizenship in 1927, the same year he was officially received into the Anglican Communion; the nationalistic character of his faith and Eliot's determination to frame his faith in Catholic and Anglican terms are both apparent in the Andrewes essay.

Eliot grew increasingly uncomfortable with the Anglican notion of via media altogether. He argues in "Thoughts After Lambeth" for a position that defines his Anglo-Catholicism not as a faith that splits the difference between Puritans and Catholics, but one that represents the Catholic Church in England. "I believe that in spite of the apparently insoluble problems with which it has to deal, the Church of England is strengthening its position as a branch of the Catholic Church, the Catholic Church in England."[60] Eliot completely disregards the existence of the recusant Catholic tradition in England. He believed that the Anglo-Catholic Church was not some sort of imaginary branch of Catholicism, but that it was every bit as apostolic and Catholic as the Catholic Church in any other country. He solidifies this judgment when he claims, "I believe that the Catholic Church, with its inheritance from Israel and from Greece, is still, as it always has been, the great repository of wisdom."[61]

Despite this belief, Eliot somewhat defensively insists that the Anglican Church should not reestablish commitment to Rome. "It is easier for the Church of England to become Catholic, than for the Church of Rome in England to become English; and if the Church of England was mutilated by separation from Rome, the Church of Rome was mutilated by separation from England."[62] Eliot then makes another significant clarification. "I prefer to think of the Church as what I believe it is more and more coming to be, not the 'English Church,' but national as 'the Catholic Church in England.' "[63] This distinction reemphasizes Eliot's need for his church to retain a universal character within a national framework, a spiritual unity he clearly thought the Roman Catholic Church as it then existed could not provide in England. He then asserted more boldly, "With all due respect, the Roman Church is in England a sect," which is a rare comment by Eliot that recognizes the existence of the recusant Catholic tradition in England.[64] However, because Eliot believed that the church in England must be sutured to English national identity, he determined the Roman Catholic Church could not possibly preserve this relationship in twentieth-century England.

Eliot's idea that the Catholic Church in England must represent national culture and political interests was not new, but it had never earned much support among recusant Catholics. Almost a century earlier, Newman argued against the necessity of the establishment of the Anglican Church and clearly stated his view that Catholic tradition needs no national movement to preserve its existence. "Establishment is the spontaneous act of the people; it is a national movement, the Catholic people does it, and not the Catholic Church . . . but, I repeat, it is not necessary for Catholicism. Not necessary, I maintain, and Ireland is my proof of it; there Catholicism has been, not only not established; it has been persecuted for three hundred years, and at this moment it is more vigorous than ever."[65] Newman believed the Catholic Church in any country could express its own culture while maintaining unity with Rome. And while Eliot did not connect establishment of the Anglican Church to the need for it to represent a national church, he nevertheless seemed unsure of what a "national church" signified. Eliot often parses his own words regarding the matter. "We still think, and rightly, of the Church of England as the 'National Church'; but the word *national* in this context can no longer mean what it once meant . . . 'the parish church of the British Empire.' An 'imperial' Church . . . would be something more odious, because far more vulgar, than the Erastian Church of the eighteenth century."[66] England's dream of an imperial church was dying with the empire, and the flaws of Erastianism, or the notion that the state should make decisions for the church, were revealed as soon as Henry VIII took control of the Anglican Church under the 1534 Act of Supremacy. Yet Eliot clung to the "national" label, while continually revising its implications.

ASH-WEDNESDAY

Despite the seeming inconsistencies in Eliot's political and doctrinal understanding of his faith, his conversion was primarily motivated by and continued under a philosophical and even mystical understanding of religion. The mystical nature of Eliot's belief takes precedence in his verse, as is evident in his first major publication after conversion, *Ash-Wednesday* (1930). In an early review of the poem, Allen Tate wisely explains that to appreciate the poetry, a reader or critic must set aside the Thirty-Nine Articles and judge the impressive aesthetic achievement of the poem. Tate argues, "Eliot has hit upon the only method now available of using the conventional religious image in poetry. He has reduced it from symbol to image, from abstraction to the plane of sensation."[67] Eliot's use of imagery to evince religious emotion in *Ash-Wednesday*, expressed through diverse tones and voices, signifies that it remains a work of modernism. In fact, Tate's analysis earns a certain vindication for Eliot, who repeatedly insisted that a poet's beliefs must remain relatively veiled in his work: if personal beliefs are too prominent, either the critic has misread the poem or the religious poet has failed.

Dante represented the perfect model for Eliot's postconversion poetry, and Eliot's critical assessment of him provides a means from which to analyze Eliot's intention and performance as a mystical poet in both *Ash-Wednesday* and *Four Quartets*. As early as 1920, Eliot praised Dante as the preeminent philosophical poet whose philosophy and theology were expressed "not as a matter for argument, but as matter for inspection."[68] In 1929, while writing *Ash-Wednesday*, Eliot even claimed Dante held more universal relevance than Shakespeare simply because "he wrote when Europe was still more or less one."[69] Of course, Eliot grounds his notion of unity on religious tradition. Nevertheless, he stresses that a reader need not understand Catholicism to appreciate the *Divine Comedy*. Eliot's objective in *Ash-Wednesday* was to follow Dante in communicating a religious exploration and experience without creating an apologetic work.

The purgatorial theme of the poem is established by its Lenten title, and it is not presumptuous to argue that Eliot consciously had begun to fashion his own major works as a reflection of Dante's *Inferno, Purgatorio,* and *Paradiso.* With the hellfire of *The Waste Land* behind him, from which the narrator like Dante's was permitted to escape awakened, Eliot more explicitly depicts the sanctifying element of mystical conversion in *Ash-Wednesday.* In the popular Christian imagination, purgatory consists of enduring physical penalty for sin, but both Underhill and Dante (who retains some element of physical punishment) follow Catholic mystical tradition in espousing a purification process that emphasizes detachment and self-renunciation. Underhill states, "The self must be purged of all that stands between it and goodness: putting on the character of reality instead of the character of illusion or 'sin.'"[70] In *Ash Wednesday,* Eliot articulates the need for an even more dramatic detachment and follows Dante in depicting a purgation that renounces not merely illusion and sin, but even apparent "goods" that come between him and God. The speaker seeks to make an unconditional spiritual commitment:

> Because I do not hope to turn again
> Because I do not hope
> Because I do not hope to turn
> Desiring this man's gift and that man's scope
> I no longer strive to strive towards such things
>
> (1–5)

To "turn again" toward sin—or, for Eliot, even toward futile human love or unfounded hope—would cause regression in the spiritual life. The stanza also echoes Shakespeare's Sonnet 29, in which the speaker renounces intellectual ambition and envy, "this man's art and that man's scope" (7), as obstacles to his contemplation of his beloved. "Haply I think on thee, and then my state, /

Like to the lark at break of day arising / From sullen earth, sings hymns at heaven's gate" (10–12).[71] In contemplating his beloved, Shakespeare's speaker models the mystic's contemplation of God.

Throughout the first section of *Ash-Wednesday*, the speaker confronts his own confusion and inadequacy. "Because I do not hope" (2); "Because I know I shall not know" (12); "Because I cannot drink . . . for there is nothing again" (14–15); "Because these wings are no longer wings to fly / But merely vans to beat the air" (34–35). This doubt-filled sentiment echoes the theology of Pascal, whose work Eliot studied diligently while writing *Ash-Wednesday*. In "The '*Pensées*' of Pascal" (1931), Eliot explains that the theologian's "despair, his disillusion . . . are no illustration of personal weakness . . . for the type of Pascal they are the analogue of the drought, the dark night, which is an essential stage in the progress of the Christian mystic."[72] Pascal, a scientist, theologian, and social critic, would have refused the title of mystic, but Eliot capitalizes on his theological effort to confront and even embrace despair as a necessary stage of development for the mystic. Eliot's struggle with despair concludes with the last line of the "Hail Mary": "Pray for us now and at the hour of our death" (42), a petition that points toward the focus on the "Lady" in the following sections. On one level, the "Lady" represents Mary, the Mother of God, but she also embodies Beatrice who accompanies Dante in the *Paradiso*.

Ash-Wednesday is not merely a mystical reflection untainted by personal experiences: while Eliot composed the poem, Vivien had been committed to a mental health hospital, and Eliot had become reacquainted with Emily Hale, a young woman from Boston for whom he still held much affection. But Eliot could not commit himself to Emily, and the tension between his unwilling resistance, his utterly failed marriage, and his veneration of the Virgin culminate in a transcendent vision:

> The single Rose
> Is now the Garden
> Where all loves end
> Terminate torment
> Of love unsatisfied
> The greater torment
> Of love satisfied

(II.33–39)

The beatific Garden effaces both Vivien ("love satisfied," a "greater torment" because of the demise of his marriage) and Emily ("love unsatisfied," a "torment" because their love was never realized), who are relegated to the memory of obstacles in the unredeemed world. Eliot renounces his futile efforts at romantic love in the world and will humbly submit to the guidance of the Virgin who is "withdrawn . . . to contemplation" (II.16–17). Mary's presence fills much of the rest of the poem. Like Beatrice, she serves as a mystical model who teaches humility, self-sacrifice, and prayer, while the speaker endures the "turning" from the desert to the garden, symbols that reflect the rhythm of spiritual fulfillment and emptiness. This turning characterizes the contemplative experience and likewise resembles the twisting road Dante ascends in purgatory.

The poem concludes with a prayer to Mary requesting the disposition that makes contemplation possible:

> Blessed sister, holy mother, spirit of the fountain, spirit of the garden
> Suffer us not to mock ourselves with falsehood
> Teach us to care and not to care
> Teach us to sit still
> Even among these rocks,
> Our peace in His will
>
> (VI.25–30)

Eliot's silent waiting renounces even expectation of God's verifiable action, but he also confronts the paradox of wanting to be free of desire to be purified, which reflects his Eastern-influenced approach to faith and prayer. In his 1929 essay on Dante, Eliot permits this sole desire for purification, and he argues that "the souls in [Dante's] purgatory suffer because *they wish to suffer,* for purgation."[73] As at the end of *The Waste Land,* the narrator in *Ash-Wednesday* still survives in a vacuous spiritual environment, "among these rocks," but now believes with certainty that peace and the fruit of redemption can grow out of the seemingly infertile land of personal suffering.

Ash-Wednesday represents Eliot's first laborious and yet largely successful attempt at treating mystical contemplation as his poetic subject, a method he would continually practice and master in *Four Quartets.* The poem also reflects the state of a spiritual mind influenced by and participating in a spiritual tradition that disregards the strict confines of the Anglican tradition Eliot professed loyalty to at the time of his conversion. After publishing *Ash-Wednesday,* Eliot exhibited some willingness to modify his rigid and often untenable critical understanding of English religious and spiritual traditions, although he continued to espouse a polemically conservative vision of history and politics incompatible with the views of most of his contemporaries.

A LAY PATRIOT: LATER CRITICISM

Eliot's prose after *Ash-Wednesday* does not so much overturn his critical objectives as it redefines the obstacles in his way. The short first paragraph of the preface to *After Strange Gods* (1934) proclaims one of its central themes. "*Le monde moderne avilit.* [The modern world demeans.] It also provincializes, and it can also corrupt."[74] If Eliot wrote as aggressively as Pound, the line would have read, "It also provincializes, and *therefore* corrupts" with no damage to the original intent. However, Eliot does not adequately articulate the difference between nationalism and "provincialization" until *Notes Towards the Definition of Culture* (1949), where he introduces and defines the term *regionalism* as "the conception of some small group of local malcontents conducting a political agitation."[75] In both collections, these local voices threaten Eliot's revised articulation of England's spiritual and intellectual traditions.

In *After Strange Gods,* Eliot continues to make connections "in matters religious, political, and literary," but asserts that he never believed "they all hang together or fall together," although in the "Andrewes" essay he rather explicitly assigns them a common fate.[76] Considering England's historical lack of religious and political cohesion, it was a necessary distinction to make (or illuminate). At the very least, this admission allowed Eliot to embrace the Roman Catholic intellectual tradition without transparent contradictions, although again it would not be until *Notes Towards the Definition of Culture* that he would confess that any nation in the "Western World . . . must recognize that the main cultural tradition has been that corresponding to the Church of Rome."[77] Of course, "culture" only found its full meaning in a religious context for Eliot. But in *After Strange Gods*, he declares "Liberalism," and not secularism, as the primary enemy for those sharing his beliefs. Liberalism, Eliot argues, has fathered humanism and intellectual relativism and imposes a more dangerous threat to the preservation of England's spiritual and intellectual tradition than secularism because it adopts religious jargon and objectives while ignoring the nation's traditional spiritual foundations.

Eliot singles out the Liberal Broad Church clergy who promoted the individualistic notion of the "Inner Light," which he calls "the most untrustworthy and deceitful guide that ever offered itself to wandering humanity."[78] Eliot's fear of systems that compromised his vision of a hegemonic English and Catholic tradition eventually forced him to distance himself even further from his previous understanding of the Anglican Church's pure intellectual tradition. As an English citizen, Eliot would never convert to the provincial sect that he believed Roman Catholicism was in England. However, had Eliot lived in and adopted the literary tradition of nearly any other country in Europe with a Catholic history, it seems a logical conjecture that he would have converted to Roman Catholicism, thus better serving "orthodoxy" and "universality." Rather than being antinationalistic, Eliot developed his conception of the preservation of culture on a nationalistic foundation. The central paradox of Eliot's later thought is that artists and intellectuals become most universal by embracing their inherited traditions. For example, Eliot reassesses Yeats's late career by claiming that "in becoming more Irish . . . he became at the same time more universal."[79]

However, Eliot commissioned only cultures with historically worthy spiritual and intellectual traditions—particularly those in Europe, Russia, and the United States—to repossess and defend their nationalistic traditions. In *Notes Towards a Definition of Culture,* he adamantly refuses to articulate "an indictment of empire itself" and only criticizes imperialists' inability to enact "a complete cultural assimilation" of those nations or areas of the world where tradition failed his test of universal orthodoxy.[80] He subsequently adds, "The failure to arrive at the latter [comprehensive cultural orthodoxy] is a religious failure."[81] The radical nature of Eliot's nationalistic and imperial political views found its voice in the antidiasporic sentiment that circled throughout Europe, especially in Germany, Italy, and England: the very cultures Eliot judged most worth preserving.[82] In the *Four Quartets,* Eliot also espouses the union between his faith and nationalism. Throughout the work, Eliot confronts the significance of his own emigration from the United States, as well as that of his ancestors from England, but he does so to render a mystical journey in which mere geographical and political associations may be revalued in favor of a more meaningful spiritual identification with God and England.

FOUR QUARTETS

On one level, *Four Quartets* is an intensely personal work: Eliot's reflection on his very public voyage as an artist, a social and literary critic, and a spiritual thinker in the first half of the twentieth century. But he manages to maintain the aesthetic form, particularly the "impersonality" of voice(s) concentrating on objects to evoke emotion, that was central to his modernist approach to art. Eliot also continues to draw on Dante and Underhill in communicating his vision, although less explicitly. Much of the work consists of Eliot's mapping the path to mystical transcendence, but *Four Quartets* does not merely contemplate the beatific revelation. In his later "Dante" essay, Eliot remarks that the prejudice that affects "the whole of the *Paradiso* . . . is the prejudice that poetry not only must be found *through suffering* but can find its material only *in* suffering."[83] *Four Quartets* confronts suffering to transcend it. Eliot's journey of suffering and transcendence is not through hell, purgatory, and heaven, but through his personal, ancestral, and national past.

To embark on this spiritual journey through the past, Eliot learns to "sit still" in the present, as he petitions through the Virgin Mary at the end of *Ash-Wednesday.* He thereby reconciles himself with the past and attains what Underhill calls "The Illumination of the Self," the final stage of mystical development, in which "the mystic . . . has now a veritable foothold in that transcendental world" while remaining in the world.[84] This spiritual development allowed Eliot to continue his path as an amateur mystic while performing his public role as poet and critic. History both fascinated and haunted Eliot, and *Four Quartets* represents his attempt to make sense of it in the context of his vocation as poet and lay mystic. Eliot establishes the transcendent objective early in the poem in claiming "all time is eternally present" (4), but this transcendent perspective can only be achieved by confronting and reconciling with the past. Therefore, the poem moves toward the concrete, present-day environment of "Little Gidding" by exploring and revaluing different aspects of Eliot's identity, a purifying process that yields him a more secure English and mystical spiritual identity.

"Burnt Norton" casts a backward glance at "what might have been and what has been" (9), but Eliot refuses to permit sentimentality to invade his mystical vision. In fact, the poem warns against the potential tyranny of past regrets. Lyndall Gordon persuasively connects many allusions in this poem to Emily Hale, whom Eliot formally rejected as a marriage partner shortly after the publication of "Burnt Norton" in 1935.[85] Eliot imagines the possibilities of such a relationship in a "world of speculation" (8), an exercise that potentially could provide relief because "human kind / Cannot bear very much reality" (42–43). However, the imagery depicted in the fire-razed eighteenth-century mansion that provides the setting of the poem—"the empty alley"; "Dry the pool, dry concrete" (32, 34)—suggests that such a world remains morally barren, provides no reason for hope, and yields no sufficient answers.

Instead, the mystic seeks "the still point of the turning world / . . . Where past and future are gathered" (62, 65). E. M. Forster claimed that this desire for stillness took precedence over Eliot's religious objectives. "[Eliot] was not a mystic. *For Lancelot Andrewes* contains several well-turned compliments to religion and Divine Grace, but no trace of religious emotion. . . . What he seeks is not revelation, but stability."[86] But Eliot's demand for stability was not independent of, but rather a necessary precursor to, his mystical reflections in *Four Quartets*. Eliot suggests that self-knowledge requires a disciplined but not inhuman spiritual focus. Yet this state of contemplation is slippery and difficult to attain, and the mystic humbly admits to these limitations when meditating on the past. "I can only say, *there* we have been: but I cannot say where" (69).

As part of the process of grasping and then relinquishing self-knowledge, Eliot accepts that his artistic vocation is incapable of supporting eternal meaning. Unlike the Word of God,

> Words strain,
> Crack and sometimes break, under the burden,
> Under the tension, slip, slide, perish,
> Decay with imprecision, will not stay in place,
> Will not stay still.
>
> (149–53)

A vocation based on such unstable material certainly cannot provide the sole foundation on which to construct a timeless vision. However, the "Word in the desert" is eternal and resists "voices of temptation" (155–56). Eliot thus reestablishes the superiority of the Word/Logos/Christ over the words of human poetry. In "East Coker," Eliot assumes a more colloquial tone when reflecting on "the intolerable wrestle / With words and meanings" (70–71) and concludes, "The poetry does not matter / It was not (to start again) what one had expected" (71–72). Of course, the poetry does still matter, or there would be no *Quartets*, but it did not yield what Eliot had first hoped it might: a means to overcome the cultural, psychological, and spiritual challenges of modernity.

The sober tone pervading Eliot's revaluation of his creative objectives and personal fantasies in "Burnt Norton"—drastically evinced in the final lines "Ridiculous the waste sad time / Stretching before and after" (174–75)—pushes toward Eliot's revaluation of his ancestral identity in England in "East Coker." As Ford returned to Germany and converted to the Catholicism of his ancestors, so a converted Eliot in "East Coker" returned to Somerset where his ancestors the Elyots once practiced their Anglican faith. Eliot explains the necessity of this return: "In my beginning is my end" (1). Both Ford and Eliot moved toward the more traditional and more formal liturgical religion of their heritage, a homecoming somewhat paradoxically reinforcing their antidiasporic ideals at that time. But Eliot sought to transcend mere political or nationalistic identifications with his family's faith.

Circular imagery dominates the first section of "East Coker," in which Eliot meditates on centuries of the Elyot family genealogy. The narrator assumes a sixteenth-century voice in describing the marriage ceremonies, claiming that "On a Summer midnight" one can hear music and observe "dancing around the bonfire / The association of man and woman / In daunsinge, signifying matrimonie—/ A dignified and commodious sacrament" (25; 27–30). But this joyful description quickly drops into a much darker description of his ancestors' unions as "The time of the coupling of man and woman / And that of beasts. Feet rising and falling. / Eating and drinking. Dung and death" (44–46). These images recall the empty sexual endeavors of the modern world that Eliot depicts in *The Waste Land*. Eliot avoids the sentimental view that the twentieth century is the first to cheapen the spiritual meaning of sexuality, but he seems unsure of how to grasp his family's spiritual significance. The second section of "East Coker" capitalizes on the notion of almost endless, mindless regenerating by emphasizing man's mortality. Eliot again consciously guards against idealizing his ancestors and the great men of history: "Do not let me hear / Of the wisdom of old men, but rather of their folly" (93–94). The sentiment is self-censuring, as Eliot inclined toward glorifying the past when condemning the shortcomings of modernity. He now realizes ancestors and even saints of the past "all go into the dark" (101), as will those still living. "And we all go with them, into the silent funeral" (110).

Nevertheless, Eliot does not imply that men should ignore the past, a decision that would be egotistical and dangerous. Instead, he writes, "The only wisdom we can hope to acquire / is the wisdom of humility: humility is endless" (97–98). For the mystic, folly contains value because it teaches humility and encourages the renunciation of one's will in favor of Providence. This renunciation surfaces in the third part of "East Coker," where darkness itself transforms into a sign of God's love. "I said to my soul be still, and let the dark come upon you / Which shall be the darkness of God" (112–13). Eliot here draws on the Roman Catholic mystical tradition in an explicit way. As in St. John of the Cross's *Dark Night of the Soul,* the mystic does not bravely yet blindly withstand darkness and death until light and birth return; instead, the contemplative finds God most purely and powerfully in the moral desert, in spiritual darkness. Eliot directly quotes St. John's mystical axioms:

Shall I say it again? In order to arrive there,
To arrive where you are, to get from where you are not,

You must go by a way wherein there is no ecstasy.
In order to arrive at what you do not know
You must go by a way which is the way of Ignorance.

(136–40)

John of the Cross's "negative way" spirituality reinforces the central purpose of the *Quartets:* the exploration of knowledge and history (poetic/personal, ancestral, national/political) to gain self-knowledge and eventually make an act of self-renunciation.

Eliot consistently grounds this mystical vision in concrete terms: through language, memories, and then the physical aspects of the sacraments. While he philosophically considers the limitations of revelation of timeless union through marriage, he physically describes the union provided by the Eucharist: "The dripping blood our only drink, / The bloody flesh our only food" (167–68). It is this sacrament, and not marriage, that provides the authentic spiritual union between him and his ancestors. Eliot's revaluation of his forefathers has taught him that, in both poetic and spiritual endeavors, there are "men whom one cannot hope / To emulate—but there is no competition" (184–85). With the lessons of "East Coker" in mind, and the accompanying observation that "Home is where one starts from" (190), Eliot directs his mystical journey toward the homes of his youth on the shores of the Mississippi and the New England coast.

In "The Dry Salvages," Eliot identifies the American obsession with technology as an obstacle to the mystic's need for stillness and self-knowledge. Images of the Mississippi River slicing through the St. Louis of Eliot's youth honor the river's natural and spiritual power that technological Americans, "worshippers of the machine" (10), attempt to turn into a docile force. However, while man ignores its presence, the river's "god" drives the Mississippi toward the ocean, "Keeping his seasons and rages, destroyer, reminder / Of what men choose to forget" (7–8). These lines likewise reflect Eliot's acknowledgment that although he often "chooses to forget" his native land, it has had a formative influence.

Eliot revisited St. Louis in the late summer of 1936, with the region in economic depression. Drawing on this experience, the second section, with its refrain "Where is there an end of it?" emphasizes that the linear motion of capitalistic progress is not inherently valuable and conceals a repetitive cycle of suffering so evident in middle America of the 1930s. As far as man is concerned, "There is no end . . . / To the movement of pain that is painless and motionless, / To the drift of the sea and the drifting wreckage" (79, 81–82). The sea imagery brings the second part of the poem to the actual Dry Salvages off the coast of Massachusetts, not far from Harvard. But here, too, despite "the moments of happiness" (90), little can be concluded except "we had the experience but missed the meaning" (93) of youth and its pleasures.

Linear movements, signified by the river, time, and advanced forms of transportation, are not the paths of the mystic. The poem warns those on the figurative "train" of modernity on which "passengers are settled / To fruit, periodicals and business letters" (132–33), that mere motion will not lead to meaningful change. Eliot implies that technologically obsessed societies have no clue how to approach history and merely cast a "backward look behind the assurance / Of recorded history" (101–2). The term *recorded* suggests that men often ignore the spiritual version of history that Eliot explores throughout the *Quartets*, one that exposes folly and teaches humility. Eliot judges the explorations of history and science made by modern men—whether it be of "the womb, or tomb, or dreams"—as "usual / Pastimes and drugs, and features of the press" (194–95). When this society does cast a "half-look" at Eliot's version of history, it is faced with a "primitive terror" that threatens its comfort with the past and its security in the technologically controlled present (102–3).

Eliot repeatedly condemns those who mindlessly participate in the modern world with an incapacity for reflection. He ironically censures such ambitious souls. "Fare foreward, you who think that you are voyaging" (149). Constant, misdirected, irreverent motion that tries to outrun time renders meditation impossible. Only contemplating the Incarnation yields man a chance at morally efficacious progress because in that phenomenon "the impossible union / Of spheres of existence is actual," and "the past and future / Are conquered" (216–19). These lines reveal Eliot's belief that contemplation of the Divine conquers the tyranny of time and mortality. Although Eliot's imaginative (and physical) return to the United States leads him to criticize the moral efficacy of rampant technological development, he nonetheless finds mystical contemplation possible within the same environment. Even in the

United States, he can still "nourish . . . / The life of significant soil" (231; 233). The mystic therefore need not extract himself from the world to encounter the Presence that will help guide him to transcend himself and time. However, Eliot's own spiritual and political identities have taken root and must be harvested in England, where he returns in "Little Gidding."

Eliot's return to England does not mean *Four Quartets* is circular or exhibits no progress. He claims the fruit of the mystical exploration of the world of possibility, and of the past and future, will be "to arrive where we started / And know the place for the first time" (241–42). Exploration gives the mystic a transcendent perspective that permits an authentic, revised self-conception, which juxtaposes the physical reality of the Second World War (and suffering in general) with the spiritual reality of the mystic's transformation. The setting for "Little Gidding," a monastic chapel destroyed by Cromwell's soldiers in the sixteenth century, symbolizes Eliot's identification with the Catholic tradition in England, especially when it suffered at the hands of Calvinistic movements. Meanwhile, Eliot wrote and published the poem in 1942 while Germany regularly bombed England. Thus, the chapel serves as an important place of prayer in a time of violent conflict. While Eliot must pray and suffer in England, his slightly less Anglo-centric worldview enables him to remember:

> There are other places
> Which also are the world's end, some at the sea jaws,
> Or over a dark lake, in a desert or a city—
> But this is the nearest, in place and time,
> Now and in England.

(35–40)

Each image refers to an intense battle location in the Second World War: the air and sea battle with Japan in South-East Asia, West Africa, London, Berlin, and Warsaw; and, as Hugh Kenner notes, each setting also refers to the homes of saints.[87] Unable to fight, the mystic must pray and thereby unite himself with those who pray in other regions, as well as with those who prayed in past centuries at this same place, "Where prayer has been valid" (48). The mystic Eliot's response to not participating in the Second World War is markedly more at peace with his spiritual and even national purpose than when he did not fight in the Great War.

The fire and water imagery of the second section corresponds with Germany's fiery destruction of London, as well as with the baptismal and purgative themes that dominate Eliot's mature poetry. The purification process Eliot describes transforms him into a more secure poet, Englishman, and mystic, and he systematically confronts his old identity. First, he encounters in a timeless world "some dead master," an embodiment of Yeats, who counsels, "My thoughts and theory which you have forgotten. / These things have served their purpose: let them be" (91, 112–13). Eliot thereby acknowledges as well as transcends the influence of tradition, and he can more confidently become his own self-sufficient spiritual poet. He also reassesses his nationalism and its tradition and recognizes that speaking in the name of England can quickly devolve into speaking for oneself:

> Love of a country
> Begins as attachment to our own field of action
> And comes to find that action of little importance
> Though never indifferent.
>
> (159–62)

The passage shows an awareness of the dangers of nationalism without condemning it. Nationalism is "never indifferent" when absorbed properly as a means to cultural understanding (for Eliot as a poet and critic) and spiritual identity.

These subtle revisions of his earlier views on the relationship between faith and nationalism signify Eliot's resistance to idolizing his own version of tradition, which now serves rather than directs his spiritual transformation. Eliot likewise accepts a slightly less polemical political approach. "We cannot revive old factions / We cannot restore old policies / Or follow an antique drum" (185–87). He explicitly delineates the purpose of his exploration of the past throughout the *Quartets*, "This is the use of memory: / For liberation / . . . From the future as well as the past" (156–59). For the mystic, only the present yields freedom from history and access to the sacred. Yet the present is often a place of violence as it was in wartime England. Eliot describes, "The dove descending breaks the air / With flame of incandescent terror" (200–201), in which the "dove" paradoxically alludes to the Holy Spirit and the German bombs setting London aflame. From the mystic's perspective, England must endure despite the tragedy of another almost inconceivably destructive war, and then, as the English Catholic Saint Juliana of Norwich once assured, "And all shall be well and / All manner of thing shall be well" (255–56).

Yet Eliot offers no sentimental assurance of comfort or success at the end of *Four Quartets*. In fact, he suggests that God permits human suffering within the context of free will that pain may teach men to turn to him. "Who then devised the torment? Love. / Love is the unfamiliar Name" that will try mankind "by either fire or fire" (207–8; 213). This imagery signifies the consuming fires of lust or even hell and the purifying fires of purgatory. Eliot's use of the word *devised* is somewhat unorthodox because it seems to imply that God creates suffering rather than permits it, a notion that conflicts with traditional Christian belief that suffering is engendered entirely by man and only allowed and used by God for his own purposes. Because Eliot fixates on the redemptive means of suffering in his spiritual thinking, it is not surprising that he would lean toward the unorthodox notion that God authors suffering. Accordingly, he concludes the *Four Quartets* with an emphasis on the price of belief: faith grants "A condition of complete simplicity / (Costing not less than everything)" (253–54). The parentheses enclose the crucial purgatorial process of which *Four Quartets* represents yet another stage, but one that also offers a view of the simplicity of paradise that transcends the necessary sacrifice.

CONCLUSION

Although the *Four Quartets* would be Eliot's final major verse publication, he continued his career as a playwright and social critic for more than two decades until his death in 1965. The plays are not as formally modernist or technically experimental as his verse, but they do model Eliot's emphasis in the *Quartets* on sacrifice as the path to self-knowledge and humility, vocation, and redemption. Just before the *Quartets*, Eliot undertakes the theme of martyrdom in his depiction of Thomas Becket in *Murder in the Cathedral* (1935). His willingness to focus on a Catholic saint who died defending the rights of the papacy against those of an English monarch suggests the extent to which Eliot imagined his heritage as Catholic and not Anglican—or, as he clarified, his Anglo-Catholic faith was "a branch of the Catholic Church, the Catholic Church in England." In the play, Thomas tells the knights who will enact his martyrdom, "I submit my cause to the judgement of Rome. / But if you kill me, I shall rise from my tomb / To submit my cause before God's throne."[88] Yet, ultimately, Thomas's sacrifice is not made in the name of any doctrinal or political position, but to place his own life in service of God rather than that of a man—even if that man be the king of England. As in the *Quartets*, Eliot's portrayal of Thomas does not signify a rejection of a national loyalty but a recasting of its purpose in service to Christianity.

In *The Cocktail Party* (1949), Eliot addresses the notion of contemporary sanctity, which rarely concerns national-religious conflicts, by depicting the difficulty of the two primary means to sanctification in modern society: marriage and the religious life. The marriage of Edward and Lavinia Chamberlayne is saved when they accept their own limitations and inability to love each other or even know each other very well. Celia Coplestone, one-time mistress of Edward, leaves the London social scene entirely to enter a Christian religious order where she is savagely killed by "natives." On the surface, neither fate appears appealing, let alone glorious. But Sir Henry Harcourt-Reilly, a psychologist whose insight directs these characters to the proper vocation, understands that it is the tedious processes of each day that purify one's intentions and life. For each of these figures, the initial steps taken to follow the proper vocation seem to compromise their social integrity; but Reilly insists, "You will find that you survive humiliation / And that's an experience of incalculable value."[89] Reilly believes that humiliation eradicates pride and leads to the humility to fulfill one's vocation.

For most, this vocation does not require the martyrdom of a Thomas Beckett or Celia but the working out of one's salvation in mundane conflicts. This process, too, has eternal consequences and leads to the glory of salvation, as Eliot argues in the *Quartets*. Because this theme is so essential to the latter half of Eliot's career, it is not surprising that he believed *Four Quartets* was his supreme contribution not only to his own corpus, but also to England's spiritual and creative tradition. However, despite his insistence that "I rest on [the *Four Quartets.*] I stand or fall on them," *The Waste Land* remains his most formative and influential work of modernism and of English literature.[90] Even a man with Eliot's critical weight does not possess the privilege of determining his own place in the tradition, and *The Waste Land* offers a vision quite simply more common to the shared experience of humanity in modernity than does the mystical vision of the *Four Quartets*.

As Eliot's career waned, the voices of those hostile to his notions of tradition, religion, and politics grew in number and in volume, motivated by Eliot's sometimes bitter condemnations of former friends and his allegedly unrepentant anti-Semitism.[91] Unlike Hopkins, Eliot anticipated and accepted his own failure to transform the spirituality of literature or English society. As early as 1931, Eliot pronounced in his typically ominous tone, "The World is trying the experiment of attempting to form a civilized but non-Christian mentality. The experiment will fail; but we must be very patient in awaiting its collapse; meanwhile redeeming the time."[92] *Four Quartets* portrays his personal effort to "redeem the time." It is a public disclosure of a very private spirit. While Eliot brought a significant amount of resistance on himself, his prejudices are discernible if problematic, and his verse and prose remain important in aesthetic, spiritual, and political contexts. He may have loved "his doom," but only that it might purify and not consume.

4

Evelyn Waugh: The Economics of Salvation

*He had too-great expectations of his fellow creatures and too-
great expectations even of his Church.*
—Graham Greene on Evelyn Waugh

LIKE T. S. ELIOT, EVELYN WAUGH'S FATHER, ARTHUR, PRACTICED HIS
Anglican faith dutifully, edited and wrote for various journals, and
aligned himself with the Tory party. But Arthur denounced *The
Waste Land* as "premature decreptitude" and refused to alter his
judgment even of Eliot's later work, which was influenced by Eliot's conversion to Anglicanism and publicly professed support of
"royalist" politics.[1] Arthur's quarrel with Eliot was aesthetic, and
many religiously and politically conservative Englishmen of his
generation—as well as Evelyn's generation—believed their traditions could not be adequately articulated or defended in the experimental aesthetic forms chosen by the literary modernists. G. K.
Chesterton likewise criticized Eliot's poetry and wrote a parody of
The Hollow Men that concluded, "And *they* may end with a
whimper / But *we* will end with a bang."[2] Chesterton's "*we*" presumably includes conservative Catholics like himself and excludes
all modernists. In a more subversive attack on Eliot, C. S. Lewis,
a conservative Anglican, composed a parody of modernist verse
and submitted it to T. S. Eliot's journal, *Criterion*. Lewis revealed
his uncharitable intentions to fellow poet William Force Stead,
calling his piece "very nonsensical, but with a flavour of dirt all
through," sent "in the hope that [Eliot] will be taken in and publish it."[3] Eliot refused Lewis's bait. While both Lewis and Chesterton later maintained cordial relationships with Eliot, neither
reassessed their aesthetic criticisms of his work.

If there was a cohesive Catholic revival in English literary circles
in the early twentieth century, high modernist converts kept a

measured distance. Evelyn Waugh and Graham Greene were rare artists conversant with both the modernists and the other less aesthetically experimental literary converts, including Chesterton, Hilaire Belloc, Christopher Dawson, and Dorothy Sayers. A young Greene insisted, "Poetry would indeed be dull if all were revolutionaries, none conservatives."[4] Of course, neither Greene's politics nor his art were conservative; thus, the more intriguing rift lay between the politically conservative modernists and the equally conservative proponents of traditional aesthetics. Waugh straddled this chasm. A Chesterton speech at Oxford proved one of the early influences on Waugh's conversion; meanwhile, he championed Eliot's poetic technique, even if he could not apply it successfully himself.[5] Although Waugh's aesthetic practices were somewhat less experimental than Eliot's, his project as a novelist was similar to Eliot's as a poet and essayist: both aimed to portray highly liturgical Christianity as a vestige of religious, political, and cultural traditions in a provocative manner that revealed the potential of faith as a relevant social force.

As modernist forms of art became less shocking to public sensibility, the gap between the modernist converts and aesthetically conservative Catholic converts began to close. A mistrust of capitalism, particularly because of its negative influence on the moral health of English culture and assault on traditional class divisions, bound these artists together politically. For example, Belloc repeatedly warned of the dangers of usury and, more broadly, identified capitalism as a symptom of the Protestant Reformation—echoing Max Weber's thesis in *The Protestant Ethic and the Spirit of Capitalism*.[6] C. S. Lewis sounded a similar alarm concerning usury-based modern economic systems in *Mere Christianity*, while characteristically avoiding Catholic-Protestant distinctions.[7] Eliot probably gives the most succinct and eloquent statement summarizing this group's suspicion of capitalism in *The Idea of a Christian Society* (1939): "Surely there is something wrong in our attitude towards money. The acquisitive, rather than the creative and spiritual instincts, are encouraged. . . . I am by no means sure that it is right for me to improve my income by investing in the shares of a company, making I know not what, operating perhaps thousands of miles away, and in the control of which I have no effective voice—but which is recommended as a sound investment."[8] Eliot's statement reverberates with Waugh's and

Ford's mistrust of the globalized economy that was fast diminishing the last remnants of the English aristocracy after the devaluation of land in the wake of industrialism.

Following suit, Waugh's primary interest in economics was to protect the traditions of the landed class, even if that effort looked increasingly quixotic after each world war. Although Waugh's nationalism hardly reached Eliot's pitch, he nonetheless felt that the preservation of England's landed class and the maintenance of its traditions in the modern world were essential to preserving English identity. As late as 1959, Waugh still clamored, "The most dismal tendency I see is that with our class system we are fast losing all national character. . . . There were different vocabularies and intonations of speech; different styles of dress. Now all those things that gave salt to the English life . . . are being dissolved."[9] Ironically, Waugh was not born into the upper class, but he behaved like an aristocrat as soon as he possessed the means. Like Ford and Eliot, Waugh's conservative Christian faith partially stemmed from a desire to preserve cultural tradition. He believed that because England was Catholic for most of its history and had in the nineteenth century turned agnostic, "The Catholic structure still lies lightly buried beneath every phase of English life; history, topography, law, archaeology everywhere reveal Catholic origins."[10] Waugh's conversion hardly meant an abandonment of an important strain of national identity as it did for Hopkins and other converts from High Church Anglicanism, but it did complicate his desired social ascent.

Waugh's fascination with the upper class can be traced to the somewhat stubborn but inarticulate right-wing approach to politics he developed at Oxford. He confesses in his autobiography, "I proclaimed myself a Tory but could not have defined Tory policy on any current topic."[11] Even his involvement in various politically based social groups such as "The Hypocrites" and the Oxford Carlton Club stemmed from his desire to rise socially rather than an intention to become informed politically. Waugh's casually conservative approach to politics at Oxford mirrored his religious practices, both of which he inherited in part from Arthur. According to Waugh, his father "had a brief Anglo-Catholic phase" but he eventually returned to a more standard form of Anglicanism; Waugh explains, "[My father's] complaint against Catholics was their clarity of dogma and I doubt whether he had a genuine intellectual conviction about any element of his creed."[12] Waugh later mocked his family's vague faith, although he blamed figures such as the "preposterous parson" of his Low Church home parish who "when he felt festal . . . decreed a feast, whatever the season or occasion marked on the calendar."[13] Such behavior appeared ridiculous to Waugh as a devout Catholic (as it would to a High Anglican) who followed the strict ecclesiastical calendar.

Waugh also found humor in his own immature faith and political views. "I, the professed Christian, merely scorned industrial and commercial capitalists and relished the arguments that proved them villains," although he neither devised nor fully grasped them.[14] Although Waugh generally retained these views in his adult life, he by then could articulate concrete historical and political support for them. His religiously inspired political views aligned him with many conservative intellectuals of the period. Eliot, for example, really did "scorn industrial and commercial capitalists" because he was a "professed Christian." Eliot warns in *The Idea of a Christian Society,* "And as for the Christian who is not conscious of his dilemma . . . he is becoming more and more de-Christianized by all sorts of unconscious pressure: paganism holds all the most valuable advertising space."[15] The connection between liturgically formal, conservative Christian beliefs and the anticapitalist political views that Eliot's comment highlights is implicit in Waugh's preconversion novels and partially explains his eventual conversion to Catholicism.

SATIRICAL NOVELS

Waugh's steadfast identification with England's landed class late in his life contrasts conspicuously, at least on the surface, with his criticism of the dwindling aristocracy in his preconversion satirical novels, especially *Decline and Fall* and *Vile Bodies.* However, the satire in these works is more critical of capitalism and its proponents than it is of the aristocracy who lose their integrity by association with it. Waugh mocks the upper class's decadence and vulnerability to superficial advertising, as well as their neglect of the historical social roles he believed they were entrusted to preserve. Ultimately, the satire in these novels is more explicit and in many ways less complex than that of other modernist novels that critique the upper classes; for example, in E. M. Forster's *Howards End* and even Ford's *Good Soldier,* the satire is woven into the narrative more seamlessly than in Waugh's novels, in which the humor takes precedence over the social commentary. These works also betray some of Waugh's sense of inferiority with the upper class, or at least a lingering sense of exclusion from it.

In Waugh's first successful satirical novel, *Decline and Fall* (1928), he takes aim at British education and the Anglican Church's failure to provide any sort of meaningful instruction in religious matters during his youth. After earning his degree at Oxford in 1925, Waugh reluctantly accepted a position as a teacher at Arnold House, a small boarding school in Denbighshire. Although he remained only three semesters, he despised the work so much that, according to his own account, he attempted to drown himself but eventually swam back to shore.[16] The school and its various teachers and students proved fertile ground for Waugh's satire of English religious education.

Mr. Pendergast, the chaplain at Llanabba, Waugh's fictional boarding school, previously served as an Anglican clergyman; however, he left his position in the church because, as he explains, "I had *Doubts.*"[17] Pendergast's vague religious conflict highlights Waugh's criticism of the lack of doctrinal and religious knowledge possessed by many Anglicans in positions of authority. It is significant that Waugh formulates this complaint well before his own conversion. Furthermore, the inadequate response of the Anglican hierarchy to the chaplain's difficulties in the novel satirically echoes the apathetic answers of church leaders to basic spiritual and theological questions that continued to surface among the men of Waugh's generation. Pendergast explains, "[A]fter my *Doubts* began . . . I asked my bishop. He said that he didn't think the point really arose as far as my practical duties as a parish priest were concerned."[18] The irony is pointed because the bishop's statement is not evasive but honest: the problem with the Anglican Church, Waugh suggests, is that fundamental spiritual concerns such as prayer or belief in the efficacy of the sacraments play negligible roles in the Anglican parish's daily functions.

Seven years before the publication of *Decline and Fall,* Waugh professed, "I have ceased to be a Christian. . . . I have realized that for the last two terms I have been an atheist in all except the courage to admit it to myself."[19] Waugh's stage of unbelief would prove to be relatively short, but in his autobiography, he blames the Anglican Church for causing it by failing to catechize its students. "I think at least half the Upper Sixth in my time were avowed agnostics or atheists. And no antidote was ever offered us. I do not remember ever being urged to read a book of Christian philosophy."[20] Students were presumed to be Christian without being exposed to any formal intellectual Christian instruction; and when they renounced the faith, they were never questioned. Instead, the influences of modern psychological and scientific advances were blamed for ruining Christian education or triumphed for disproving its efficacy. In *Decline and Fall*, Waugh metaphorically explores the consequences of the Anglican Church's catechetical neglect. Pendergast becomes a prison chaplain because he has been imprisoned symbolically by his own lack of religious understanding. He is grotesquely murdered by a cultish psychotic who believes God has called him to kill others. His life thus is ended pathetically by a fanatic who pursues his own religious ignorance with zeal rather than apathy.

The main character of the novel, Paul Pennyfeather, holds sincere and well-informed religious beliefs, but he is prevented from studying to become a minister because of his ill-fated encounters with the upper class, the other major object of Waugh's satire. After being expelled from Oxford as a scapegoat for infractions committed by an upper-class club that the administration protects, Paul teaches at Llanabba and unwisely proposes to Margot Best-Chetwynde, an upper-class mother of one of the students, who subsequently involves the ignorant Paul in an international prostitution ring. His eventual arrest follows the pattern set earlier in the novel: Paul suffers for the errors of the rich who escape punishment. Waugh increases the irony at Paul's trial when his prison sentence is extended because he allegedly attempted "to drag down to his own pitiable depths of depravity a lady of beauty, rank, and stainless reputation."[21] Because Waugh was struggling for his own livelihood at the time he wrote the novel, he trashes the aristocracy, who waste an opportunity to be productive, through his depiction of their decadent behavior.

Through Paul's experience, Waugh also ironically imagines prison as one setting where he might have the freedom to write. Paul's monthlong solitary confinement proves to be "among the happiest of Paul's life" owing to the regular schedule, the freedom to follow spiritual and intellectual interests, and protection from the upper class.[22] The similarities between monasteries and prisons cannot be ignored: Sebastian Flyte in *Brideshead Revisited* desires similar freedom from his own aristocratic family so that he might become a contemplative. Paul's vocation, however, is not to the monastic life but to the Anglican priesthood; he gains his freedom to follow this path when a guilt-ridden former Oxford club member arranges for Paul's "official" death during a staged appendicitis operation. Although Paul has regained freedom, Waugh implies that those trying to associate with the aristocracy may lose their identity, especially if they are not familiar with the unjust components of the social system.

In *Vile Bodies*, Waugh's comic turn grows more absurd and the social implications more serious than in *Decline and Fall*. His writing of the novel coincided with his own brief courtship and briefer marriage in 1928 to Evelyn Gardner, herself a child of wealth and a dysfunctional home. Evelyn and "She-Evelyn," as she was affectionately (or derisively) known, were introduced to each other through the London party scene and attempted to maintain that social circle while married. The two were divorced shortly after Waugh's wife admitted to her adulterous relationship with another mundane and shallow partier. Although Waugh willingly participated in this frivolous lifestyle, he also recognized its moral vacuity and exploited that very issue in *Vile Bodies*. Ostensibly, the novel centers on Adam Fenwick-Symes, a young journalist who covers the upper class in London and embellishes stories—or even constructs entirely false ones—for a tabloid press. Adam intends to marry the wealthy and ignorant Nina Blount, but he cannot garner enough money from his writing of books and his journalism. Yet Adam's story actually is secondary to Waugh's portrayal of the party scene itself and the media, the language, and the attitude toward life that surround it.

Waugh ridicules the media for promoting this empty lifestyle and setting it up as an ideal to which all classes should aspire. The media's influence extends beyond its cycle of propping up one social hero or heroine while defaming another: it also controls the public's attitudes toward politics and art. For example, one of the first columns Adam fabricates concerns "a sculptor called Provna, the son of a Polish nobleman, who lived in a top-floor studio in Grosvenor House" and allegedly creates constructions made of "cork, vulcanite and steel."[23] Naturally, Adam claims all of his work is "in private hands" and therefore cannot be shown, but the author insists the Metropolitan Museum in New York "had been negotiating for some time to purchase a specimen, but so far had been unable to outbid the collectors."[24] Waugh's satire mocks the public's opinion of art, which is driven by superficial values. These values include false perceptions of rarity, which leads Adam to claim his fictional artist is a Pole named Provna; modern aesthetic form, as is indicated by the unique combination of materials in these imaginary sculptures; and the collections' rumored monetary value, which is determined by unseen forces in the public and private art spheres. In *Decline and Fall,* Waugh makes a similar attack on modern forms of art through his portrayal of a German architect Otto Friedrich Silenus, who states, "The problem of architecture as I see it . . . is the problem of all art—the elimination of the human element from the consideration of form. The only perfect building must be the factory, because that is built to house machines, not men."[25] Although Waugh boldly mocked modern architecture, he refused to make such an attack on modernist poets or novelists—although he did disdain the Dadaists, Futurists, and other groups of the avant-garde—probably because he understood the broader message of the high modernist's fragmented forms in the novel and in poetry and believed it contained a redemptive aspect that he could not identify in most examples of modern art.

The media also defined, or possibly more often parroted, the chic vocabulary employed by the wealthy dilettantes of the period. Waugh creatively uses this corrupted language throughout much of his narrative, a classic modernist move perfected by Joyce and Eliot. The term *divine* serves as the most excessive and frequent example of verbal decadence in *Vile Bodies,* and the characters apply it to almost any mundane occurrence. Waugh deliberately uses a word that originally held spiritual significance to highlight the characters' lack of spiritual sensibility. His most satiric and pathetic application of the term occurs when Nina responds to her first sexual experience with Adam by observing, "I don't think that this is divine at all. . . . It's given me a pain."[26] The irony here is characteristically more tragic than humorous. In particular, Waugh's satirical depiction of sex and marriage gives *Vile Bodies* the gravity not present in his earlier works of satire, and it reinforces his disillusion with the urban social scene of the 1920s.

The one prominent Catholic figure in the novel, the Jesuit priest Father Rothschild, issues a penetrating assessment of the state of this energetic but morally hollow generation: "I don't think that people ever *want* to lose their faith in religion or anything else. I know very few young people, but it seems to me that they are all possessed with an almost fatal hunger for permanence. I think all these divorces show that."[27] Waugh's willingness to place this perceptive observation in the mouth of a Jesuit gives evidence of his growing interest in Catholicism. Waugh was exposed to Catholicism through Teresa Jungman and Olivia Greene, two of Waugh's infatuations at Oxford who both converted to Catholicism before Waugh. But his encounters with the Jesuit Father Martin D'Arcy, a well-known priest in upper-echelon English society (and Master of Campion Hall, Oxford, from 1932 to 1945) who influenced the conversions of many wealthy and important young men and women, likely inspired Waugh's positive portrayal of the insightful Father Rothschild.

Unfortunately, Adam does not have the moral integrity to turn toward Catholicism or reform his life. The only significant event that might save him from a life of futility is war. When the outbreak of another war is announced, the narrator refers to the event as "the most terrible and unexpected thing."[28] But Waugh implicitly satirizes this reflexive description, because war was certainly not unexpected (although it would be delayed for another decade); and for men like Adam, the news was not "terrible," because it gave him a chance to break free from the boredom of his life. In 1924, Waugh himself confessed to a friend, "You know . . . what we want is another war. I become more and more convinced of that everyday. . . . We also know that when there is a war the fighting people at least have moments of really intense enjoyment and really intense misery."[29] Waugh's search for meaningful experience, which his trivial, wealthy social circle could not provide, lies behind his satirical portrayal of his own corner of society in *Decline and Fall* and *Vile Bodies*. However, religious conversion, and not war, ultimately would provide Waugh a means of reaching his objective.

CONVERSION

After separating from Evelyn Gardner less than a year after their marriage, Waugh plummeted into severe depression. Richard and Elizabeth Plunkett Greene, a married couple who had recently converted to Catholicism, offered Waugh a vacant room in their flat in Holland Park and became a source of psychological and spiritual comfort. Although circumstantially important, neither Waugh's relationship with the Greenes nor the depression resulting from his divorce was the most influential factor in his conversion. What Waugh sought, much like Eliot, was a fortifying spiritual answer to the more comprehensive problem of the amorality of modern urban life. Waugh was disgusted with the spiritual state of society; his frustration with the capitalistic culture that suddenly took such a strong hold on all classes of English society surfaces throughout his satirical novels. For instance, in *Vile Bodies*, Adam cannot convince Nina's father, Colonel Blount, that he is not in fact a vacuum cleaner salesman. The colonel cannot comprehend why anyone would come to visit him without making a sales pitch.[30] The humor of such scenes should not conceal Waugh's serious attention to the absence of noneconomic human interaction in modern society. After his divorce, Waugh concluded that only a universal and unified church could resist the stultifying spiritual and psychological influences of modernity, and he determined to convert to Catholicism on what he (somewhat dubiously) insisted were entirely intellectual and not emotional grounds.

Other artists and intellectuals issued a similar diagnosis of modern society's ills in the first decades of the twentieth century. Max Weber's 1904 sociological treatise *The Protestant Ethic and the Spirit of Capitalism* represents the best-known articulation of the theory that modern man's difficulties stemmed from religious change. Although Weber never converted to Catholicism, he regarded the Reformation as the key event that propelled the alienating economic and social systems of the early twentieth century. He blamed the Reformation for causing man to experience "a feeling of unprecedented loneliness" owing mostly to the fact that, "[In] the most important thing in his life, his eternal salvation, he was forced to follow his path alone to meet a destiny which had been decreed for him from eternity. No one could help him. No priest, for the chosen one can understand the word of God only in his own heart. No sacraments . . . they are not the means to the attainment of grace, but only the subjective *externa subsidia* of faith. No Church . . . even no God."[31] Weber blames Calvinistic Protestantism specifically, with its emphasis on predestination and its pseudomonastic approach to social and economic life, for fueling Europe's depersonalized modern economic machine.[32] Since its publication, Weber's work has been judged important but in many ways simplistic, yet his argument remains valuable in reflecting the way men like Waugh living in the period assessed their own condition in relation to the social world. [33] As Weber's analysis suggests, and as Waugh came to believe, the Catholic sacraments provide a material answer to the moral corruption caused by materialism.

For Waugh, Catholicism also presented an adequate answer to what he determined were the monetary and aesthetic excesses of the Anglican Church. In the *Daily Express* column Waugh wrote announcing his conversion in 1930, he defensively insists that his conversion had nothing to do with the seductive beauty of Catholic religious art and architecture. "In this country, where all the finest ecclesiastical buildings are in the hands of the Anglican Church . . . the purely aesthetic appeal is, on the whole, rather against the Roman Church."[34] The essay reveals little about Waugh's personal reasons for conversion, although he resolutely contends that he did not convert because "the Jesuits have got hold of him," because "he is captivated by ritual," or because "he wants to have his mind made up for him"—all stock explanations of the English public for twentieth-century conversions to Catholicism.[35] Waugh, however, does highlight his understanding of the difference between his conversion and that of Eliot and C. S. Lewis's to High Church Anglicanism by insisting that Catholicism's claims to universality must be honored over nationalistic identification: "Those who regard conversion to Roman Catholicism as an unpatriotic doctrine—a surrender to Italian domination—seem to miss the whole idea of universality."[36] While such comments might seem to align Waugh with the ultramontanes, who emphasized the Vatican's authority over Catholics in England, the faith Waugh practiced in the following decades mirrored that of the recusant tradition in England: he preferred a simple liturgy, was an intellectual Catholic who rarely evangelized with any sort of fer-

vor, and believed the landed gentry, not emotional converts or
Continental immigrants, were the rightful preservers of English
Catholicism. Waugh's description of his conversion reveals the extent to which he simply read his way through history and theology
into the Catholic Church: there was to be no blinding or falling off
horses. Father D'Arcy, who oversaw Waugh's conversion,
claimed, "I have never myself met a convert who so strongly based
his assents on truth . . . with only an intellectual passion."[37]

Despite this reserved approach to the faith, Waugh's first novel
released after his conversion, *Black Mischief,* ignited friction in
Catholic circles for passages some clergy and lay readers misread
as indecent condemnations of Catholic thought. Seth, a twenty-
four-year-old Oxford graduate, is summoned home to become emperor of Azania, a fictional island nation in the Indian Ocean. He
intends to transform his barbaric and cannibalistic country into a
modern nation-state. To begin this process, Seth hires as his "Minister of Modernization" a fellow Oxford graduate, the English
Basil Seal—who makes appearances in numerous Waugh novels
as a staple dandy character, most notably in *Put Out More
Flags.*"[38] Waugh's irony here stems from his postdivorce travels in
Africa, where European colonial efforts ranged from unreasonable
and cumbersome to downright ridiculous. The irony intensifies
when it becomes clear that Basil's original intention in traveling to
Africa was to escape the confines of modernity, but he gladly accepts a position that requires him to impose that same modern system on an "undeveloped" nation.

But the controversy in the English Catholic press regarding the
novel did not directly concern Waugh's depiction of colonization.
It began when Cardinal Bourne, Catholic archbishop of Westminster, wrote a letter in *The Tablet* condemning Waugh's irreverent
treatment of the Catholic teaching on birth control. Bourne misread Waugh's satirical intentions in having Seth conjure up a governmental program for modernization that would encourage the
nation to use contraception. Waugh satirizes proponents of birth
control when Seth creates an absurd "Birth Control Pageant"
(which he promotes through an "encyclical"!) taking the form of
a parade complete with "Azanian beauties with typewriters, tennis
rackets, motor bicycling goggles, telephones, hitch hiking outfits
and other patents of modernity inspired by the European illustrated papers."[39] The women also carry signs with messages, in-

cluding, "WOMEN OF TOMORROW DEMAND AN EMPTY CRADLE" and "THROUGH STERILITY TO CULTURE."[40] Waugh's intention was to mock both the colonizers and those loyal to them among the colonized who celebrated the technological advances and progressive moral beliefs they thought would assuage modern social ills. Not surprisingly, Waugh found it mind-boggling and disconcerting that the archbishop could so blatantly miss that progressive capitalists were the intended object of satire.

In fact, Waugh underscores his point in the novel when he portrays the resistance group "Nestorian Catholic Action," whom he describes as "muscular Christians who for many weeks now had been impatiently biding their time to have a whack at the modernists."[41] This passage demonstrates that Waugh understands the Catholic position on these social questions and draws the lines of battle between "modernists" and Catholics. In his letter responding to the archbishop's condemnation, Waugh insisted, "Like all Catholics I regard Birth Control as a practice which is a personal sin and an insidious social evil," while at the same time admitting, "It is painful to have to explain one's jokes."[42]

Black Mischief would be the last of Waugh's unapologetically over-the-top satirical novels, and it is unfortunate if the Catholic response to the novel made him reluctant to engage in such provocative works again. His next publication, *A Handful of Dust*, likewise takes aim at the social consequences of modernity, but the comedy is more subtle and deliberately tragic than in *Black Mischief*. Ultimately, Graham Greene assumed the role of the twentieth century's most controversial Catholic novelist, and, ironically, Waugh sometimes censured him for his potentially scandalous portrayal of Catholics in his novels.[43]

Marriage and the English Country Estate

Waugh published *A Handful of Dust* in 1934 while awaiting a decision on his application to the Catholic Archdiocese of Westminster for annulment of his marriage to Evelyn Gardner, a process overseen by none other than the same Cardinal Bourne who so incautiously denounced *Black Mischief*. Originally, Waugh was reluctant to submit the request because of the painful and often embarrassing intrusion of privacy each trial necessitated, not because of his relationship with the cardinal, whose death in 1935 only slowed the seemingly interminable process. Ultimately, the annulment was not granted until July 4, 1936, almost three years after Waugh's initial application was submitted. Years later, Waugh deemed the annulment process one of the most urgent matters in need of reform in the Catholic Church, and this frustration, along with the emotional scar from his divorce, likely informs his cynical presentation of modern marriage in *A Handful of Dust*.[44]

The novel consists of a multifaceted attack on the shallowness of both the privileged and middle classes in modern England, and the title echoes Eliot's line from the "The Burial of the Dead" section of *The Waste Land:* "I will show you fear in a handful of dust" (30). Waugh thereby implies that he reads *The Waste Land* as a similar attack on modernity; however, Tony Last, the apparent victim of the modern environment in *A Handful of Dust*, does not appear on the verge of redemption as does Eliot's narrator at the end of *The Waste Land*. Tony represents the prototypical English aristocrat: he marries the beautiful and wealthy Brenda Last, lives in his beloved country home, and regularly attends Anglican services at his nearby parish. Yet while Tony cherishes each of these aspects of his life, he ultimately proves himself to be a superficial man who cannot penetrate into the deeper historical or spiritual significance of his social position.

Despite the highly suspicious and adulterous behavior of his wife Brenda, Tony takes their marriage for granted and attends to her complaints concerning the state of their relationship as he might those of a servant. Brenda succumbs without resistance to the dazzling but superficial appeal of modern London, produced by the social parties, tabloid coverage, and advertisements that Waugh derided in *Vile Bodies*. Although Tony is not susceptible to the enticements that lure his wife, Waugh depicts him as a man mindlessly enjoying traditions he does not comprehend. For example, Tony's Anglican faith has little to do with spiritual commitment, as he merely mimics a pattern of behavior passed on from more spiritually engaged generations: "Tony invariably wore a dark suit on Sundays and a stiff white collar. He went to church, where he sat in a large pitch pine pew, put in by his great-grandfather. . . . When service was over he stood for a few minutes and chatted affably with the vicar's sister and the people from the village. . . . That was the simple, mildly ceremonious order of his Sunday morning, which had evolved, more or less spontaneously, from the more severe practices of his parents."[45] The narrator assumes Tony's perspective if not his voice and reveals that he has little interest in prayer or the liturgy, the elements of the service that might actually give him a meaningful experience rather than merely a convenient way to pass a few quiet weekend hours. Waugh also intends to use such passages as attacks on what he saw as the lack of depth in Anglican spirituality. In *Edmund Campion*, Waugh's biography of the English saint published the year after *Handful of Dust*, he again emphasizes his belief that the Anglican faith had its basis in empty forms of spirituality. Waugh condescendingly portrays the nature of the queen's faith after the Reformation. "Elizabeth's personal inclinations were towards something mildly ceremonious in public worship; she kept a cross and candles in her chapel . . . she liked to think that her church had retained something from the tradition of her ancestors."[46] This description highlights Waugh's distance from nationalistic Anglicans like Eliot, who probably would have considered such statements to be moderately treasonous. But Waugh was more concerned with his faith than his country, and he believed the Tony Lasts of England were the inevitable offspring of the illegitimate and uninformed faith planted by Elizabeth.

Waugh's portrayal of Tony Last anticipates the type of Englishman that many readers likely assumed was the social antidote to the raucous club members in *Decline and Fall*, Adam Fenwick-Symes and his frivolous cohorts in *Vile Bodies,* or the champions of modernity, Emperor Seth and Basil Seal in *Black Mischief.* But Waugh demonstrates that upstanding but ignorant gentlemen like Tony are not much better than those reprobates, and Tony has no power to defend his marriage or any other remnant of his life. Brenda decides on a divorce in which Tony passively accepts a monetary settlement to avoid a degrading court battle, in spite of the fact that the payment causes him to lose his beloved estate, Hetton. While the Lasts settle their divorce, their only son dies in a hunting accident with a servant—significantly neither parent is present—and Tony responds by fleeing to Brazil in search of an ancient, lost city. The "ancient city" represents Tony's New Jerusalem, "the city shining on hill." Tony's secular effort to find redemption fails, however, after a mentally deranged European named Todd traps Tony in the Brazilian wilderness and forces him to read Dickens novels aloud each day. This dark, exaggerated comedy befits Waugh's earlier satires and suggests that no escape from England and its suffocating culture will succeed if it is not accompanied by serious effort at internal reform.

Waugh never believed that the country home and the lifestyle it procures are inherent social evils; in fact, he deliberately constructed such a life for himself. But Waugh knew the English estate would become obsolete if English gentlemen did not grasp the historical significance of its social function. Waugh therefore depicts Tony envisioning his lost city in the same manner as he thinks of his estate, with "Gothic in character . . . a transfigured Hetton."[47] But a sober Tony later admits, "There is no city. Mrs. Beaver has covered it with chromium plating and converted it into flats. Three guineas a week with a separate bathroom. Very suitable for base love."[48] For the first time, Tony accurately diagnoses a problem in a manner that accords with Waugh's own judgment: Hetton no longer adequately serves the modern economy and is therefore vulnerable.[49] Tony's own relatives ultimately occupy Hetton after his death and manage a profitable silver fox farm in the backyard stables. For Waugh, Tony's losing Hetton represents one of the central English tragedies depicted in the novel: the dismantling of the great houses of the English aristocracy. Michael Gorra has argued that the loss of Hetton is a necessary "accession to modernity" because the home and the aristocratic system that made its existence possible provide "inadequate protection against the inhumanity of Brenda's modern world."[50] But Waugh portrays the Lasts' fate as one that might have been avoided had they comprehended the significance of their social position. If Tony had run his house properly and been knowledgeable about his faith, and if Brenda had not been lured by London's false promises, then Hetton might still represent a bastion of English culture and history in the countryside.

With substantial royalties from the successful sales of *A Handful of Dust,* a reissue of *Decline and Fall,* and slavish service to various periodicals, Waugh found an estate of his own and determined to prove that a man might protect it from the onslaught of the modern economic system. With characteristic deliberateness, Waugh married a young and relatively devout Catholic named Laura Herbert in 1937, bought a home in the country named Piers Court (complete with a coat of arms!), and set about turning him-

self into the English aristocrat he always dreamed he might become—at least until the Second World War escalated, and he
could not resist the call to battle. For Waugh, the protection of
the country home, and the aristocratic ideal it embodied, was a
nationalistic matter: "It may be a good or a bad thing to be class-
less; it is certainly un-British. The most dismal tendency I see is
that with our class system we are fast losing all national character.
It was thought absurd by many and detestable by some, but it was
unique and it depended for its strength and humour and achieve-
ments on variety: variety between one town and another, one
country and another; one man different from another in the same
village in knowledge, habits, opinions."[51] Although Waugh does
not explicitly assert that the maintenance of the English class system is a moral matter, he certainly invokes moral language in defending it. Furthermore, he indirectly explains and defends his
satire of the upper class in his earlier novels by calling the system
that preserves their existence "absurd," "detestable," and a
source of"humour." Waugh never suggested the class system
should be abolished in his satirical novels, even when he aimed
the brunt of his criticism at the upper classes.[52] But the most interesting element of the passage is the way Waugh connects the protection of the class system to his views of nationalism. For in
becoming an English landowning Catholic, Waugh joined an ever-
dwindling class of landed recusant Catholics and well-endowed
converts who still held land in some parts of rural pockets of England.[53] At the conclusion of *Campion*, he argues that such saints
died to preserve the Catholic families in England who, after the
Reformation, "survived here and there in scattered households,
regarded by the world . . . like a ghost or a family curse. . . . Their
only ambition was to live quietly in their houses, send their children to school abroad, pay the double land taxes, and, as best they
could, avoid antagonising their neighbors."[54] Not surprisingly,
Waugh would depict one of these families in his next and most
successful novel, *Brideshead Revisited* (1945).

BRIDESHEAD REVISITED

Waugh structures *Brideshead Revisited* in a manner that positions the Brideshead estate as the emblem of all that is worth pre-

serving in the modern world. The fact that its owners are Catholics who maintain a chapel with the consecrated Eucharist on the estate grounds distinguishes it from Tony Last's Hetton, which possesses only a superficial majesty unable to withstand the social and economic transformations of the twentieth century. Charles Ryder, the first-person narrator, returns to Brideshead with his military company during World War II after having known the Flytes, Brideshead's owners, well before the war. Although raised a middle-class agnostic, Ryder eventually becomes the unlikely defender of the recusant family tradition in England and assumes the voice and social perspective of the remnants of the landed Catholic gentry. The form of the novel also speaks to the significance of the Catholic estate. The central narrative describing Ryder's experiences with the Brideshead's owners, the Flytes, is bookended by a prologue and epilogue Ryder narrates during World War II while at Brideshead with his company.

In the prologue, Ryder singles out Hooper, a young subaltern in his unit, as an embodiment of modern culture: "Hooper became a symbol to me of Young England," with his modern approach to religion, politics, and language.[55] Hooper is a child of amoral capitalism. Waugh's presentation of young Englishmen in the novel models Max Weber's assessment of modernized Europeans: "The people filled with the spirit of capitalism to-day tend to be indifferent, if not hostile, to the Church."[56] Hooper's pragmatic observations of the Catholic estate and his utilitarian assessment of its worth seem irreverent when contrasted with Ryder's reflective, vigilant mood once on Brideshead's grounds. Ryder later elaborates on his animosity toward Hooper, whose beliefs threaten the existence of landowning English Catholic families like the Flytes: "The [Flyte] family history was typical of the Catholic squires of England; from Elizabeth's reign till Victoria's they lived sequestered lives among their tenantry and kinsmen, sending their sons to school abroad; often marrying there—intermarrying, if not, with a score of families like themselves. . . . These men must die to make a world for Hooper; they were the aborigines, vermin by right of law, to be shot off at leisure so that things might be safer for the travelling salesman."[57] Ryder's fatalistic language assumes Waugh's unmistakable polemical tone when discussing social problems. The passage also echoes Waugh's increasingly radical belief that the Protestants and atheists who control England are little more than colonists occupying a once proud Catholic country."[58]

Ryder is saved from an unenlightened future by his encounter at Oxford with the eccentric Sebastian Flyte, the youngest Brideshead heir, who leads a social crowd of decadent and Catholic aesthetes with homosexual undertones. Clearly, Waugh's novel does not portray an upright and innocent Catholic family that falls helpless victim to the evils of Hooper's modern world. Instead, the novel's central message is that while Catholic families like the Flytes, "half paganised themselves" in Waugh's words, inevitably succumb to modernity in many ways, their faith will redeem them and allow them to serve God's "divine purpose," even if the circumstances under which that will is realized are far from ideal.[59] Like Hopkins, Ford, and Eliot, Waugh depicts the preservation of tradition in less-than-glorious terms. Despite Waugh's insistence that the novel explores "the operation of divine grace" through flawed Catholics in the modern world, critics such as Humphrey Carpenter have argued "the novel is very little concerned with God" until "the last chapters" when Lord Marchmain, the Flytes' father, dramatically repents and accepts the Catholic sacrament of Extreme Unction before his death.[60] But such a reading disregards Waugh's portrayal of the characters' enactment of their divine vocation despite their own failures and the obstacles in the modern world.

Sebastian offers the prime example of this pattern. Waugh insisted to a friend more than a decade after the publication of the novel that he intended to portray Sebastian as "a contemplative without the necessary grace of fortitude."[61] Sebastian's vocation explains why he insists on preventing Ryder from getting involved with the rest of the Flyte family, who intrude on Sebastian's yearning for isolation. Sebastian's monastery of choice is none other than Brideshead itself, complete with a chapel and vast gardens. He only invites Ryder there when he knows his family will be absent. Although Ryder is permitted to meet the housekeeper, Nanny, he notes that she "did not particularly wish to be talked to; she liked visitors best when they paid no attention to her."[62] Nanny represents a necessary but unintrusive part of Sebastian's private Brideshead.

Ryder initially dismisses Sebastian's desire to be alone and assertion that his Catholic faith sets him apart from others, although he later acknowledges that the Flyte family's Catholic faith is precisely what distinguishes them from other English aristocrats. Yet Ryder never fully grasps that Sebastian's descent into alcoholism stems from his inability to follow his vocation as a contemplative. Ryder only casually notes that Sebastian's "constant, despairing prayer was to be let alone," and when Sebastian shuns him, Ryder perceives, "I was no longer part of his solitude."[63] The language of "solitude" and "prayer" signify the nature of Sebastian's true vocation, but the only way he can find peace in this crowded environment is to drink himself into isolation.

Only Sebastian's younger sister, Cordelia, understands Sebastian's conflict. The most devout Catholic of the Flytes, she possesses an uncanny ability to see through social façades and penetrate into the true character of those about her. Rather than joining the efforts of the family in hopelessly attempting to deny the cunning Sebastian access to alcohol, Cordelia assists him in his addiction. Rex Mottram, an ignorant, social-climbing Canadian engaged to the eldest Flyte sister Julia, complains to Ryder, "That kid's a walking marvel—she'd been feeding Sebastian whiskey right under our noses for a week."[64] But the unperceptive Rex misunderstands Cordelia's strategy: as a young woman discerning her own vocation to the religious life, she perceives Sebastian's vocation and therefore the nature of his addiction, and she decides that keeping her brother from the only means to solitude presently available to him might prove fatal.

Cordelia's strategy proves vital in guiding Sebastian to a monastery, which reinforces Waugh's intended message that Catholics achieve God's divine purposes in the modern world, although often through tortuous circumstances. Sebastian wanders drunkenly through Europe until he lies unconscious on the steps of a monastery in Algiers where the brothers deny his desperate requests for entrance into the community but permit him to remain on the cloistered grounds. Thus, in a twisted way, Sebastian fulfills his vocation. Ryder laments his friend's fate, but Cordelia accepts it contentedly and speaks of her brother's future as if it fit a pattern with which she and other English Catholics were familiar:

> He'll be a great favourite with the old fathers, something of a joke for the novices. Everyone will know about his drinking; he'll disappear for two or three days every month or so. . . . They'll bring him forward to

act as a guide, whenever they have an English-speaking visitor; and he will be completely charming. . . . He'll develop little eccentricities of devotion. . . . Then one morning, after one of his drinking bouts, he'll be picked up at the gate dying, and show by a mere flicker of the eyelid that he is conscious when they give him the last sacraments.[65]

In Waugh's unashamedly romantic vision of Catholic redemption, this mere act of blinking signifies consent to receiving the church's final anointing. Waugh's decision to narrate Sebastian's predicted fate remotely through Cordelia shows her foresight in comparison to non-Catholics, and it also depersonalizes Sebastian's narrative to make its effect more universal. English Catholics, Waugh implies, are as flawed and seemingly hopeless as the rest of the country, but God persistently works through them and guides them to his intended end. Ryder listens to Cordelia's narrative and offers a conventional, rhetorical response. "I suppose he doesn't suffer?" But Cordelia rebukes his clichéd reply. "Oh, yes, I think he does. . . . No one is ever holy without suffering."[66] The exchange highlights the extent to which a Catholic like Cordelia and Ryder differ in their judgment as to what constitutes a meaningful life. For Ryder, the primary objective of life is to cherish pleasure and avoid pain, but Cordelia seeks more transcendent answers and understands that the path to holiness for most is neither straight nor narrow.

The conclusion of Sebastian's narrative marks a key step in Ryder's own conversion to Catholicism, a conversion narrative often critically neglected, probably because of Waugh's vague and sentimental way of describing it.[67] Ryder confesses that at Oxford he assumed the "view implicit in my education . . . that the basic narrative of Christianity had long been exposed as a myth."[68] But Ryder is converted, ironically, by his resistance to the Flytes' priest's attempts to coerce Lord Marchmain, who unexpectedly returns from Italy where he had lived with his American mistress, into consenting to receive the Last Rites. Ryder emotionally appeals to his own moderate understanding of the necessary conditions for an efficacious final sacrament. "Let's get this clear . . . he has to make an act of the will; he has to be contrite and wish to be reconciled; is that right?"[69] Waugh intends (and succeeds dubiously) for Ryder's wrestling with Catholic ideas to reflect a battle concerning the faith that has commenced in Ryder's own soul. In a scene not unlike the one Cordelia foresees for her brother Sebastian on his deathbed, Lord Marchmain silently assents to receiving the sacrament, and a curiously relieved Ryder admits, "I suddenly felt the longing for a sign."[70]

Lord Marchmain's reconversion inspires the Flytes to become more assertive Catholics. For example, before Lord Marchmain's death, Ryder and Julia, both divorced, intended to marry; however, her father's death forces the lapsed Catholic Julia to reassess her own spiritual life, and she determines that she cannot remarry, an act that the Catholic Church would not recognize as legitimate. Julia explains, "I can't shut myself out from His mercy. That is what it would mean; starting a life with you, without Him."[71] After Ryder and Julia part, Waugh writes in the last paragraph before the epilogue, "The avalanche was down, the hillside swept bare behind it; the last echoes died on the white slopes; the new mound glittered and lay still in the silent valley."[72] Is this image a metaphor for Ryder's newfound acceptance of Catholicism, with his views and assumptions being washed in a "glittered" avalanche of faith? If so, Waugh's attempt to be poetic engenders as much confusion as clarity with regard to the plot.

Ryder's implicit conversion in the epilogue does little to resolve the novel's vague resolution. In the epilogue, Ryder muses on the light in the chapel that indicates the presence of the consecrated Eucharist in the chapel's tabernacle: "Something quite remote from anything the builders intended has come out of their work . . . something none of us thought about at the time: a small red flame—a beaten-copper lamp of deplorable design . . . the flame which the old knights saw from their tombs, which they saw put out; that flame burns again for other soldiers, far from home. . . . I found it this morning, burning anew among old stones."[73] Ryder apparently believes that Christ's presence redeems Brideshead and the men and women it hosted, and he is therefore not particularly interested in the fate of the Flytes or the army's abuse of the estate. His description of the chapel unites him with England's Catholic past, with the image of knights connecting him to a time before Henry VIII and Elizabeth and the establishment of the Anglican Church. Such passages reinforce Waugh's identification with the recusant tradition in England. However, Ryder may overstate his case when he claims "none of us thought" about the importance of the chapel, for both Sebastian and Cordelia treat the chapel as the center of Brideshead. Furthermore, Ryder's change of heart toward Catholicism seems sudden and forces the reader to scour the text for earlier evidence of his possible conversion: clues can be discerned, but they are so subtle and dubious that the epilogue still reads as an excessively romantic section.[74]

Despite the tone of the epilogue and the circumstances surrounding Ryder's conversion, Waugh's portrayal of the Flyte family's struggle to find identity in the modern world is far from romantic. In fact, in periodicals where Waugh defends the traditions of the recusant English Catholics, Waugh's voice actually sounds more nostalgic than in his fiction.[75] In its theme and form, *Brideshead* should be considered a modernist work. As in many modernist novels, there is little hope for the characters' temporal future. If there is a central moral, it is only that Waugh thinks Catholicism is true and that redemption is made possible through the Catholic Church; but for men, this redemption will have to wait. Furthermore, *Brideshead* assumes the nostalgic and desperate tone—achieved through a moderately inconsistent narrative voice that reconstructs the narrative via flashbacks—that characterizes most modernist authors. Waugh's novel defended the class and the faith with which he had by then formally aligned himself, and the permanence of the red lamp contrasted with the dismantling of Brideshead by the British military demonstrates that Waugh suspected Catholicism might be the only tradition capable of surviving the destruction of the Second World War.

WORLD WAR II AND THE *SWORD OF HONOUR* TRILOGY

Brideshead Revisited represents Waugh's eulogy for the upper-class English Catholic estates that he had come to accept would not survive the twentieth century, except in the case of isolated families like his own. But even that peculiar sector of English society could only be maintained within the broader context of a conservative approach to social and political issues, and from the 1930s until his death, Waugh repeatedly articulated his defense of conservative movements in England and throughout Europe. As with his understanding of Catholicism, Waugh viewed the conservative movement as one that crossed national borders and transcended history. In his 1939 "Conservative Manifesto," Waugh outlines a platform of beliefs that defines his conservative political philosophy. His creed includes the following professions: "I believe that inequalities of wealth and position are inevitable and that it is therefore meaningless to discuss the advantages of their elimination; that men naturally arrange themselves in a system of classes; that such a system is necessary for . . . keeping a nation together. . . . I do not think that British prosperity must necessarily be inimical to anyone else, but if, on occasions, it is, I want Britain to prosper and not her rivals. I believe that war and conquest are inevitable."[76] Waugh issued this statement on the threshold of the Second World War, and it explicitly conveyed his desire to protect England's class structure and her empire if they were threatened by Communist or Fascist governments. But Waugh's nationalism remained somewhat tempered because he suspected England might be so degraded socially by modern culture it would become a nation not worth defending. He briefly considered moving to Ireland, as an unapologetically modern England was to Waugh "no country in which to bring up children," but that assessment was not made until after the war.[77]

On the eve of the Second World War, Waugh insisted that communism was a more dangerous long-term threat to European tradition than Fascism.[78] He also consistently censured the English government for not giving adequate protection to Poland, Hungary, and Serbia from Germany during the war and Russia after it. In Waugh's war trilogy *Sword of Honour,* the narrator explains, "In the world of high politics the English abandonment of their Serbian allies—those who had once been commended by the Prime Minister for having 'found their souls'—was determined and gradually contrived."[79] Waugh's intense fear of the Communists stems from their refusal to permit religion a place in the social system. It is not coincidental that the nations Waugh most vocally defended were historically Catholic countries for which he held affection. For example, after walking through the streets of Budapest in 1938, Waugh noted the strange dress, language, and architecture and concluded, "Nothing could have been more 'foreign' in the popular sense of the word (even the street names defied pronunciation) but I do not think that anyone could have felt a stranger, for the atmosphere was permeated through and through with Catholicism."[80] Waugh's Catholic loyalties provided the foundation from which he articulated his conservative political views, even when allegiance to his faith worked implicitly against his nationalism. His position with regard to his faith and his nation is evident throughout Waugh's fictional account of World War II in the *Sword of Honour* trilogy.

Waugh's portrayal of the British Army and the Second World War in the trilogy is informed by his brief experience in battle and his overwhelming sense of alienation as a Catholic not just in the military, but in modern Europe. Considering that Waugh had a young family, finally ruled over his country estate, and had gained enough popularity as a novelist and columnist to earn financial security, it initially seems surprising that he would want to join the military in any mobile capacity. But his love of travel, coupled with his increasingly polarized conservative political opinions, motivated Waugh to serve England. Furthermore, the quiet country life did not always deliver on the promise of peace and fulfillment Waugh had expected. He and his wife had numerous children, and he frequently expressed his frustration with them: "I abhor their company because I can only regard children as defective adults, hate their physical ineptitude, find their jokes flat and monotonous."[81] The war provided Waugh a means to escape Penelope's lair after he had worked so hard to reach it.

Like Ford Madox Ford, Waugh had difficulty finding a position in the army, due in part to his limited physical capabilities. The Ministry of Information denied Waugh's application in 1940, and he was finally commissioned by the Royal Marines at the end of the year. But if Ford was a figure of sympathetic mockery to many of his comrades once he found an outfit, Waugh was a source of disdain—a characteristic Waugh does not assign to the hero of *Sword of Honour,* Guy Crouchback. Waugh could not relate to the working-class men who comprised a great proportion of the military, and he brashly advertised his advanced education and higher social standing when among them.[82] He later blamed his outcast status on his faith, but it was more likely a result of his behavior. Waugh engaged in sparse action on the island of Crete in 1941, but he was quickly removed to London as an office assistant so that he would not get "accidentally" shot by his own men in battle.[83] Although the work in London bored him, it freed Waugh to write much of what would become *Sword of Honour,* while at the same time satisfying his desire to participate in the English war effort.[84]

The trilogy is less modernist in its form than Waugh's satirical novels or *Brideshead Revisited*. Although it is still nostalgic and often ironic, the narrative voice and the structure are unified, with fewer flashbacks or intrusions of fragmented memories that characterize Waugh's earlier novels. Nevertheless, many of the same conflicts and themes resurface, including the demise of a Catholic family under the pressures of the modern world, ridicule of the upper classes, which simultaneously (and more emphatically) shows Waugh's deference to their social position, and the hero's fulfillment of God's will through seemingly less-than-holy means. Ostensibly, the central focus of the novel is Guy Crouchback's experience in World War II, but Waugh's broader objective is to portray how Catholics can still successfully navigate the war-torn modern world.

Guy is a flawed Catholic with an implicit vocation to marry and produce an heir who can preserve the Crouchback name and inherit their Catholic tradition. The Crouchback family might dissolve for the same reasons the Flytes had by the end of *Brideshead:* loss of wealth due to the decrease in the value of land, intermarriage with non-Catholics, and the diaspora of young men made necessary by the modern economy and the war. Waugh once again implies that the existence of the upper class is in jeopardy in part because of its own actions. For instance, Guy's sister Angela marries an Anglican, his older brother Gervase dies while serving in the Irish Guards, his devout brother Ivo starves himself to death for unstated reasons (a protest against modernity?), and Guy himself marries a lively, secular English girl named Virginia (in the mold of *Vile Bodies'* Nina Blount and *A Handful of Dust's* Brenda Last), who quickly divorces him.

Waugh's portrayal of Mr. Crouchback, Guy's father, resembles his depiction of Cordelia in *Brideshead Revisited;* both are knowledgeable Catholics who admirably practice their faith in a humble way. The Crouchbacks serve as eloquent spokesmen for the other Catholics in the novel, who are isolated social misfits, including a quixotic young Scottish nationalist named Katie who awaits the return of the Stuart reign and a dead English Catholic soldier whose family Guy unsuccessfully tries to help by sending them their son's identification tags. Waugh thus highlights the outcast condition of Catholics throughout Europe, but he contrasts their fate with Mr. Crouchback's moral strength. In one of Mr. Crouchback's rare appearances—Waugh forms his character primarily through Guy's memories and letters—he visits Guy in Europe and leaves his rented apartment early to accommodate the owners. The couple who owns the complex is suspicious even of his gratitude. "There's something about people like him. They were brought up to expect things to be easy for them and somehow or other things always *are* easy."[85] Waugh contends that Mr. Crouchback's charity is motivated by his firm Catholic faith. In a letter written before his death, Mr. Crouchback explains to his son, "The Mystical body doesn't strike attitudes and stand on its dignity. It accepts suffering and injustice."[86] Such principles contrast starkly with modern society's approach to life, in which suffering and injustice usually spawn more suffering and injustice—a cycle Mr. Crouchback, and eventually Guy, determine to stop.

Although much of the novel concerns Guy's comic experience with his ragtag military outfit, the Halberdiers, the more serious narrative traces Guy's development from a thoughtless Catholic with little appreciation for his genealogy to a man capable of making simple but heroic decisions in defense of his faith and family.[87] Mr. Crouchback's death and burial at Broome, the family's Catholic estate in England, marks a turning point for Guy in his transformation. After the novel was published, Waugh told a friend, "'Crouchback' (junior: not so his admirable father) is a prig. But he is a virtuous, brave prig," who learns from his father how to conduct himself as a Catholic in the modern world.[88] The means through which Guy demonstrates his worthiness and fulfills God's will for him to raise a Crouchback heir prove to be as undignified as the drunken Sebastian finding a monastery at the end of *Brideshead Revisited*. Virginia provides the heir after she becomes pregnant from one of her many affairs, and Guy arranges for his Uncle Peregrine, Mr. Crouchback's brother and another devout although somewhat socially awkward Catholic, to provide her with money so that she can support the child. Uncle Peregrine's skill in articulating his faith in a manner relevant to modern women like Virginia leads her to convert to Catholicism, although her ulterior objective—to convince Guy to help raise the child—is not lost on the Crouchbacks.

Yet Waugh wanted to avoid the widely criticized romantic conclusion of *Brideshead Revisited*. Unlike Ryder's humble and nostalgic conversion, Virginia considers her newfound faith to be relatively trivial. She announces after her first confession, "Why do people make such a *fuss*? It's all so easy. But it is rather satisfactory to feel that I shall never again have anything serious to confess as long as I live."[89] Waugh's irony turns sinister after a German bombing raid over London kills Virginia but spares her newborn child, making Virginia's impudent prediction quite possibly true. Guy completes his transformation by abandoning his position with British Intelligence and returning to England to raise Virginia's son, the long-awaited heir to the Crouchback name.[90] Underlying Guy's decision to raise the child are the words of Mr. Crouchback in an earlier letter to his son. "Quantitative judgments don't apply. If only one soul was saved, that is full compensation for any amount of 'loss of face.'"[91] Although the conclusion does contain a moral element—and that moral is explicitly Catholic—Waugh disagreed with those who considered the novel uplifting. He explained to his friend Anthony Powell, "I am disconcerted to find I have given the general impression of a 'happy ending.' This was far from my intention."[92] Yet Guy, in a way, is rewarded for his sacrifice, for he eventually meets a Catholic woman in England who becomes his wife, and, in the first edition of the novel's conclusion in *Unconditional Surrender*, he has legitimate children with her.

Waugh takes the blame for making a hopeful reading of the novel tenable: "The mistake was allowing Guy legitimate offspring. They shall be deleted in any subsequent edition."[93] As promised, Waugh grants Guy no biological children in the compiled *Sword of Honour* trilogy. But if Waugh was committed to a definitively modernist style that underscored God's ability to manifest his will by providing Guy an heir despite innumerable social obstructions, Guy might have raised the illegitimate heir on his own. The danger in such a scenario would have been that excessively sensitive Catholic readers might have protested Waugh's decision to have a single male raise a child, and Waugh probably feared having to explain his artistic intentions as he did after the publication of *Black Mischief*. Waugh knew his sales after *Brideshead* would rely a great deal on finding a Catholic readership, and he desired to write complex, inventive novels and sell them while he still lived. This desire necessitated a certain degree of self-censorship.

CONCLUSION

In his 1964 preface to the first publication of *Sword of Honour* trilogy, Waugh admits that the collection of novels came to express a different objective in their final form than he had initially intended, and he also argues that the Second Vatican Council eventually gave the trilogy a new significance: "I had written an obituary of the Roman Catholic Church in England as it had existed for many centuries. All the rites and most of the opinions here described are already obsolete. When I wrote *Brideshead Revisited* I was consciously writing an obituary of the doomed English upper class. It never occurred to me, writing *Sword of Honour* that the Church was susceptible to change. I was wrong and I have seen a superficial revolution in what then seemed permanent."[94] Waugh's refusal to even name the Second Vatican Council as the event that proved the church "susceptible to change" points to his disgust with the reforms initiated by Pope John XXIII and enacted by church leaders throughout the early 1960s. But Waugh's insistence on professing his opinion regarding the council somewhat exaggerates the effect it had on his work. What characters, scenes, or passages in the trilogy are materially changed by the decisions made at Vatican II? None immediately come to mind. Furthermore, the "rites" and opinions in the novel still seem relevant today, which suggests that Waugh's response was rather melodramatic.

The two elements of Vatican II that disturbed Waugh most were the permission given clergy to say the Mass in the vernacular and the emphasis (albeit not clearly defined at the actual council) on allowing the laity a more pronounced role in the liturgy. Waugh was not as concerned with other central issues of the council that were extensions of movements that had already gained popularity throughout the church before the council; these include the council's emphasis on ecumenical dialogue, Catholic socio-economic justice, and the use of historical-critical methods in biblical exegesis. Waugh's focus on the more tangibly liturgical elements of change makes sense, because those were the reforms that most directly affected his experience of the faith. The liturgical adjustments broke the silent unity of participants in the Catholic Mass in Latin that Waugh cherished, and he disliked the tone of collegiality and commonality between the priest and his flock the changes instilled. In his first public response to the council, "The Same Again Please" he insists, "Anything in costume or manner or social habit that tends to disguise that mystery is something leading us away from the sources of devotion."[95] Those common devotions were the ties that bound together the Catholic faithful throughout the world and a source of identity that Waugh found necessary in post-World War II European culture.

Waugh felt that the modern world had breached the walls he once thought impenetrable, and he feared that the church's desire for inclusion—be it of modern ideas or of the spiritual notions of other faiths—would damage Catholicism's distinct international identity. As early as 1949, Waugh had asserted, "I am afraid catholicism is the enemy of Catholicism," and in his mind, Vatican II was a step toward blurring the lines between the two terms.[96] Waugh's increasingly conservative theological views in his final years mirrored the development of his right-wing political views as a youth. Furthermore, just as Waugh's conversion to Catholicism led him to seek a home (literally and figuratively) on the outskirts of English society in a Catholic country estate, his response to Vatican II placed him in a similar position in relation to the rest of the church, as he desired to practice his faith only in the few churches that preserved the Latin Mass and generally disregarded the suggestions of the council.

Waugh's frustrations with England's social atmosphere, developments in Cold War politics, and the direction of Catholicism were many, and his death after suffering a heart attack directly after Mass on Easter Sunday in April of 1966 seems providential. In the *Times*, Graham Greene responded to the death of his fellow English Catholic writer. "Evelyn Waugh was the greatest novelist of my generation. . . . We were deeply divided politically, we were divided even in our concept of the same church . . . but [he] had an unshakeable loyalty to his friends, even if he may have detested their opinions and sometimes their attitudes."[97] Greene wrestles with committing to the superlatives he wants to grant Waugh, and Waugh himself would probably have been uncomfortable if Greene had professed that their political objectives were somehow compatible. It remains intriguing, however, that while Waugh was so rigidly conservative politically and theologically, he both practiced and remained interested in relatively experimental artistic forms.

If one flaw were to be assigned to Waugh justly as a writer, it is that he was too sure of what he believed and not always graceful in expressing his views; but this brash style, too, is often his greatest asset as a novelist whose cutting satirical voice admirably attempted to eulogize the character of English Catholicism in the mode of his generation.

5

Graham Greene: Toward a Postmodern Catholicism

There are different kinds of fear. One of the most terrible is the sensation that you are likely to become, at any moment, the protagonist in a Graham Greene novel: the man who tries to be virtuous and who is, in a certain sense, holy, and yet who is overwhelmed by sin as if there were a kind of fatality about it.

—Thomas Merton, *The Sign of Jonas*

GRAHAM GREENE ONCE OFFERED AN EXPLANATION FOR EVELYN Waugh's conversion that accounts for his friend's resentment toward the Second Vatican Council. "He needed to cling to something solid and strong and unchanging."[1] Although Greene likewise admired the church for obstinately defending its core doctrines (even if he could not accept them all) and questioned some of the church's changes implemented at the Second Vatican Council, he certainly never "needed" the church in the emotional and spiritual sense that Waugh did. Among English Catholic modernists, Greene most admired Ford Madox Ford, on whom he conferred high praise: "No one in our century except [Henry] James has been more attentive to the craft of letters."[2] Nonetheless, Ford's adamant defense of the British Empire and conservative belief in the cultural importance of nationalism—views he shared with the other Catholic modernists—could never be reconciled with Greene's anti-imperial political perspective.

Neither Greene's conversion nor his art stemmed from a desire to preserve religious or cultural traditions: he spent so little time in England it is impossible to extensively connect him to any branch of English Catholicism. His conversion process began with a romantic interest in his future wife, Vivien Dayrell-Browning. Without conscious intention of converting, he privately sought the spiritual guidance of Father Trollope, an English priest and spiri-

160

tual leader among the upper classes—and of the reserved, intellectual, recusant tradition type—who led Greene to accept the teachings of Christ as espoused by the Catholic Church. In spite of his religious instruction, Greene claims that these dogmatic matters "came nowhere near the core of my disbelief. I didn't disbelieve in Christ—I disbelieved in God. . . . It was on the ground of a dogmatic atheism that I fought and fought hard. It was like a fight for personal survival."[3] These were certainly not the terms on which most converts from Anglicanism over the previous century entered the Catholic Church. Greene's conversion in 1926 at age 21 was a personal and internal confession to a God whose existence he questioned and that Greene periodically abandoned later in his life. It never inspired him to defend the cause of English Catholics or to promote the evangelical mission of the church through his art.

Furthermore, at no point in his career do Greene's novels express nostalgia for a previous spiritual or sociopolitical period, as do the works of Waugh or other Catholic novelists. While Waugh wanted England to return to Catholicism and Ford argued that the British Empire should guide the world to peace as nationalism preserved religious and aesthetic culture, Greene was never tempted by such fantasies. Nevertheless, in the first half of Greene's writing career, he presented Catholicism as an irrevocable and universal truth system that his characters do not so much question as unsuccessfully try to reconcile with their social reality. Not until Greene revised the presentation of the Catholic faith in his novels into a belief system that is more doctrinally flexible and not universally applicable can his novels be firmly distinguished from those of the Catholic modernists.

THE "CATHOLIC" NOVELS

After graduating from Oxford in 1925, Greene worked for the *Nottingham Journal* and then the *Times* as a late-shift copy editor, and he began writing novels in his free time at the office. His first publication, *The Man Within* (1929), is a type of psychological thriller that seems to owe a substantial debt to G. K. Chesterton's *The Man Who Was Thursday*.[4] Both novels center on a conflicted young man caught in a confusing web of friends, enemies, and suspicious characters. Chesterton's novel concludes with a Christian revelation that transforms the protagonist's strange experiences into a complicated *Pilgrim's Progress* for the modern Catholic. In Greene's novel, the protagonist never experiences such a neat resolution of his identity crisis. Francis Andrews, the son of an urban smuggler who has inherited the family business, betrays his accomplices and seeks refuge with a pure young woman in her rural home. Although Andrews tries to convince the anonymous woman of the impurity of his heart, she insists on finding in him morally redeeming qualities. He cannot determine whether to accept her view of him or to admit that he lacks the moral strength and will to live honorably. While wrestling with this question, Andrews confesses to her, "It is as though . . . there were about six different people inside me. They all urge different things. I don't know which is myself."[5] The nameless lady symbolizes both the church and his wife, and the entire novel speaks to Greene's discomfort with his recent professions of loyalty to his wife in marriage and to the Catholic Church in conversion.

But while Greene, like Andrews, might find the offer of domestic and eternal salvation appealing on one level, he knew his wife and the church demanded a commitment he would never be able to offer. Greene despised tranquility, and a quiet Catholic marriage was not an effective weapon in what he deemed his "lifelong battle against boredom."[6] The unexpected popular success of *The Man Within* earned him a contract to write three more novels for Heinemann Publishers, which gave him the money necessary to leave the *Times* and write full-time. But Greene would soon regret his decision to stop editing because his three subsequent novels, *Stamboul Train* (1932), *It's a Battlefield* (1934), and *England Made Me* (1935), were all popular and commercial failures that led Greene and his family of four into financial difficulty.

Greene required a varied range of experiences to employ a more complex approach to his art that would improve the quality of his work and help his novels sell. His mystery and suspense works failed or succeeded on the unquantifiable whims of popular readers, and these genres stultified his development as a serious novelist. Not until his 1937 trip to Central America to write a nonfiction report on the state of the persecuted church in Mexico did Greene find his calling as a man and novelist. Late in his career, Greene defined how this excursion changed his approach to writing. "My subject is rootlessness—but then my subject matter is my life, so there's no paradox."[7] His obsession with travel and his inability to commit to one woman effectively ended his marriage, although he and Vivien would never formally divorce. The church, however, proved a more difficult lady to abandon. In *Brighton Rock* (1938), Greene worked Catholic psychology into the thriller genre and finally broke through the monotony of his earlier works, and sales of the novel were encouraging. In *The Power and the Glory* (1940) and *The Heart of the Matter* (1948), Greene found the fullest expression of his art, as these works evidence his talent for conveying suspense, recreating his impressions traveling in remote and politically unstable regions, and exploring the depths of Catholic psychology in the modern world.

In *The Power and the Glory*, Greene could not with any historical accuracy portray a vibrant, pious saint-hero who saves Mexican Catholics from their apathy in the face of Socialist persecution. Instead, Greene wisely envisions a flawed, unwilling martyr rising above religious and cultural indifference in Catholic Mexico. The cowardice and despair that grip the whiskey priest accurately reflect the spiritual state of many Mexicans when Greene visited. In *Another Mexico*, the travel book Greene composed while touring the country in the late 1930s, he notes that "the Catholics died out slowly—without Confession, without the Sacraments, the child unbaptized, and the dying man unshriven."[8] The Mexican-Catholic population's lethargic response to the crisis hindered any chance of creating an organized rebellion. Greene portrays this problem in *The Power and the Glory* when the anti-Catholic government raids a small mountain town and fear prevents the priest from confessing his identity, prompting the police to arrest an innocent father named Montez. The priest later confesses it was "a damnable mockery that [the Catholic townspeople] should sacrifice themselves for a whiskey priest with a bastard child."[9] The priest's humiliation at such moments, set against the pride of the Socialists, eventually inspires his desperate repentance and guides him to a worthy martyrdom.

Greene parallels the priest's route to sanctification with the mostly absurd legend of the saintly Juan, a martyred priest who in his youth prepared "himself for the evil days ahead with the most rigorous of mortifications."[10] A Catholic mother narrates Juan's story to her children, and Montez offers a similar narrative of a young Catholic girl, dying of consumption, who on her deathbed sees a man "with a golden crown" standing next to her parish priest.[11] Although Greene lightly satirizes such embellished legends, he also realizes that they preserve Catholicism in the imagination of younger Mexican generations. After the priest's death at the end of the novel, the mother who told the story of Juan explains to her daughter that she must not say the whiskey priest "had a funny smell" because "he may be one of the saints."[12] And the storyteller's husband laments, "There were no more priests and no more heroes."[13] Although such seemingly absurd hagiographies invoked a mixture of ridicule and admiration in Greene, a typically reserved English Catholic, he accepted that they concealed a deep, realistic understanding of sainthood for the cultures that preserved them.[14]

By contrast, Greene offers a ruthless satire of the Socialist police force. While the children inherit the story of Juan and the redemptive whiskey priest from bedtime stories, the lieutenant on the priest's trail catches the interest of children on the street by brandishing his pistol. A little child observes the weapon, and the lieutenant reflects, "It was for these he was fighting. He would eliminate from their childhood everything which had made him miserable, all that was poor, superstitious, and corrupt. They deserved nothing less than the truth—a vacant universe and a cooling world, the right to be happy in any way they chose."[15] This ideology, Greene implies, is more ignorant and harmful to children than the one formed by the saint's embellished legend. The Catholics and the Socialists in Mexico continually fight for the emotional support of the children who will inherit the spiritual and political fate of the country and play an important role even in the violent present. Although the priest is a deeply flawed man, he plays a heroic role in protecting the children from this violent form of socialism, which is every bit as hostile to cultural development and freedom as a colonial power.

Greene also underscores the importance of the priest's role by drawing structural parallels to the Gospel. The priest unwittingly thinks when being chased by a mestizo bounty hunter, "He knew. He was in the presence of Judas."[16] The mestizo uses the supposed need for confession of a Catholic-American murderer, who has been captured and is dying, to draw the priest toward his own arrest. Recognizing his own sinfulness and, like Christ, accepting his vocation in his final hours, the priest acquiesces to this false request, even though he suspects its maliciousness. Paired with this American criminal, the priest's immediate Gospel equivalent is not Christ but the good thief executed along with the unrepentant thief next to Jesus on the cross in the Gospel of Luke. In the biblical narrative, Christ promises the good thief salvation for his admission of guilt and need for mercy, and this connection underscores the possibility of the priest's salvation in the novel.[17]

In a form less romantic than the novels of Waugh or Ford, *The Power and the Glory* argues for the social value of Catholicism through the priest's narrative. Greene underscores the importance of defending and publicizing the role of the Catholic faith in oppressed societies in *Another Mexico*. "Perhaps the only body in the world today which consistently—and sometimes successfully—opposes the totalitarian State is the Catholic Church."[18] Even later in his career, when Greene wavered in his belief in Christ and the church, he continued to defend the Catholic Church's political activity and to honor worthy priests in his essays and fiction. Like James Joyce, he found a connection between the creative work of priests and novelists. Yet while Joyce linked the two vocations through the power of imagination and transformation, Greene focuses on a different aspect of their brotherhood by asking how the rest of the world can know "that for a writer as much as for a priest, there is no such thing as success."[19]

The Power and the Glory eventually brought Greene success and lasting fame, but the novel did not become widely popular until after the Second World War. Greene served in the war primarily as a British intelligence officer, a mobile assignment that granted him access to the dangerous, unstable worlds that became the primary setting of his later fiction, a fictional landscape some critics have called "Greeneland."[20] His first novel published after the war, *The Heart of the Matter*, is set in a British Empire outpost in Africa, where he worked as a British intelligence officer in 1941–1942. With *The Power and the Glory* and *Brighton Rock*, *The Heart of the Matter* most readily earns Greene the Catholic modernist label. Although "rootlessness" adequately describes the subject of these novels, the truth of Catholicism is taken for granted by the main characters who supply the narrative voices and perspectives throughout the novel. Each protagonist's conflicts and psychological strain arise from his difficulty reconciling his unshakable Catholic beliefs with his own moral failures and with the chaotic modern world, a condition also found in the characters in Ford's and Waugh's novels, and an internal conflict reflected in the voices of Eliot's and Hopkins's verse.

The possibility of redemption for Greene's flawed characters, who renounce their own salvation, relies solely on the mercy of God. Both Pinkie in *Brighton Rock* and Scobie in *The Heart of the Matter* commit suicide, convinced that they are sending themselves to a hell they deserve. According to Catholic doctrine, they are both objectively correct. Pinkie, who kills himself in part because he does not believe he can be forgiven for fornicating—though he has little moral problem with the murders and illegal trafficking he commits as a precocious gangster in Brighton—argues that he is doing God a favor by removing himself from the world. But when his young wife Rose fails to join him in suicide and speaks with a priest about the probability that Pinkie is damned, the priest assures her, "You can't conceive, my child, nor can I or anyone the . . . appalling . . . strangeness of the mercy of God."[21] The priest's counsel does not violate Catholic orthodoxy; it only allows for a more subjective judgment of Pinkie's culpability.

Similarly, at the conclusion of *The Heart of the Matter*, a priest assures Scobie's wife, who is insistent that her husband should be in hell for suicide in accordance with Catholic teaching, "The Church knows all the rules. But it doesn't know what goes on in a single human heart."[22] Like Pinkie, Scobie believes his suicide will relieve the world of a damned soul that might only cause destruction. But the priest's comment again suggests the possibility of mercy once the soul is extracted from the complexities of the world. Even in *The Power and the Glory*, the anonymous priest's fear that he "had to go to God empty-handed," seems unfounded because Greene presents his final actions in heroic terms.[23]

By emphasizing the possibility of mercy for these characters, Greene does not question the truth of Catholic orthodoxy. Instead, he demonstrates that a Catholic's adherence to orthodoxy can only be judged in God's mercifully subjective eyes and not man's objectively merciless ones. According to Alan Warren Friedman, the reader is "meant to look past the priest's fornication and cowardice, Scobie's and Sarah's adultery—and even Pinkie's murders—in order to discern the true worth of these characters."[24]

With the exception of Sarah Miles, the female protagonist in *The End of the Affair* whose death is neither voluntary nor self-condemning, each of these characters' unbending belief in Catholic doctrine ultimately leads them toward misguided acts of self-sacrifice in which they die to help others. Greene implies that the charitable intent behind these misdirected acts of love, while contributing very little good to the temporal world, establishes the possibility of divine mercy. These characters' "true worth" only can be assessed in a salvific context. Although Greene's conclusions are not cast in nostalgic or ironic language, they do present Catholic redemption as an answer to the complexities of modernity, a motif characteristic of the other Catholic modernists, who likewise do not so much attempt to solve the moral problems of modernity as point to the Catholic salvation that lies beyond them.

The Heart of the Matter would mark the last time Greene explored the notion of suicide and subsequent condemnation as potential acts of charity. Greene privately continued to maintain a rigid view of Catholic doctrine, but he emphasized the creative need to part ways with orthodoxy to be a significant writer. Greene once commented on the reasons for this decision. "I belong to a group, the Catholic Church, which would present me with grave problems as a writer if I were not saved by my disloyalty."[25] This statement in part explains his portrayal of his main characters' destructive commitment to orthodox Catholicism. However, Greene stubbornly refused to learn the apparent lessons of his novels and consistently applauded the church for its adherence to its core beliefs, even if he had no intention of following them.

THE POSTMODERN TURN

Greene's inflexibility with regard to Catholic doctrine accounts for his definitive (and to many critics surprising) negative response to the liturgical and theological changes implemented at the Second Vatican Council in the 1960s. Greene lamented the loss of the Latin Mass particularly and mocked "the freedom given to priests to introduce endless prayers" into the liturgy, "for the astronauts or what have you."[26] His close relationship with Waugh makes more sense in light of these views, although Greene's response to the changes was not nearly as caustic. After his friend's death, Greene reflected that Waugh had "too-great expectations of his fellow creatures, and too-great expectations even of his Church."[27] The primary conflicts between Waugh and Greene stemmed from the unorthodox notions Greene was willing to explore in his art. Accordingly, Greene consistently expressed his discomfort with readers who looked to his novels for insight into their faith, while Waugh took such expectations for granted.[28]

The other major difference between the two was that Greene did not feel he had the moral capacity or will to remain a practicing Catholic. Whereas Waugh's conservative beliefs inspired him to increase his devotion, Greene ultimately grew tired and abandoned the effort. In 1947, having long since permanently separated from his wife, Greene fell in love with Catherine Walston, another married Catholic, and he determined that this long, taxing affair disqualified him from staying in communion with the church. Greene was unwilling to adopt a personal version of Catholicism to practice his faith, but orthodoxy proved too burdensome for him. After meeting Padre Pio in 1949 and professing to witness the stigmata on the priest's hands, Greene refused an invitation to speak with him. He later explained, "I didn't want to change my life by meeting a saint."[29] Near the end of his life, Greene's language similarly invokes this exhaustion with the moral exertion necessary to retain religious faith. "With the approach of death I care less and less about religious truth. One hasn't long to wait for revelation or darkness."[30] However, at the same stage in his life, he also admitted, "I hope that [God] is still dogging my footsteps."[31]

In *The End of the Affair* (1951), Greene explores God's resilient and disruptive presence in the modern world. Greene's portrayal of Catholicism as an intrusive and archaic belief system throughout the novel points to his personal and artistic fatigue with his status as a Catholic writer. Many critics have identified *The End of the Affair* as a novel that marks a new direction in Greene's corpus, but what constitutes that change or whether the change only occurs after Greene finished the novel has found little critical consensus. In one of the earliest and most effective analyses of the difference between *The End of the Affair* and the novels that precede it, Frank Kermode argues that Bendrix, the main character and narrator of the novel, "is not a Scobie but the hero Mr. Greene has needed: a natural man who sees this God as a natural man would, as unscrupulous rival, corrupter of human happiness, spoiler of the egg; and a novelist who hates Him as a superior technician."[32] Unlike Pinkie, Scobie, and the Mexican priest, Bendrix is not concerned with his status in relation to God, but rather he questions God's purpose in interfering in human affairs. To Bendrix, God should confine himself to a certain time and place, and that place should not be in the heart of a woman who has an extramarital relationship with him, leading her to break off their affair. Ultimately, Bendrix's attempts to understand God and his role in determining fate exhaust him and leave him not so much seeking answers as a way out of the entire question of God's existence and purpose. Bendrix's parting shot, the last sentence of the novel, expresses this moral fatigue. "O God, You've done enough, You've robbed me of enough, I'm too tired and old to learn to love, leave me alone forever."[33]

The apathetic, even despondent, attitude toward faith Greene invokes through his characters in later novels, evident in his portrayal of Bendrix and fully realized in the character of Querry in *A Burnt-Out Case* (1961), parallels a turn in the modernist movement highlighted by Irving Howe in *Decline of the New*. Howe notes, "The problem of belief appears with great force in the early phases of modernism. . . . Later there arises a new impulse to dissolve the whole problem and to see literature as beyond opinion or belief, a performance or game of surfaces. Weariness sets in, and not merely with this or the other belief, but with the whole idea of belief. Through the brilliance and fervor of its straining, modernism begins to exhaust itself."[34] Howe's observation complements Jean-François Lyotard's distinction between modernism, which reinforces metanarrative, or a transcendental ideological system that must be evangelized aggressively for the supposed good of the entire globe, and postmodernism, which questions and/or discards the truth and efficacy of metanarrative. In Lyotard's seminal text *The Postmodern Condition*, he defines postmodernism, in its most reduced version, as "incredulity toward metanarratives."[35] The exhaustion of modernism inspires the rejection of metanarratives, especially those embodied in transcendent religious systems that might provide adequate answers to the challenges of modernity. The development of apathy toward metanarratives also helped bring about the postmodernist period in English literature, and the transition can be traced within the context of Greene's corpus.

Greene should be considered a Catholic modernist until the publication of *The End of the Affair* precisely because his early novels never question the metanarrative of Catholicism. But in *The End of the Affair* and in Greene's subsequent novels, the narrators and/or the main characters through whom the novels are presented do not take Catholic truth for granted, and the aesthetic, spiritual, and political consequences of this change reflect Greene's turn toward a postmodern mode of expression.[36] Using Lyotard's delineation, *The End of the Affair* represents Greene's first postmodernist text because in it Greene conveys exhaustion with faith and directly questions the metanarrative of Catholicism.[37] Greene's characters no longer wrestle with individual points of doctrine—what Howe terms "this or the other belief"—but with "the whole idea of belief," a question that never concerns the main characters of his earlier novels.

When Bendrix and Sarah commence the adulterous affair that provides the central external conflict of the novel, neither maintains any sort of religious belief. Bendrix notes that, before Sarah began to take interest in her Catholic faith, "We had agreed so happily to eliminate God from our world."[38] Sarah likewise initially discounts the possibility of turning to religion for moral assistance. In her diary, which constitutes Book Three of the novel, she recalls observing a man publicly attacking Christianity and claims, "He was attacking something dead already."[39] However, as Bendrix pieces together the story of his relationship after Sarah has died of a violent bout with what appears to be little more than the common cold, he recognizes that Sarah's Catholic faith is eventually what disrupted their affair. Yet breaking with the pattern of Greene's more unambiguously Catholic works, *The End of the Affair* does not then reinforce the metanarrative of faith or emphasize God's mercy as the truth that eventually will overcome all temporal problems.

Although Sarah's faith leads other characters to potential conversions (including her husband, Henry Miles; Parkis, an investigator of adulterous affairs, whose son is miraculously cured; and Richard Smythe of the Rationalist Society, who spends his life as an apologist for atheism, but wavers when the hideous spots on his face suddenly disappear after Sarah's death), these subplots can distract the reader from Bendrix and the primary battlefield on which his fight with God commences: the right to control narrative. Bendrix assumes a defensive position with regard to this authority in the first lines of the novel: "A story has no beginning or end: arbitrarily one chooses that moment of experience from which to look back or from which to look ahead. I say 'one chooses' with the inaccurate pride of a professional writer who—when he has been seriously noted at all—has been praised for his technical ability, but I do in fact of my own will *choose* that black wet January night on the Common, in 1946."[40] As later becomes evident, Bendrix's emphasis on "choosing" the beginning of his narrative is a deliberate and strategic move in his fight with God over the right to tell, and therefore interpret, Sarah's story. Lyotard insists that the right to control a narrative correlates with interpretive capacity and power. He calls transcendent systems of belief "narratives" regardless of whether they are of an aesthetic, political, or economic nature. "Narratives, as we have seen, determine criteria of competence and/or illustrate how they are to be applied. They thus define what has the right to be said and done in the culture in question, and since they are themselves a part of that culture, they are legitimated by the simple fact that they do what they do."[41] What Catholicism does for Bendrix, and presumably for Greene on some level as a novelist, is primarily interpretive in nature; in this novel, Catholicism interprets Bendrix's "hate" as love, his peace as divine presence, his survival as an act of divine mercy, Sarah's death as providential, and various healings as the power of prayer after death. Throughout the novel, Greene quite consciously confronts the Joycean conflict between faith and art: either artist or God has the right to create and manage narrative development, and, as Lyotard explains, to function as interpreter. In *The End of the Affair*, only Bendrix, and possibly the priest who knows of Sarah's conversion, is fully aware of the real grounds on which his battle with God occurs.

Bendrix knows he fights an invincible foe, and this knowledge interferes with his creative vocation. He confesses, "My book wasn't going well (what a waste of time the act of writing seemed, but how else could time be spent?)" and even admits, "If Sarah is right, how unimportant all the importance of art is."[42] Bendrix's only chance for victory is that God does not exist, or at least only that he exists only as an idea or an ineffable and unknowable figure that does not impose himself on the narrative of life. Sarah herself confronts this possibility when she prays to be released from her vow to believe in God if Bendrix is preserved after being injured from a German bomb. She thinks, "I said I hate you, but can one hate a vapour? I could hate that figure on the cross."[43] But if Sarah can hate the God represented in the tacky crucifix above the church altar, she knows that she can also love him. Bendrix undergoes a similar process. After reading her diary and being assured of Sarah's love, Bendrix finds Sarah praying in a Catholic church, and the images of bad religious art fill him with patient confidence. "I could have waited years now that I knew the end of the story. . . . If there is a conflict between an image and a man, I know who will win."[44] Bendrix assumes that the poor quality of the art in the Catholic church indicates the lack of power of the God it represents. But the incarnational faith of Christianity, and the sacramental life of Catholicism in particular, make it difficult for Bendrix to call Sarah's God a mere vapor or image. Because the Catholic God became man, he threatens to wrest interpretive power from artists like Bendrix. Therefore, it is in conveying the significance of Sarah's story that Bendrix realizes he can lose his power to God early in the novel when he laments, "Now I am betrayed by my own technique."[45] The betrayal occurs when Sarah's faith and death lead others to the point of conversion, while Bendrix attempts to interpret her final days as a testament to the power of their own love.

But unlike the (anti-)protagonists of Greene's earlier novels, Bendrix vows to fight this God even after he accepts his existence and despite knowing the hopelessness of his position. While acknowledging the absurdity of his predicament, Bendrix determines to defend the integrity of his art, and in particular Sarah's narrative, against the narrative authority of his creator. He sets out quite deliberately to destroy evidence that Sarah's story is one of conversion, redemption, and grace. As Parkis and Henry submit to the control of this God, Bendrix plans his moves, although not without vestiges of the irony that becomes the quintessential voice of Greene's later works. He knows Sarah's diary describes the circumstances of her conversion, and thinks, "I remembered the journal in my drawer upstairs and thought, That has to go too, for that could be interpreted in their way."[46] "Their way" refers to the Catholic interpretation of her story. Bendrix's most cunning foe is Father Crompton, the priest who counsels Sarah during her conversion, because this Catholic clergyman perceives Bendrix's strategy better than the other baffled characters, who do not see much harm in accepting Sarah's conversion or giving her a Catholic burial. Nothing enrages Bendrix more than the priest's self-assured attitude when he states, "Oh don't worry, Mr. Bendrix. Nothing you can do will affect her now."[47] This statement suggests that the story of Sarah's life and death has been fashioned within a Catholic sensibility. This Catholic "infection" spreads various and powerful narratives that a mere artist cannot write against.

Yet Bendrix is not motivated simply by an obsessive desire for control of narratives: he also fears God will usurp the right to aesthetic judgment from the artist. With the exception of saints like Sarah, Bendrix contends that the enactment of God's will in a sinner's life is mundane. "[Saints] stand outside the plot, unconditioned by it. But we have to be pushed around. We have the obstinacy of nonexistence. We are inextricably bound to the plot, and wearily God forces us, here and there, according to his intention, characters without poetry."[48] Bendrix, like Greene, apparently does not believe he has grace to become a saint, but fears living life as if he were a flat character in a novel, one of the characters who "will not come alive" in his own works.[49] Even worse, Bendrix realizes that belief might eventually lead to the end of his life as an artist and thinks, "If I begin to love God. . . . I'd lose even my work, I'd cease to be Bendrix."[50] This identity conflict points to Greene's tenacious fight for creative control and the artistic integrity of his own work, and it generates novels such as *A Burnt-Out Case*. The fact that the motif of faith becomes much less central in Greene's subsequent works, which are increasingly concerned with political conflicts in the third world and often depict the Catholic faith with a sense of tragic irony, suggests that *The End of the Affair* represents something other than a mere rehashing of the preceding Catholic works in which faith and mercy speak the final word. Despite the contentions of some critics, I find it somewhat disingenuous to read Bendrix's petition, "leave me alone for ever," in the final line as an almost mirthful indication that he will soon convert and begin the process of sanctification.[51] Instead, by this comment, Greene underscores Bendrix's exhaustion with metanarratives, even those that seem impossibly true, that Greene believes characterize the condition of man in a postmodern world.

Yet, if the novel is read as a work that expresses an "incredulity toward metanarrative" and represents Greene's movement toward a postmodernist mode of expression, one must still account for Sarah's conversion. Bendrix wants to believe that she has simply interpreted and enacted certain cultural signposts and superstitions—such as praying when faced with death or seeking a church as a place of emotional refuge—and followed them to Catholicism. Lyotard identifies how the cultural remnants of metanarratives contain powerful if latent social power. "Consider the form of popular sayings, proverbs, and maxims: they are like little splinters of potential narratives, or molds of old ones. . . . The narratives' reference may seem to belong to the past, but in reality it is always contemporaneous with the act of recitation."[52] Despite the supposed widespread religious ignorance of Bendrix and Sarah, both quite readily access powerful traditional Catholic verbal signifiers. For instance, Bendrix once reflects, "What do I know of phrases like 'the dark night' or of prayer, who have only one prayer? I have inherited them," and the reader is left to wonder from whom he has inherited St. John of the Cross and the language of Catholic mysticism.[53] Later, as Bendrix tries to resist recognition of God's existence, he prays, "I believe in magic even less than I believe in You: magic is your cross, your resurrection of the body, your holy Catholic church, your communion of saints" and seems capable of reciting the entire Nicene Creed.[54] Of course, as a novelist who engages in careful study of characters, it is possible that Bendrix would learn these prayers and theological traditions for intellectual purposes; still, Bendrix sounds more believable when he calls God "an infinite tide," an "eternal pimp," or simply "X."[55]

Sarah also rather easily invokes the language of Catholic tradition. The most striking example is her conception of the spiritual battlefield as taking place in a desert, which refers to John the Baptist's preparations for the Messiah in the desert, Christ's temptation period before he begins his ministry, and the Catholic "desert fathers" and mystics who were emptied of the world and purified in the desert. In her journal, Sarah asks a notably orthodox question. "What can one build in the desert? . . . If one could believe in God, would he fill the desert?"[56] Her eventual "yes" to this question makes conversion inevitable. It is striking that Sarah—and to an extent Bendrix—have been prompted into their contention with faith by Catholic signifiers that prove not to be lifeless remnants of the dead metanarrative but cultural catalysts with power that is, as Lyotard insists, "contemporaneous with the act of recitation."

But these acts do not signify the restoration of a metanarrative. According to Lyotard, the "breaking up of the grand Narratives" that once promised transcendental meaning does not mean that these metanarratives are permanently eliminated from social consciousness; instead, each of these narratives survives as a "little narrative [*petit récit*]."[57] A petit récit signifies a system of beliefs held by individuals or groups whose adherents either do not argue that their economic or spiritual system would be effective in all parts of the globe or do not aggressively or violently attempt to impose the tenets of their system on the rest of humanity. The adherents of such "little narratives" tolerate coexistence with other systems, even when living among competing narratives. Sarah's Catholicism represents this mode of belief, for she never publicly confesses her faith. It is only when Bendrix lies unconscious after a bombing raid that she prays to God, "Let him be alive, and I *will* believe . . . I'll give him up forever,"[58] and that she converts—or, more precisely, reconverts. The only evidence is in her diary. Sarah's faith is a private belief in a personal God, which will only influence a handful of others, even with its spiritual drama. The legends that gather around her conversion still do not constitute any widespread reimposition of the Catholic metanarrative in England. Her faith still has the power to evangelize a small circle, but it does not have the power to again transcend the culture.

Naturally, this diminution of the dominant metanarratives disrupts the continuity and threatens the doctrinal integrity of universal social traditions, a condition most modernists lamented and postmodernists characteristically accept and sometimes celebrate. Furthermore, a world devoid of controlling, culturally shared religious metanarratives inevitably poses its own challenges for the individual psyche. Lyotard notes that, in the increasingly globalized world, "Each individual is referred to himself. And each of us knows that our *self* does not amount to much."[59] Thus, Sarah's private confession silently rearranges her approach to the world and in some ways leads to her alienation from others. Nevertheless, tolerating this sometimes isolating condition causes less violence than inflicting a totalizing system on an unwilling world.

At the end of his treatise, Lyotard addresses his fear of those who proclaim new metanarratives—usually politically and economically based narratives grounded in the remnants of religious rhetoric—that allegedly will solve all modern problems. Because such systems constitute "the desire for a return of terror" for Lyotard, he exclaims in response to those who endorse them, "Let us wage a war on totality; let us be witnesses to the unpresentable" and accept the postmodern condition.[60] Greene's *Quiet American* anticipates Lyotard's call to arms by heavily criticizing the destructive metanarrative of American capitalism and democracy, while also implicitly suggesting that Catholicism, functioning as a petit récit, provides a viable response to the American approach to foreign conflicts.

THE QUIET AMERICAN

In *The Quiet American,* Greene reveals the damage the United States could potentially inflict in Vietnam by trying to implement the metanarrative of American democracy in an environment that has no use for it. Sergeant Alden Pyle, a young, naïve member of the American intelligence services that covertly support French efforts to defeat the Communist Viet Minh advance from North Vietnam, articulates the metanarrative of American democracy. He quixotically bases his resolution for the conflict on the introduction of a "Third Force" in Vietnam, a theory first propounded by a marginal political thinker named York Harding, whose views Pyle follows unquestioningly. Pyle values Harding's theory because it lies politically under the larger umbrella of his central metanarrative: American democracy. Thomas Fowler, a British reporter who perceptively identifies and condemns Pyle's beliefs and actions, narrates the novel and transforms what might be a comic satire into a tragic exploration of American political behavior overseas. Fowler ridicules the underpinnings of Pyle's ideology. "There was always a Third Force to be found free from Communism and the taint of colonialism—national democracy he called it; you had only to find a leader and keep him safe from the old colonial powers."[61] As a sort of reflection of Greene's revised, postmodernist ideology, Fowler supports neither the metanarratives of the British Empire nor of communism, but he discerns a more threatening and destructive problem in Pyle's "aggravating views on what the United States was doing for the world."[62]

Pyle functions as an imperialist whose most effective weapon is knowledge. He personifies Lyotard's prediction that "nation-states will one day fight for control of information, just as they battled in the past for control over territory."[63] In the provisional skirmishes of the Cold War, this battle for information and the imposition of ideology already coexisted with the fight for territory. The novel, in true postmodernist fashion, ultimately rejects any potential metanarrative that might solve complex regional conflicts such as the one in Vietnam. Accordingly, Fowler adopts a humanistic approach to the conflict, mercilessly criticizing Pyle's conception of the Vietnamese position on both sides of the dividing parallel, while simultaneously explaining the actual situation of the Vietnamese whom Pyle takes for his enemy. "They don't want Communism. They want rice."[64]

Initially, Fowler treats Pyle's seemingly innocuous ignorance with a mixture of playful disdain and pity. Fowler confesses, "That was my first instinct—to protect him. It never occurred to me that there was greater need to protect myself."[65] But Pyle's ignorance—fueled by his defense of American democracy and its global interests—proves extremely dangerous, in accordance with Lyotard's arguments concerning the threat of metanarratives in a postmodern context. The American metanarrative of worldwide democracy inspires Pyle to engage in the conflict by secretly organizing a series of coordinated bicycle bombs that kill women and children in the streets of Saigon. As Fowler uncovers Pyle's central role in the bicycle bombing plot, he realizes that his American acquaintance "belonged to the skyscraper and the express elevator" and wishes he would have remained in that protected, ignorant world.[66] Greene portrays Fowler as a character who transforms from one who tolerates metanarratives without professing one himself, to one who realizes their incompatibility with the globalized world. After reassessing Pyle's innocence as "a kind of insanity," Fowler determines that the world must confront the innocent—especially those with global power like the representatives of American capitalistic democracy—and "control them or eliminate them."[67]

Fredric Jameson identified American-sponsored democracy and capitalism as destructive metanarratives more definitively than Lyotard.[68] In *Postmodernism, or the Cultural Logic of Late Capitalism*, Jameson calls Vietnam the "first terrible postmodernist war" and, in a later essay, he argues that American suburbanites-turned-politicians, of which Pyle is a representative example, frequently complicate violent international conflicts because of their well-intentioned but ignorant intervention.[69] Jameson claimed not to dislike such people personally, but he remained wary of their potential for harm. "There is nothing particularly disgraceful in having lived a sheltered life, in never having had to confront difficulties . . . but it is nothing to be particularly proud of either. Moreover, a limited experience of life normally does not make for a wide range of sympathies with very different kinds of people."[70] Consequently, American global economic success and influence engendered a dangerous spirit of negligence and hubris in American foreign policy and in private economic activity that reignited and, in some cases, created violent conflicts. Jameson later issues a more definitive condemnation of America's transnational involvement. "American postmodern culture is the internal and superstructural impression of a whole new wave of American military and economic domination throughout the world: in this sense, as throughout class history, the underside of culture is blood, torture, death, and terror."[71] Jameson's observations and assessment of American foreign activity as informed by a transcendent belief in the universal benefits of American democracy and capitalism mirror Lyotard's (and Greene's implicit) concerns about those who attempt to impose metanarratives on the postmodern world.

According to Jameson, even disapproving silence constitutes political participation in the complex and increasingly interconnected world. He explains that because of the globalized nature of the capitalistic, postmodern world, "every position on postmodernism in culture . . . is also at one and the same time, and *necessarily*, an implicitly or explicitly political stance on the nature of multinational capitalism today."[72] Greene's novel anticipates this politically charged rhetorical environment and reveals the dangers of this spreading predicament through the voice of Fowler. For example, Fowler's objective of avoiding participation in the conflict—remaining *"disengagé,"* as he calls it—proves impossible when he witnesses Pyle's violence. Fowler's refrain, "it wasn't my war," proves inadequate; he must admit that, as a reporter, "even an opinion is a kind of action."[73] Therefore, given the option to participate in an elaborate plot designed to murder Pyle, contingent on Fowler's inviting him to dinner, Fowler hesitantly complies. An investigator who suspects the truth disregards Fowler's guilt and Phuong returns to his side, but Fowler neither enjoys nor feels satisfied by his participation. He does, however, accept its necessity. Fowler learns that everyone shares responsibility in a globalized world and even silence functions as a form of collaboration.

Fowler's action, however, is not committed in the name of communism or British imperialism. Through Fowler, Greene explores how humanists might influence international politics: by obstructing those who wish to impose metanarratives. Therefore, Fowler determines to thwart Pyle's covert campaign of violence by which the young American tills the field in Vietnam for the introduction of American-sponsored capitalism. Jameson notes the ability of this new metanarrative to permeate beyond political contexts. "There is a certain way in which this system [of American-sponsored democracy and capitalism] . . . is as effective a vehicle for depoliticization as religion may once have been."[74] Not coincidentally, proponents of metanarratives in the twenty-first century who want to inflict their own metanarrative on the rest of the globe—in American and other contexts—have frequently adopted fundamentalist religious systems and rhetoric to justify their violent activity. In *The Quiet American,* Greene depicts how religion also can be corrupted in the modern world and, through Fowler, mocks shallow forms of faith. He undercuts Pyle's hollow claims to Methodism, while simultaneously dismissing the Caodist's religion syncretism—mixing Buddhism, Christianity, and other faiths in a fantastic display of meaningless liturgy—as "play-acting."[75] A religious petit récit for Greene does not translate into tolerance of self-constructed forms of faith; a petit récit is the same historically grounded religious tradition, defended with patience and eloquence rather than with force.

Although Greene suggests that no single faith should aim to conquer the world, he makes it clear throughout *The Quiet American* that religious systems should not be abandoned or desecrated in the name of tolerance and replaced with silly conglomerations and hollow forms of religious expression. Although a professed atheist, Fowler expresses a consistent respect for Catholicism, not least because Catholic leaders refuse to adopt a partisan position in the internal conflict in predominately Catholic Vietnam. When Pyle suggests that Catholics might support his endeavors, Fowler joyfully refutes him, "[The Catholics] trade with the Communists. . . . I wouldn't say they were exactly York

Harding's Third Force."[76] Yet Fowler's admiration for Catholicism extends beyond a mere political sympathy; in fact, his calling one religion "play-acting" implies that some faiths might possess authentic efficacy. He consciously observes that, in moments of intense violence, people of every religion flock to the Catholic Cathedral: "They believed, whatever their religion, that here they would be safe."[77]

Through Fowler's peculiar admiration for Catholicism, and Catholicism's positive portrayal throughout the novel, Greene suggests that the Roman Catholic faith, reduced from a metanarrative to a petit récit, represents one worthy response to Pyle's deadly democratic capitalism. Almost subconsciously, Fowler continually positions himself as a firm but quiet Catholic apologist. He begins to attribute proper conduct to the Catholic faith; Fowler thinks his favorite leader, Dominguez, a South Vietnamese man who distrusts the French allies, "was a Roman Catholic," although Fowler possesses "no evidence for it beyond his name and the place of his origin . . . he might have worshipped Krishna."[78] Although Fowler's interest in Catholicism has little basis in doctrinal differences with other faiths, he admires the church for the way it functions as a spiritual (and at times physical) safe haven for the war-torn people of South Vietnam. The Catholic Church's appeal is established because it is not a faith that is trying overtly to conquer the country, nor is it some concocted system of belief that has no basis in history and therefore no lasting meaning for the people seeking answers in a time of pain and confusion.

While planning *The Quiet American*, Greene wrote to Waugh, "It will be fun to write about politics for a change, and not always about God."[79] And yet, as is evident in the novel, Greene cannot entirely distance himself from at least recognizing the potential value of a Catholic worldview. Like *The End of the Affair*, *The Quiet American* avoids endorsing Catholicism while keeping open the possibility of its validity. As a postmodern and still Catholic novelist, Greene could abandon and even attack metanarrative, while preserving the integrity of his own Catholic petit récit.

POSTMODERN TRAGICOMEDY

Greene earned a popular reputation as a Catholic-turned-Communist after *The Quiet American*, but he accurately insisted that he did not maintain "the slightest coherence in his political vision."[80] In making this claim, Greene intentionally distanced himself from identification with any political or even religious system—any form of metanarrative—that would effectively solve all political strife. He conveniently adopted the rhetoric and tenets of Catholic social teaching or Communist thinking in certain situations, but he did not believe any single theory always would function adequately. For example, in 1957, he spied on the Communists in China because of the atrocities its government committed. A decade later, he wrote a bitter letter in *The Times* virulently condemning the Soviet Union's treatment of authors and other intellectuals who spoke out against their government.[81] Such actions call for a reassessment of Greene's political reputation as a polemical anti-American Communist.

It is nevertheless true that, more than other systems of thought, Catholicism and communism frequently provided Greene with the means to articulate his humanistic approach to international conflicts. In 1966, he boldly "argued for the possibility, not of a mere chilly co-existence, but cooperation between Catholicism and Communism."[82] The inherently antireligious strain in communism combined with the Catholic Church's refusal to support explicitly one economic or political system to the exclusion of another made reconciliation impossible. However, the church and Communist thinkers have consistently echoed similar criticisms of the dangers of global capitalism, which allowed Greene to continue to draw on these systems for rhetorical support. Greene avoided widespread criticism for his views in England, where neither Catholics nor Communists garnered much popularity, by living primarily in France after 1960 and moving there permanently in 1966. Greene's emigration from England coincided with the deterioration of his long affair with Catherine Walston. Although he would establish new love relationships while he lived in France, most notably with Yvonne Cloetta, Greene loved Catherine more than any woman and regretted that their relationship never became more permanent than an indiscreet affair. The pain and instability of his personal life paralleled the violent, conflict-ridden social world that he so persistently continued to explore even in the last stages of his life. Greene admitted that, after *The End of the Affair,* "I felt myself used and exhausted by the victims of religion," which explains why that novel in many ways renounces the transcendental value of Catholicism.[83]

Ultimately, Greene turned to irony and comedy as an answer to his despair, although not to the nostalgic irony that pervades the work of other Catholic modernists. Instead, Greene employs a postmodernist irony that would become the most recognizable feature of his last works. In *Horizons of Assent,* Alan Wilde argues that postmodernist irony, in contrast to modernist irony, "is suspensive: an indecision about the meanings or relations to things is matched by a willingness to live with uncertainty, to tolerate, and, in some cases, to welcome a world seen as random and multiple, even, at times, absurd."[84] Greene tolerated more than welcomed the inevitably quixotic condition of postmodern man trying to make sense of his identity in the impossibly complex and conflicted, yet increasingly interconnected world. He had attempted to reconcile the inflexibility of Catholic doctrine with his moral reality, as well as his sympathy for Catholic and communistic social thinking, with little success. Despite these conceptual failures, Greene's art and his political writings could contribute to the promotion of justice. As Greene announced in *Ways of Escape,* the second volume of his autobiography, "I found myself . . . in that tragicomic region of La Mancha where I expect to stay."[85]

Although Greene cites *A Burnt-Out Case* as the novel that most explicitly represents this turn toward tragicomedy, he honed his comedic voice in *Our Man in Havana* (1958). The most effective comedy in the novel centers on the melodramatic Catholic faith of Milly, the daughter of a nonpracticing Catholic mother who leaves her English husband, Jim Wormwold, a middling English vacuum cleaner salesman. Wormwold recalls that, as a young child, Milly responded to her classmates' pestering by setting a young boy on fire. She then defended herself by rationalizing that he "was a Protestant and if there was going to be a persecution Catholics could always beat Protestants at that game."[86] She later explains to her unbelieving father, "You are invincibly ignorant. . . . It's only theology. You'll be saved like the good pagans," thereby employing a more astute catechetical logic than many desperate characters in Greene's earlier Catholic novels.[87] Milly also believes she is "about the age" where it would be appropriate to hear divine voices, as did St. Thérèse or St. Joan of Arc, and she uses novenas as threats to coerce her father to buy her a horse. Greene's lighthearted portrayal of Catholicism through Milly serves two functions: it distances him from his tired reputation as a tortured Catholic writer and redirects the readers' attention to the political satire, where Greene's more serious criticisms are at stake.

Greene first mocks the British Secret Intelligence office that he once served. An agent named Henry Hawthorne hires the ignorant and uninterested Wormwold to become a key component in the British government's expanding undercover agency throughout Latin America. Hawthorne justifies Wormwold's selection in a statement that satirizes the intelligence agency's political strategy and rhetorical style. "Patriotic Englishman. Been here for years. Respected member of the European Traders' Association. We must have our man in Havana, you know."[88] The final sentence reinforces Greene's criticism of the convoluted and ubiquitous teams of government spies and petty criminals in environments that are as tedious as Scobie's mundane colonial outpost in *The Heart of the Matter*.

If *The Quiet American* argues that political participation cannot be renounced in the postmodern world, then *Our Man in Havana* demonstrates that this participation must be engaged cautiously. For example, when Wormwold senses impatience from the central office in London to keep this absurd system relevant, he determines to fabricate observations based on real men he knows in Havana. The alleged volatility in Havana earns Wormwold a secretary from London, Beatrice, to help him manage his growing network. However, his plans go astray when his falsified activity leads to action by agents from other countries spying in Havana, and an alcoholic pilot whose identity Wormwold had used in his false reports is murdered. Even Wormwold's best friend, Dr. Hasselbacher, turns out to be a real German secret agent, a remnant from World War II exiled to do menial work in Havana. Hasselbacher is unnecessarily killed by Carter, another member of British Intelligence who does real undercover work and sees through Wormwold's deceptions.

Wormwold's loyalties are tested when he must choose to either sacrifice himself for his nation by staying in Havana or flee to England with his daughter. He decides to leave, which underscores Greene's antimetanarrative turn. But before Wormwold exits, he must kill Carter in preemptive self-defense. Wormwold justifies this solitary act of violence by explaining: "I wouldn't kill for my country. I wouldn't kill for capitalism or Communism or social democracy or the welfare state—whose welfare? I would kill Carter because he killed Hasselbacher."[89] Greene thus implies that the abandonment of belief in metanarrative does not constitute pacifism. Wormwold must act if he wants to protect his family from Hasselbacher's fate. Beatrice, who promises to marry Wormwold back in London after his assessment trial—where he is pardoned to cover up the inane decision to hire him in the first place—also confesses her mistrust of grand systems. "I don't care a damn about men who are loyal to the people who pay them, to organizations. . . . I don't even think my country means all that much. There are many countries in our blood—aren't there?—but only one person."[90] Even Milly relaxes her inflexible Catholicism and condones the future marriage of Beatrice and her father even though both have been separated from living spouses, a marriage the Catholic Church would not recognize as legitimate. The novel emphasizes Greene's unwillingness to commit completely to any single economic, political, or spiritual system, while suggesting that comedy may provide the medicine that helps one survive the inevitable tragedies of contemporary existence.

But the much more cynical comedy of *A Burnt-Out Case* indicates that *Our Man in Havana* did not adequately assuage Greene's frustration with being labeled a Catholic novelist who might contribute to the salvation of humanity. In his autobiography, Greene examined his spiritual and artistic struggle during this period. "I had no apostolic mission, and the cries for spiritual assistance maddened me because of my impotence. . . . I was like a man without medical knowledge in a village struck with plague. It was in those years, I think, that Querry was born, and Father Thomas too. He had often sat in that chair of mine, and he had worn many faces."[91] Querry, the main character in *A Burnt-Out Case*, flees his life as a famous English Catholic architect and seeks moral and emotional shelter in an obscure African leper hospital run by the Missionaries of the Sacred Heart, a Catholic religious order. The premise, based on a trip Greene actually took to a leper colony in Yonda, West Africa, provides the ground for a dark and tragic comedy. Greene admitted to Waugh that Querry had a substantially autobiographical foundation, and that the character's desperate submersion deep into the third world in order to abandon the life of boredom engendered by his own reputation and responsibilities reflect the primary personal conflicts in Greene's life and career.[92] Like Greene, Querry cannot escape his reputation and the expectations produced by his artistic success. Querry insists that he is a "retired" Catholic and clarifies that his buildings were not charitable endeavors. "The use of what I made was never important to me. I wasn't a builder of council-houses or factories. When I made something I made it for my own pleasure."[93] Querry rhetorically adds (as if Greene's intentions were not yet evident), "A writer doesn't write for his readers, does he?"[94] Querry's venture into the leper colony represents a voluntary purgation meant to cleanse him of his past; if successful, it might purify him in his vocation.

Greene's purpose in writing the novel can be drawn from Querry's attempt to rid himself of his Catholic reputation and his publicly assigned redemptive role. But Querry's failure, and possibly also Greene's, results not from his inability to undergo this self-imposed purgatory, but from the interference of the same forces that drove him to the leper colony. The identity conflicts resurface for Querry through various other expatriates: Montague Parkinson, a relentless journalist who constantly reminds Querry of his past; Fr. Thomas, a hero-deprived Catholic priest; and Rycker, a local factory worker and fellow English Catholic. In his unsolicited interviews of Querry, Parkinson parrots the questions Greene so despised in his own career. "Do you consider that the love of God or the love of humanity is your principal driving force, M. Querry? What in your opinion is the future of Christianity? Has the Sermon on the Mount influenced your decision to give your life to the lepers? Who is your favorite saint? Do you believe in the efficacy of prayer?"[95] The most problematic of these darkly humorous questions may be the one that characterizes Querry's exile as a self-sacrificial pilgrimage, which is precisely how Parkinson constitutes Querry's actions in a lengthy *Post* magazine article that he maliciously publishes despite Querry's firm request that he not do so. Greene demonstrates that artists can create public works of art and present a self-styled personality, but they possess almost no control over how the public interprets their decisions, let alone their work.

Greene's object of satire is not only the media, but also those who accept its concoctions at face value. Parkinson's article ironically convinces Fr. Thomas that Querry is a saint, a belief he predetermines to hold for spiritual rather than commercial reasons. Fr. Thomas repeatedly asks to hear Querry's confession and creates a false spiritual kinship in which he serves as Querry's unsolicited comforter. "Those doubts you have. I can assure you I know them, too. But couldn't we perhaps go over together the philosophical arguments . . . to help us both?"[96] The deluded priest even considers Querry's quest a parallel to St. John of the Cross's mystical journey; Fr. Thomas represents the myriads who seek a road to salvation in the person of a "retired" Catholic artist like Greene.

Yet Querry's death ultimately comes at the hands of a vengeful Rycker, whose neglected wife Marie provokingly claims to have a child by the former architect—an event that Greene depicts in order to lament the general vulnerability to pernicious accusations of all public figures, regardless of creed or vocation. The chaste Querry has no way to refute this false claim. While Greene mocks Rycker, who legitimates his manhood by Querry's murder, and Parkinson, who unapologetically moves on to another assignment, he reserves an equally sinister criticism of Fr. Thomas, who responds to Querry's defamation. "We gave you a warm welcome here, didn't we? We asked you no questions. We didn't pry into your past. And in return you present us with this—scandal. Weren't there enough women for you in Europe?"[97] Fr. Thomas quixotically attacks Querry for not being the saint Querry never wanted to be. In light of the priest's tragicomic reaction, Querry's earlier renunciation of sainthood demonstrates that the man he most consciously intended to protect was not himself, but men like Fr. Thomas who place their spiritual trust in unwilling and unworthy people. Greene presents a less scathing image of the Catholic priesthood through Father Joseph, who works in the leper colony and hardly views Querry as a spiritual model. This emotional distance allows him to make a perceptive judgment of Marie Rycker's accusation. "We mustn't forget that it's only her word against his."[98] Yet Father Joseph's voice is quickly silenced by the others' panic, and Querry has little possibility of deliverance.

Due to the novel's nearly hopeless portrayal of humanity, Waugh refused to review it, and in his diary he called Querry a "bored, loveless, voluptuary," adding somewhat equivocally, "There is nothing I could write about it without shame one way or the other."[99] Yet Waugh (probably aware that his diary might one day be public property) confessed, "I am not guiltless as one of those who put him in the odious position of 'Catholic artist,'" thereby implying Greene never deserved the burdensome title.[100] Greene even admits that the very act of writing the novel fostered despair. "Never before had a novel proved more recalcitrant or more depressing."[101] The central redemptive scene in which Querry instinctively hunts down his leprosy-ridden roommate, Deo Gratias, and pulls him from a jungle pit cannot override the pervasiveness of misery in the novel. It is a singular, heroic act hidden from public view that alone cannot transcend the tragedy of Querry's fate. Instead, Greene's depiction of Querry's purgatorial march into the leper colony collapses into a tired exploration of hell on earth.

The popular and artistic failure of A Burnt-Out Case compelled Greene to return with new vitality to the strongest aesthetic elements of the latter part of his career: writing works of tragicomedy that are often humorous and not devoid of hope, lightheartedly portraying Catholicism in a manner that preserves its importance as a petit récit, and continuing to explore third-world conflicts with immediate political implications. Each of these components surfaces in The Comedians (1966), in which Greene recreates the brutal tyranny imposed on Haiti by "Papa Doc" Duvalier and his bogeymen police, the Tonton Macoutes. Greene also successfully balances a subtle anti-American undercurrent by referring to American support for Papa Doc because he served as a deterrent to communism, while distancing himself from a comprehensive endorsement of communism as a legitimate metanarrative. The native Haitians in the novel mix their Catholicism with voodoo-ism, which renders the Catholic faith impotent politically. But it still functions as a source of hope for individual men.

The first-person narrator, significantly given the mundane name Brown, exemplifies the rootless condition of postmodern man. Born in Morocco to an unknown father presumed to be British and a wayward Catholic mother who leaves him to be raised and educated by the Jesuits, Brown renounces his potential vocation to that order (à la Joyce's Stephen Dedalus) along with his faith. He instead determines to save his deceased mother's Haitain hotel, the Trianon. Brown acknowledges his peripatetic social position that is simultaneously isolating yet liberating. "The rootless have experienced, like all the others, the temptation of sharing the

security of a religious creed or a political faith, and for some reason we have turned the temptation down."[102] Brown lives not for
any metanarrative, but for the success of his hotel and the love of
Martha, the German wife of an obtuse ambassador to Haiti. Martha likewise expresses the "incredulity toward metanarrative" that
embodies the postmodern condition. She once explains to Brown,
"I used to think you were . . . a Protestant nothing, not a Catholic
nothing. I am a Protestant nothing. . . . I even thought you might
be a Communist nothing."[103] Through such passages, Greene suggests that spiritual and political systems are best used as means to
various ends and not systems worthy of respect in and of themselves.

Dr. Magiot, Brown's brave Haitian friend and a political agitator, models Greene's approach to communism. Initially, he confidently professes, "I believe in the future of Communism."[104] But
when he writes to Brown just before he is slain by the Tonton Macoutes, Magiot modifies his commitment to communism. "I believe of course in that economic plan—in certain cases and in
certain times, here in Haiti, in Cuba, in Vietnam, in India."[105] In
the typical pattern for late Greene novels, Dr. Magiot revises his
belief in communism as a nation-saving metanarrative to a belief
in its potential effectiveness as a petit récit, to be employed only
"in *certain cases* and in *certain times.*" Although communism
may have helped bring economic stability to Haiti, Greene argues
that the American influence on the island prevents this possibility.
Captain Concasseur, the only Tonton Macoute who reveals his
face, explains to Brown the regime's fearlessness with regard to
the Communists. "Oh, there's no danger from them. The Americans would land Marines if they ever became a danger."[106] The
United States's capitalistic enterprise that makes Papa Doc's reign
possible proves to be the most resilient and harmful metanarrative
functioning in the novel. When Brown suggests that even the capitalists may lose their faith just as he lost his belief in religion, Concasseur, more familiar with American political strategy, responds,
"They lose their lives but never their faith. Their money is their
faith."[107] Greene's depiction of the callous greed of the imperial
capitalists in *The Comedians* serves as an indictment of American
international political behavior that is as profound as his portrayal
of Pyle's ignorant violence in *The Quiet American.*

Yet Greene's persistent attention to comedy prevents the appropriately titled novel from spiraling into the ubiquitous sense of despair that characterized *A Burnt-Out Case*. Two men who sailed with Brown back into Haiti—Mr. Smith, a failed American presidential candidate in the 1948 race, and Major Jones, supposedly an American war hero in Burma—provide comic relief that extends beyond their ludicrously mundane names. Mr. Smith, completely controlled by his witty, uncontainable, outspoken wife, travels to Haiti with the dream of opening up a vegetarian restaurant in the tyrannized country. Vegetarianism is this couple's petit récit. They reason that because "wars are made by politicians, by capitalists, by intellectuals, by bureaucrats, by Wall Street bosses or Communist bosses" while the other "ninety-five percent" of humanity "can't afford meat or fish or eggs," vegetarians may help save the world.[108] Despite their dubious views, the Smiths represent Greene's only mildly positive portrayal of Americans in his corpus, for they are sincere and extremely sensitive to the plight of the rest of humanity.

Major Jones presents an even more authentically tragicomic figure than either of the Smiths. He constantly refers to his exploits in the Burmese jungle and begins to organize an elaborate coup against Papa Doc. But Brown quickly discerns the truth that "Major" Jones is little more than a pathetic confidence man self-exiled from the United States because of pressing legal trouble. Jones essentially wills his lies into reality when a collection of authentic guerillas rally around him to stage a revolt on Papa Doc's regime from the mountainous jungle along the Dominican border. The Tonton Macoutes sabotage the party before Jones can be revealed as an imposter, and the surviving guerillas who meet Brown in the Dominican Republic complain because they had great hope for their fallen leader. Jones's fate is at once comic, tragic, and somehow redemptive, for he dies with men giving him the attention and praise he worked for so diligently throughout his life.

Through Jones, Greene challenges readers to consider whether a sober response to tragedy is adequate. Comedy certainly holds a higher place in this novel and functions as a more soothing way to endure the postmodern world's innumerable tragedies. Unlikely sources articulate the defense of comic sensitivity throughout the novel. For instance, Martha's husband, a thick-headed ambassador, wisely counsels, "We mustn't complain too much of being comedians—it's an honourable profession. If only we could be good ones the world might gain at least a sense of style. We have failed—that's all. We are bad comedians, we aren't bad men."[109] One implication of this speech is that taking a comic approach to the world may help men handle pain and possibly slow the political ascent of men like Papa Doc—who is full of seriousness and fear, and never leaves his palace—from spreading terror. Even Captain Concasseur, the chief Tonton Macoute, makes an apology for humor, "I am in favour of jokes," although he abuses their value somewhat in claiming, "They have political value. Jokes are a release for the cowardly and the impotent."[110] However, he may unknowingly possess more wisdom than he realizes, for Concasseur is just such an impotent coward, who needs a sense of humor to justify committing atrocities while wearing a mask.

Despite these surprising validations of comedy, Greene's voice surfaces most recognizably through the temperate Brown, for whom comedy functions not merely as an anesthetic, but as the catalyst for a potentially renewed understanding of his Catholic faith. Recalling his time as a believer with the Jesuits, Brown observes, "Life under [God's] shadow was a very serious affair; I saw Him incarnated in every tragedy."[111] He determines that this approach to faith cannot withstand the conflicts of the postmodern world. Comedy therefore helps Brown revise his conception of God's role in the world. "Now that I approached the end of life it was only my sense of humour that enabled me sometimes to believe in Him. Life was a comedy, not the tragedy for which I had been prepared."[112] Yet, for Catholics, what ultimately renders life a comedy is not that the innumerable tragedies are sometimes mixed with humorous moments and circumstances, but that the conclusion—the redemption which Brown is far from accepting but may have at least turned toward—overcomes life's relentless pain. With these hints of comedy, manifested in the novel in both a comic and redemptive Catholic sense, Greene reestablishes and revitalizes his authentic "tragicomic" voice.

CONCLUSION: GRAHAM GREENE, *MONSIGNOR QUIXOTE*

The 1966 publication of *The Comedians* coincided with the death of Waugh, Greene's best literary friend and possibly his closest male companion. In Greene's autobiography, he fondly recalls

Waugh's words to him in 1952: "Our friendship started rather late. Pray God it lasts," leaving Greene to assert confidently over a decade after his friend's death, "It did."[113] Waugh's death, along with Greene's separation from Catherine and his move to France, distanced him even further from England. He continued his obsessive travels, confessing in 1973 after the publication of *The Honorary Consul*, yet another political novel concerning a fallen away British Catholic in Latin America, "I saw myself living abroad. I even wanted to feel homesick for my native England—but all these dreams came to nothing . . . and though I live abroad I'm not homesick."[114] Greene found a way to accept and even embrace the rootless condition of a truly postmodern man. He let humor guide him through danger, as is illustrated in his response to Fidel Castro's suggestion that he should be dead "according to the estimate of probabilities": "Well, I always was bad at mathematics."[115]

In the 1980s, Greene reinvigorated his attempts to promote a better political relationship between Catholics and Communists. He announced during a 1987 trip to Moscow, "Roman Catholics are fighting together with the Communists and working together. We are fighting together against the death squads in El Salvador. We are fighting together against Contraras in Nicaragua. We are fighting together against General Pinochet in Chile. There is no division in our thoughts between Roman Catholics and Communists."[116] Greene's dream never materialized, probably because having common enemies does not necessarily make two organizations allies, especially in this case, considering the wide disparity between the Catholic and Communist visions of the future. Yet Greene never let such politically motivated idealism seep into his novels. In *Monsignor Quixote* (1982), one of his last publications, he humorously explores the relationship between Catholics and Communists by drawing parallels with the relationship between Don Quixote and Sancho Panza. Fr. Quixote, a simple-minded but sincere priest at a rural parish in El Toboso, Spain, is unexpectedly joined on a pilgrimage by the deposed Communist mayor of El Toboso, the novel's Sancho figure. Their attempts at reconciling their respective ideologies prove mildly humiliating for both sides. The mayor painfully attempts to excuse the cruelties committed by Communists around the globe, while Fr. Quixote must answer absurd theological questions, such as whether a dog's soul can be saved or whether it is acceptable to listen to the confession of a man in an adjacent stall in a public restroom. Greene seems to suggest that mixing these two metanarratives produces more comedy than results.

Both characters also observe that the principles of each organization take precedence over the bureaucratic obedience demanded by the hierarchy. Fr. Quixote claims, "It seems to me . . . that you have more belief in Communism than in the Party," which prompts the mayor's response, "And I was just going to say almost the same, father, that you seem to have more belief in Catholicism than in Rome."[117] Greene has moved from presenting Catholicism as a metanarrative in his early novels, to a petit récit, and now finally to an organization that merely provides guidelines for living. However, while one may adopt the principles of an economic and political system like communism and express sympathy with them, it is more problematic to lay claim to a mere theoretical Catholicism. Catholicism without liturgy or doctrine, without even spirituality, is only a glorified form of humanism.

Greene apparently recognizes this problem and does not permit Fr. Quixote's and the mayor's peaceable but relativistic exchange to stand as the novel's final message. Returning home from the pilgrimage, a defrocked Fr. Quixote (who was mistakenly given the title of respect "Monsignor" and is then persecuted by the envious conservative clergy) interferes with a pagan ceremony in which a statue of the Virgin Mary coated in Spanish currency is paraded through the city. He successfully prevents this desecration and unintentionally starts a riot, thereby proving his constancy to the church. Greene underscores this loyalty when Fr. Quixote dies saying Mass, albeit without the actual bread and wine, which his bishop withholds from him. An old priest defends the efficacy of Fr. Quixote's final sacramental act, and he challenges his more learned counterparts. "Do you think it's more difficult to turn empty air into wine than wine into blood? Can our limited senses decide a thing like that? We are faced by an infinite mystery."[118] Fr. Quixote's comic role as an unexpected hero again transformed into humbled defender of the Catholic faith reflects Greene's commitment to postmodern, tragicomic narratives.

Like Fr. Quixote, Greene would die with a complicated relationship to the church. In the decade before his death in 1991 of leukemia, Greene formed a meaningful relationship with Fr. Leopoldo Durán, a priest from Spain. According to Greene, Fr. Durán had "permission to say Mass in Latin and say it anywhere," which satisfied Greene's desire for a pre-Vatican II liturgy and allowed him to attend Mass while traveling without making his attendance a public event.[119] Greene even once admitted that he went to confession and took the Eucharist "to please Fr. Durán," although he quickly recanted this revelation.[120] It is at least verifiable that Fr. Durán gave Greene the Anointing of the Sick—a Catholic sacrament given before death to forgive the sins of believers and anoint them for burial—and a Catholic Mass was said for Greene at his funeral. Fr. Durán proclaimed in his homily at the funeral, "I do beseech you to be convinced that Graham Greene was a real Catholic Believer."[121]

Although he joined the church without compulsion, Greene was haunted by the church rather than enmeshed in its sacramental life. He certainly did not support an evangelical form of Catholicism that attempted to spread the faith as an essential global metanarrative. And yet, it served resiliently as his petit récit. The psychology of Catholics in the twentieth century provided the foundation of Greene's best novels, and his aesthetic shift from a modernist to a postmodern novelist both influenced and was influenced by his relationship with the church. In 1951, Greene visited the Vatican and contemplated the church's spiritual and political inadequacy, but, at the conclusion of a Mass celebrated by the Pope Pius XII in St. Peter's Square, he confessed, "It was not after all the question, can this Thing survive? it was, how can this Thing ever be defeated?"[122] Greene could not imagine the course of human history continuing without the Catholic Church, and, once converted, he certainly could never shake its presence from his own consciousness.

Conclusion: Impossible Temptations

*The Church . . . will assume different forms. She will be less
identified with the great societies, more a minority Church;
she will live in small, vital circles of really convinced believers
who live their faith. But precisely in this way she will, bibli-
cally speaking, become the salt of the earth again.*
—Joseph Cardinal Ratzinger (Pope Benedict XVI),
The Salt of the Earth

I HAVE DISTINGUISHED GRAHAM GREENE FROM THE OTHER ENGLISH
Catholic converts in this study in part because he faced a post-
metanarrative social reality in a more developed form than the others. Yet each of these converts—even Hopkins, who died before
the worldwide catastrophes of the twentieth century—on some
level faced the end of the metanaratives of the British Empire and
the Catholic faith, at least in their traditional historical forms. Of
course, only Greene believed the end of metanarrative essential
and useful; for other Catholic modernists, it signified a tragic cultural loss. Greene once complained that in England "Catholicism
which should produce revolutionaries produces only eccentrics"
and that "Conservatism and Catholicism should be impossible
bedfellows."[1] Certainly in the former point Greene is accurate
with regard to Hopkins, Ford, Eliot, and Waugh, who were more
eccentric than revolutionary, but to the conservative mind, that
was a necessity and only superficially a failure. That Catholicism
and conservatism are not compatible is a more contentious notion.
Although these artists had difficulty conflating their religious and
political views in some matters, in others these views comple-
mented each other. The same can be said with regard to Greene's
faith and his liberalism. Yet Greene accepted these incompatibili-
ties more easily than the others, or at least he responded with
irony and not bitterness or nostalgia.

The predictable inability of these artists' modernist works to re-

194

claim pre-Reformation English Catholicism or to reestablish an impermeable British Empire does not signify the end of the Catholic faith in England or the loss of a meaningful English national identity. If that was true from a Catholic perspective, then the movement from metanarrative to petit récit would reflect the triumph of moral relativism. Such a result would be heretical. The transformation of Catholicism from petit récit to metanarrative says nothing of its truth value—believers still hold that the Catholic faith contains the fullness of religious and moral truth as it has been revealed. But the way that faith and its believers function when these beliefs come into conflict with those outside of its system is transformed: instead of demanding that all adopt the same position or be excluded, ignored, or even attacked, the (ideal) postmodern Catholic witnesses his faith by faithful practice, political and interreligious dialogue, and efforts at promoting peace.

As Greene insisted with regard to the travesties caused by totalitarianism and certain agents of communism in Latin America and Eastern Europe—and also in the worldwide abuses caused by American capitalism—the Catholic Church plays an important political and moral role in the world, even when functioning as a petit récit. This role is made possible in part because the Catholic Church's relevance on the international scene is derived largely from its moral influence on its more than one billion members and not on the veracity of its religious dogma (although the two are not unrelated). This development correlates with Lyotard's understanding of the effects of the movement from the modern to the postmodern. He explains that, in a postmodern world, "The question (overt or implied) now asked by the professionalist student, the State, or institutions of higher education is no longer 'Is it true?' but 'What use it is?' "[2] Accordingly, in the postmodern world, the Catholic Church typically is judged based on the usefulness of its political and social platforms and on the truth of its religious dogma only when it directly influences the former.

And yet this postmodern condition need not constitute a failure for the Catholic Church and its mission, because these political and social platforms can be occasions for implicit evangelization of the Catholic faith. The Catholic modernists may have grasped this better than Greene; Hopkins's "Terrible Sonnets," Ford's *Parade's End* tetralogy, Waugh's *Sword of Honour* trilogy, and Eliot's *Four Quartets* and dramas are all works that simultaneously accept the demoted place of faith (and empire) while seeking a re-formulation of religious and national identity in the postmodern world. Not surprisingly, there is sometimes a defeated tone in each of these works, because the failure of these artists' somewhat outlandish religious and political objectives provoked an amount of humiliation—even if their art was largely an aesthetic success. Greene preempted this reaction through his characteristic irony, and certainly clinging to a petit récit that was once a metanarrative invites an ironic response. But humiliation can also transform into humility, and a tone of humility surfaces in each of these artists' final major works and words.

Ford's humility is probably closest to Greene's in that he also found an amount of irony in the loss of his religious and political notions. In fact, Ford judged his own views archaic while formulating them and anticipated the negative response of his contemporaries. Although Ford's political and religious stance is evident in his implicit identification with the sentimental Edward Ashburnham in *The Good Soldier,* his admiration often seems as deliberately pathetic as it is sincere. In *Parade's End,* Tietjens's defense of the estate at Great Groby likewise underscores Ford's dream of a Catholic, feudal England. But this nostalgia sometimes sounds purposefully ridiculous, such as when Tietjens imagines the ideal future for his son. "Christopher wished he would be a contemplative parson farming his tythe-fields and with a Greek testament in folio under his arm."[3] The irony here somewhat undermines the seriousness with which Ford held to his beliefs. Ford risks the temptation to misread Tietjens's vision as evidence of the absurdity of his hopes, but Ford thought it was only the faulty values of the modern world that made this idyllic scene absurd, not the scene itself.

After the Great War, Ford blamed Cervantes for ruining "the gentle ideal of chivalry," a code that contained all that "might have saved our unfortunate civilization."[4] Clearly, the modern world and the beginning of the end of metanarrative for Ford was not initiated by the First World War, but a process that began in the sixteenth century may have culminated in that tragedy. Although Ford never really believed a reinstitution of the old system was possible, he did try to defend its merits when he could—a characteristic of those who defend a petit récit rather than a metanarrative. When Ford's daughter by Stella Bowen, Julie, announced that she was leaving the Catholic faith, he responded famously, "You see, if you will think of it, I am the kind of person whose truths eventually swim up to the surface. They seem silly to you now as they seem to the press and public of [England]. But if you think of the persons whose truths, historically, have eventually swum up to the surface of public consciousness and have prevailed you will see that it is the lonely buffaloes, ploughing solitary furrows who have generally produced those truths."[5] Ford's claim that his truths might "seem silly" to the British public is paradoxical, because Ford plays the part himself: through characters such as Ashburnham and Tietjens and in various editorials, he portrays his views as being so anachronistic they sound mildly preposterous. But again, Ford chose to defend these values behind this self-created cloud of irony. Because Julie is his daughter and the letter concerned with the message rather than the form, the irony in this passage drops away, and Ford's serious tone reinforces the gravity with which he approached his Catholic faith and the umbrella of his social and political views.

Ford's voice is especially powerful when it is serious, in part because it is so often playful. Although the language is certainly different, the sentiment in such passages echoes Hopkins when defending his beliefs despite the absence of another soul with the same ones from both a political and religious standpoint. Because Ford's Catholic faith, when not tied to his socioeconomic system, still held a great deal of relevance, he occasionally defended it shamelessly. He once rebuked Anthony Betram for his careless treatment of the faith in a novel. "Christianity isn't you know a Sunday supper with the maids given the evening off; it is eating flesh and drinking blood."[6] The direct nature of this criticism is striking. When Ford's purpose outweighed his art, he renounced irony and his role as the "lonely buffalo" in favor of a more forthright apologist for his truths.

While Ford accepted the incompatibility of his beliefs early in his career but asserted them with more boldness in his final years, the opposite pattern might be traced in Waugh's career. Waugh's tenacious ironic voice in his early novels yields to the sentimental tone of *Brideshead Revisited,* in which he laments the irrevocable loss of the landed Catholic aristocracy. In *The Sword of Honour* trilogy and Waugh's later essays, an ironic voice returns, but much of its earlier vindictiveness is muted. Here Waugh assumes an almost defeated tone worthy of Ford's best novels. Unlike Ford, Waugh truly hoped on some level that the aristocracy might regain its power and the church sustain a new power in Europe, if not in England. He believed the church was a worthy foe to fascism or communism after the Second World War. But Waugh's portrayal of Guy Crouchback as an isolated, misunderstood Catholic outcast wandering the Continent suggests that he had come to terms with the diminished role of English Catholics. Waugh's great comfort was what he viewed as the immutability of Catholicism. He insisted, "The function of the Church in every age has been conservative—to transmit undiminished and uncontaminated the creed inherited from its predecessors."[7] Of course, Waugh thought the Second Vatican Council jeopardized this mission.

Waugh's rejection of the council's changes is not surprising, but the subjugated tone of his opposition is. As much as the end of the empire or the Catholic aristocracy frustrated him, it was the liturgical changes to the Mass that shattered his will to continue. Instead of firing back at those instituting the changes, he meagerly retorted at the advent of the council: "By all means let the rowdy have their 'dialogues,' but let us who value silence not be completely forgotten."[8] The "silence" here refers to attitude of the congregation during worship, but Waugh's request simply to "not be completely forgotten" sounds much different than the caustic voice in which he usually delivers his criticisms. Part of this change may be explained by the fact that his enemies in this instance were mostly clergy, but Waugh rarely tempers his rhetoric regardless of his audience.

At the end of his life, Waugh was addicted to pain killers and alcohol, insomniac and rheumatic, and bored by the tedium of suffering and life. By most accounts, he was a bitter man in his final years, but he clung to his belief in Catholicism even after the council. With regard to the church, he tried to comfort himself. "In her inspired wisdom, she will come out right but not in our time" and even revealingly commented that the council was "destroying all that is *superficially* attractive about my Church."[9] The adverb suggests that he still believed entirely in the dogmatic core Catholicism, although Waugh would probably never accept its fate as a petit récit—it would remain for him a metanarrative that the Continent was foolishly abandoning as his country had centuries before.

Hopkins is the other figure in this study who would never accept Catholicism, or the British Empire for that matter, as a petit récit. And also like Waugh, Hopkins hoped for a Catholic spiritual revival that went far beyond the bounds of the Oxford Movement converts. As the "Terrible Sonnets" indicate, he knew he would die without seeing this dream come to fruition, and he probably also deduced that a Catholic reconversion of England and the empire was not imminent. Because few of his poems were published or widely read, he did not have Waugh's advantage of gauging the public response to his political views; yet, because his great hopes for Catholic England also diminished at the end of his life, the tone of his poetry follows a similar pattern as Waugh's novels. Hopkins was humbled more by the increasing impotence of English Catholicism and the empire than by the inability of his works to revive these metanarratives.

But his later rhetoric reveals that he was not so detached from the fate of his poetry as he may have wished. In 1883, five years before his death, he wrote in his diary, "Also in some med[itation] today I earnestly asked our Lord to watch over my compositions, not to preserve them from being lost or coming to nothing, for that I am very willing they should, but they might not do me harm through enmity or imprudence of any man or my own; that he would have them as his own and employ or not employ them as he would see fit. And this I believe is heard."[10] The humility in this passage is sincere, but it is a forced sincerity. Hopkins's unstated desire that his poetry gain an audience can be heard in the comment that God "employ or not employ" his works, a statement that echoes Christ's prayer for deliverance in Gethsemane. It is still remarkable how fully this veiled petition was answered. Yet, somewhat ironically, Hopkins's posthumous reputation grew largely due to the technical elements of his verse rather than its religious themes. But that vehicle also incidentally spreads his Catholic message.

In this pattern, Hopkins compares with Eliot, whose initial reputation was earned from a form so experimental in *The Waste Land* that it inarguably changed the course of poetry in English. Yet that work can be read as a desperate attempt to reclaim metanarrative in England, or at least salvage those petit récits worth preserving. As *The Waste Land* implies and his postconversion essays substantiate, Eliot knew this project was unlikely to succeed, but he considered the attempt not only noble but redemptive. In 1936, he asserted, "We are committed to what in the eyes of the world must be a desperate belief, that a Christian world-order, *the* Christian world-order, is ultimately the only one which, from any point of view, will work."[11] The horrors of the Second World War entrenched Eliot deeper in this position, while at the same time it confirmed the implausibility of a "Christian world-order" ever materializing. In *The Four Quartets*, Eliot delineates his acceptance of the hopelessness of an expansive reinvigoration of this metanarrative by constructing a personal mystical vision that places the past in the context of an eternity that can begin to be manifested in the present.

The plays are an attempt to articulate this revised perspective. From *The Cocktail Party* to *The Elder Statesman*, Eliot emphasizes the salvific value of the present moment. The old vision of a powerful church-led empire still haunts him, but he must leave the comprehensive reassertion of that metanarrative for the proper time. In *Murder in the Cathedral*, Eliot imagines Thomas Becket enduring the same trial. Thomas humbly accepts his martyrdom, but not without an internal fight against the hope for his desired result of his conflicts with the monarch. He defends himself against one of his tempters:

> The impossible is still temptation.
> The impossible, the undesirable,
> Voices under sleep, waking a dead world,
> So that the mind may not be whole in the present.[12]

As in the *Quartets*, these lines suggest that Eliot's desire for a "Christian world-order" were misguided. According to his beliefs, only at the redemption of the world will that order be reestablished; temporarily, metanarrative becomes merely a temptation, something "undesirable" because it is not yet willed by God. Following God's will in the reality of the present is the only way to make it possible again.

Eliot scholars often consider his marriage to Valerie Fletcher a transformative moment in his spiritual life. The love affair certainly revived him emotionally. His comments about the relationship exude a sense of joy not discernible in the preceding years. He claimed, "Before my marriage I was getting older. Now I feel younger at seventy than I did at sixty. . . . This last part of my life is the best, in excess of anything I could have deserved."[13] The marriage fulfilled him, but it is a mistake to insist that his religious perspective changed. Even in the darkest of his spiritual nights, Eliot hoped for peace and contentment; he simply thought these gifts would not be attained while he was alive. In this belief he wanted to emulate the saints, but he was wise enough to accept an early relief from this purgatorial process.

Eliot found peace only after accepting failure. Hopkins, Ford, and Waugh died feeling less satisfied with their personal lives and literary careers, but their work has endured and sometimes flourished in popularity since their deaths. None of these authors had the influence on English Catholicism (or Anglo-Catholicism) they hoped their works might prompt. Yet their works are a legacy that some have called an English Catholic revival; and while I have resisted that designation, these artists' individual efforts have modeled how Catholic literature can function when Catholicism is preserved as a petit récit. It is worth repeating that this condition for the church is not relativistic; the faithful await the universal reinstitution of this metanarrative in redemption. These authors, Greene included, died with at least a remnant of that hope, and the contrast of their faith with the fragmented reality of the modern world contributed to the genesis of an important strain of modernism in England.

Notes

INTRODUCTION

T. S. Eliot, *The Waste Land*, in *T. S. Eliot: Collected Poems 1909–1965* (New York: Harcourt Brace & Co., 1963), 53.

1. Edward Said, *Culture and Imperialism* (New York: Alfred A. Knopf, 1993), 12.

2. Kenneth O. Morgan, ed., *The Oxford History of Britain* (Oxford: Oxford University Press, 2001), 521.

3. Ibid., 541.

4. For an overview of the 1851 census and a discussion of its potential flaws see Josef L. Altholz, "The Political Behavior of English Catholics, 1850–1867," *Journal of British* Studies no. 4,1 (November 1964): 1.

5. Christopher Hollis, *Newman and the Modern World* (Garden City, NY: Doubleday, 1968), 113.

6. For further discussion of the differences between Irish and English Catholicism after the English Reformation, see John Bossy, *The English Catholic Community 1570–1850* (New York: Oxford University Press, 1976), 315–16.

7. Ibid., 127–28.

8. See Edward Norman, *Roman Catholicism in England* (Oxford: Oxford University Press, 1985), 52–56.

9. Reverend George Stebbing, C. SS. R., *The Church in England* (London: Sands & Co., 1921), 574.

10. Nicholas Atkin and Frank Tallett, *Priests, Prelates and People: A History of European Catholicism Since 1750* (Oxford: Oxford University Press, 2003), 119.

11. Susan M. Griffin's *Anti-Catholicism and Nineteenth Century Fiction* (Cambridge: Cambridge University Press, 2004) offers an insightful study of the different explicit and subversive forms of anti-Catholicism in Victorian novelists from Dickens to Henry James.

12. For an overview of the historical debate about the correlation between the Ritualists and homosexuality, see John Shelton Reed, *Glorious Battle: The Cultural Politics of Victorian Anglo-Catholicism* (Nashville, TN: Vanderbilt University Press, 1996), 221–23.

13. Norman, *Roman Catholicism in England*, 75.

14. John Henry Newman, *Second Spring: A Sermon* (London: Thomas Richardson and Son, 1852), 5.

15. Bossy, *English Catholic Community*, 85.

16. Bossy describes specific examples of these family's struggles maintaining

their Catholic traditions in the nineteenth century. Few English traditions with foundations in the landed gentry were intact after the Industrial Revolution and World War I. Ibid., 323–63.

17. Newman, *Second Spring*, 6.

18. Ian Ker, *John Henry Newman: A Biography* (Oxford: Oxford University Press, 1988), 363.

19. John Beer explains, "There was a domestic centripetality in his Catholicism that surprised his contemporaries. His fellow Roman Catholics could not understand his reluctance to proselytize." John Beer, *Romantic Influences* (New York: St. Martin's Press, 1993), 141. Newman's conduct once again mirrors that of the recusant Catholics, which makes his critical stance toward them as baffling at the end of his career as it was at the beginning.

20. Mary Heimann, *Catholic Devotion in Victorian England* (Oxford: Clarendon Press, 1995), 137.

21. Hilaire Belloc, *Europe and the Faith* (London: Burns & Oates, 1962), 108.

22. W. B. Yeats, ed., *The Oxford Book of Modern Verse* (New York: Oxford University Press, 1936), xi.

23. Ibid., xi–xii.

24. Ezra Pound, "To H. L. Menken" (1916), *Selected Letters* (New York: New Direction Publishing, 1971), 97–98, quoted in Lyndall Gordon, *T. S. Eliot: An Imperfect Life* (New York: Norton, 1998), 103.

25. Ibid., 104.

26. Pound, "Manifesto," *Blast*, 1 (June 1914): 7, quoted in Michael H. Levenson, *A Genealogy of Modernism: A Study of English Literary Doctrine 1908–1922* (Cambridge: Cambridge University Press, 1984), 76.

27. Ford, Madox Ford, "Literary Portraits XXVII: Nineteen Thirteen and the Futurists," *Outlook* 33 (January 3, 1914): 15, quoted in ibid., 59.

28. Paul Peppis, *Literature, Politics, and the English Avant-Garde: Nation and Empire, 1901–1918* (Cambridge: Cambridge University Press, 2000), 15.

29. Gordon, *Imperfect Life*, 137.

30. For a detailed analysis of the way Christianity and other myth systems began to preoccupy the consciousness of the men on the front lines see Paul Fussell's chapter "Myth, Ritual and Romance" in Paul Fussell, *The Great War and Modern Memory* (New York: Oxford University Press, 1975), 114–54.

31. Ibid., 118.

32. Andreas Huyssen, *After the Great Divide: Modernism, Mass Culture, Postmodernism* (Bloomington: Indiana University Press, 1986), vii; viii. Huyssen argues that high modernists were not nearly as divorced from capitalistic economic culture as they insisted. John Xiros Cooper's *Modernism and the Culture of Market Society* (Cambridge: Cambridge University Press, 2004) extends Huyssen's analysis and attempts to show the close relationship between the commodification of popular novels and works of high modernism. However, I believe the boundary between high and low art can be maintained even if modernist works of "high art" were marketed and sold in the same manner as popular works. In Ihab Hassan's *The Postmodern Turn*, he makes a similar distinction between high modernism and the avant-garde. Hassan claims the avant-garde, which included "Cubism, Futurism, Dadasim" was "anarchic," while high modernism

"proved more stable, aloof, hieratic." *The Postmodern Turn: Essays in Postmodern Theory and Culture* (Columbus: Ohio State University Press, 1987), 90.

33. Stephen Spender, *The Struggle of the Modern* (Berkeley: University of California Press, 1963), 76. Spender adds, "Graham Greene, Evelyn Waugh, Henry Green, Angus Wilson . . . are serious novelists of modern subject matter: but I do not write about them because I am only discussing obvious examples of modernism or anti-modernism." Ibid., xi–xii. Strangely, Spender neglects to describe why Greene or Waugh are not "obvious examples of modernism" when Spender's own definition of modernists consists of "those who start off by thinking that human nature has changed: or if not human nature, then the relationship of the individual to the environment . . . which in fact causes human beings to behave as though they were different." Ibid., xiii. Greene and Waugh certainly highlight the peculiar historical and psychological state of the twentieth-century Englishman—even if an author like Waugh (or Eliot) wished "human nature" and behavior had not changed so drastically.

34. E. M. Forster, *Aspects of the Novel* (New York: Harcourt, Brace & Co., 1927), 245. Lawrence Rainey also highlights the modernists' involvement with national and spiritual institutions and notes that the boundaries between Anglo-American literary modernism and the historical avant-garde "acknowledge the special density of the social and institutional space that bound together the authors whose works have been deemed central to discussion of the modernist moment." *Institutions of Modernism: Literary Elites and Public Culture* (New Haven, CT: Yale University Press, 1998), 6.

35. Yeats, *Oxford Book of Modern Verse*, ix.

36. T. S. Eliot, *Selected Essays* (New York: Harcourt Brace & Co., 1950), 248 (Eliot's italics).

37. Pope Pius X, *Pascendi Dominici Gregis,* Papal Encyclicals Online, http://www.papalencyclicals.net/Pius10/p10pasce.htm, 1.

38. Ford, "On a Notice of Blast," *Outlook* 36 (July 31, 1915): 144.

39. Fredric Jameson, *Postmodernism, or The Cultural Logic of Late Capitalism* (Durham, NC: Duke University Press, 1991), 75.

40. For a detailed analysis of Frazer's influence on English literature, see John B. Vickery, *The Literary Impact of the Golden Bough* (Princeton, NJ: Princeton University Press, 1973).

CHAPTER 1. GERARD MANLEY HOPKINS

Rupert Brooke, *The Collected Poems of Rupert Brooke* (London: Kessinger Publishing, 20905), 115.

1. Gerard Manley Hopkins, *Further Letters of Gerard Manley Hopkins* (London: Oxford University Press, 1956), 93.

2. Gerard Manley Hopkins, *Gerard Manley Hopkins: Selected Prose* (Oxford: Oxford University Press, 1980), 31.

3. See Alfred Thomas, S. J., *Hopkins the Jesuit: The Years of Training* (London: Oxford University Press, 1968), 15–22. Thomas surmises various reasons

for Hopkins's attraction to the Jesuits, including those mentioned above, as well as his father's documented respect for the order.

4. John Henry Newman, *The Letters and Diaries of John Henry Newman*, vol. 1 (Oxford: Clarendon Press, 2006), 73.

5. Yeats, *The Oxford Book of Modern Verse*, xxxix.

6. Alison G. Sulloway, *Gerard Manley Hopkins and the Victorian Temper* (New York: Columbia University Press, 1972), 1.

7. J. Hillis Miller, "The Linguistic Moment" in *Gerard Manley Hopkins*, ed. Harold Bloom (New York: Chelsea House Publishers, 1986), 147.

8. Ibid.

9. William Wordsworth, *The Fourteen-Book Prelude*, ed. W. J. B. Owen (Ithaca, NY: Cornell University Press, 1985), 8.296.

10. Ibid., 319–20.

11. Newman, *Letters and Diaries*, 2:10.

12. Hopkins, *Selected Prose*, 36.

13. St. Ignatius Loyola, *The Spiritual Exercises*, trans. Louis J. Puhl, S. J. (Westminster, MD: The Newman Press, 1954), 1.

14. Thomas, *Hopkins the Jesuit*, 31.

15. Miller, "The Lingusitic Moment," 155.

16. This and all subsequent poems cited from *Gerard Manley Hopkins*, ed. Catherine Phillips (Oxford: Oxford University Press, 1986). Parenthetic citations in the text refer to line numbers.

17. Wordsworth, *Prelude*, 1079.

18. Loyola, *Spiritual Exercises*, 30.

19. For discussion of Hopkins's struggle with homosexuality, see Robert Bernard Martin, *Gerard Manley Hopkins: A Very Private Life* (New York: G. P. Putnam's Sons, 1991), 80–99. Putnam also focuses on Hopkins's infatuation with Digby Doblen, a young aesthete and nearly a Catholic convert. Dolben committed suicide just before Hopkins entered the Jesuit novitiate.

20. Loyola, *Spiritual Exercises*, 12.

21. Wordsworth, *Preface to Lyrical Ballads*, 7.

22. Eliot, *Selected Essays*, 243.

23. Benedict Anderson, *Imagined Communities: Reflections on the Origin and Spread of Nationalism* (New York: Verso, 1983), 16 (Anderson's italics).

24. Ibid., 143.

25. Ibid., 17.

26. Ibid., 149.

27. Hopkins, *Gerard Manley Hopkins*, 213.

28. Martin, *A Very Private Life*, 258.

29. For example, Jill Muller argues that " '*Deutschland*' echoes the anti-German rhetoric of the major ultramontanists like Manning in his essays 'Ceasarism and Ultramontanism' and 'Christianism and Anti-Christianism.' " Muller, *Gerard Manley Hopkins and Victorian Catholicism: A Heart in Hiding* (New York: Routledge, 2003), 50. Muller also cites Sjaak Zonneveld's similar contention that Hopkins was an ultramontane Catholic in *The Random Grim Forge: A Study of Social Ideas in Gerard Manley Hopkins* (Maastricht, Netherlands: Van Gorcem, 1992).

30. Gerald Roberts, "Hopkins and the Catholics of England," *Hopkins Quarterly* 14, no. 1–4 (April 1987–January 1988): 115.

31. Hopkins, *Selected Prose*, 55.

32. Hopkins, *Further Letters*, 293.

33. In the late nineteenth century, many Catholic scholars subscribed to the theory that Scotus was from England, but later scholarship gave greater evidence that he was in fact from Scotland, as his name suggests. Martin, *Very Private Life*, 207–8.

34. Hopkins, *Selected Prose*, 84.

35. Loyola, *Spiritual Exercises*, 147.

36. Although Hopkins's scholarly language and sometimes esoteric spiritual notions prevented him from becoming a popular preacher, especially among the poorly educated working class or rural people, his nearly incessant movement from place to place had little to do with his performance. For a discussion of why the Jesuits constantly moved their young members to fill the diverse needs of the order, see Joseph F. Feeney, S. J., "Hopkins's Frequent Reassignments," *Hopkins Quarterly* 11, no. 3 & 4 (Fall 1984–Winter 1985): 106.

37. Hopkins, *Gerard Manley Hopkins*, 260.

38. Oliver P. Rafferty, *The Church, the State, and the Fenian Threat* (New York: St. Martin's, 1999), 144.

39. Joseph F. Feeney, S. J. "Four Newfound Hopkins Letters," *Hopkins Quarterly* 23, no. 1 & 2 (Winter-Spring 1996): 24

No. 3 & 4): 24.

40. Hopkins, *Further Letters*, 414.

41. Hopkins, *Gerard Manley Hopkins*, 264.

42. Hopkins, *Selected Prose*, 79.

43. Ibid., 103.

44. Hopkins himself did not give these poems either title, and there is disagreement about which poems belong in this group. However, five poems typically comprise scholarly lists: "To Seem the Stranger," "I Wake and Feel," "No Worst (Carrion Comfort)," "Patience, Hard Thing," and "My Own Heart." Nevertheless, as Catherine Phillips notes in her edition of Hopkins's poetry, the dates and order of composition of the poems is still uncertain, although all were composed in Ireland sometime during the years 1885 and 1886. Hopkins, *Gerard Manley Hopkins*, n166; 372.

45. Edward Said, *Reflections on Exile and Other Essays* (Cambridge, MA: Harvard University Press, 2000), 177.

46. Hopkins, *Further Letters*, 274.

47. Ibid., 280.

48. Ibid., 281.

49. Ibid., 194.

50. Hopkins, *Gerard Manley Hopkins*, 303.

51. Anderson, *Imagined Communities*, 144.

CHAPTER 2. FORD MADOX FORD

Quoted in Hugh Kenner, *A Sinking Island* (London: Barrie & Jenkins, 1988), 93. According to Kenner, Basil Bunting recited this quote to him in 1980.

1. Max Saunders, *Ford Madox Ford: A Dual Life, Vol. 1* (Oxford: Oxford University Press, 1996), 357.

2. Ibid., 356.

3. Ford Madox Ford, *Memories and Impressions* (London: Harper, 1911), xviii.

4. Ibid., 9

5. Allan Tate in *Ford Madox Ford: Critical Essays*, ed. Max Saunders and Richard Stang (Manchester, UK: Carcanet, 2002), 13.

6. Saunders, *Dual Life, Vol. 1*, 18.

7. Ford, Madox Ford *England and the English: An Interpretation* (New York: McClure, Phillips & Co., 1907), 301.

8. Saunders, *Dual Life, Vol. 1*, 28. Madox Brown took custody of his grandson after Ford's father died in 1891. While in his home, Ford was influenced by his aunt, Christina Rossetti, and other Pre-Raphaelite artists until Madox Brown's own death in 1893. In addition to providing a valuable aesthetic influence, Ford's association with the Pre-Raphaelites gave him an appreciation for the historical culture and art of Continental Catholicism.

9. Ford, *England and the English*, 336.

10. Saunders recounts Ford's brief determination to become a German citizen. But Ford's visit to Westminster Abbey in 1911 left him proclaiming "This is the very heart of England; this is the very heart of Britain; this is the heart of hearts of the Empire," and he took no more steps toward renouncing his English citizenship. Saunders, *Dual Life, Vol. 1*, 340.

11. Ford, Madox Ford, *Return to Yesterday* (New York: Horace Liverright, Inc., 1932), 367.

12. Ford, *England and the English*, 340.

13. Ibid., 334–35.

14. Ibid., 294.

15. Ibid., 343.

16. Ford, Madox Ford, *The Critical Attitude* (London: Duckworth & Co., 1911), 4.

17. Ibid., 7.

18. Ford, *English Review* (1909), quoted in Peppis, *Literature, Politics, and the English Avant-Garde*, 22.

19. Ford, *Critical Essays*, 99.

20. Ibid., 105.

21. See Pound's essay "Provincialism the Enemy" reprinted in *Selected Prose: 1909–1965* (New York: New Directions, 1973), 189–203.

22. Ford, *Return to Yesterday*, 399.

23. Ford, *Critical Attitude*, 5.

24. Ford, Madox Ford, *The Good Soldier* (Oxford: Oxford University Press, 1999), 7; 8.

25. Ibid., 44.

26. Ibid., 21.

27. Ford, *England and the English*, 336.

28. Ford, *Good Soldier*, 10.

29. Ibid., 177; 31.

30. Ibid., 34.

31. Ibid., 69.

32. Ibid., 171.

33. Ibid., 188.

34. Ibid., 172.

35. Ibid., 167.

36. Ibid., 157.

37. Ibid., 39.

38. Ibid., 70; 215.

39. Ford, "On Impressionism," reprinted in *The Good Soldier* (Ontario, Canada: Broadview, 2003), 274.

40. Ford regularly used the distinction between "Roman Catholics" and "Papists" as a marker of the reasons they professed the Catholic faith. For example, in Ford's "Literary Portrait" of Thomas Hardy, he recounts meeting a group at Hardy's house consisting of "a Cambridge professor of classics . . . two lady novelists—one, like our host, an atheist of the eighties; one a Roman Catholic" and "a "Servian representative of the Press . . . like myself for that matter . . . a Papist." Ford, *Critical Essays*, 169.

41. Ford, *Return to Yesterday,*369.

42. Ibid., 368.

43. Ibid., 367.

44. While Ford claims to have admired some aspects of Belloc's work and the two would later meet regularly with G. K. Chesterton, who was less brash but just as definitive about his religious views, Ford wrote conspicuously little about either figure (collectively and derisively called "Chesterbelloc" by George Bernard Shaw). Despite the fact that they were Ford's English Catholic contemporaries and held some of Ford's romantic economic views—Belloc and Chesterton tirelessly advocated for the institution of a Distributist economic system in England that was similar to Edward Ashburnham's anachronistic pseudo-feudalism—Ford kept his distance from their extremely conservative Catholic beliefs.

45. Ford, *Good Soldier,* 71.

46. Ibid., 54.

47. Ibid., 49.

48. Ibid., 53.

49. Ibid., 53.

50. Ibid., 53; 55.

51. John A. Meixner, *Ford Madox Ford's Novels: A Critical Study* (Minneapolis: University of Minnesota Press, 1962), 186.

52. Ford, *Good Soldier,* 214.

53. Ibid., 219.

54. Ibid., 234.

55. Ibid., 274; 285.

56. Ibid., 278.

57. Ford, *England and the English,* 314.

58. Ibid., 315.

59. Ford, Madox Ford, *War Prose,* ed. Max Saunders (New York: New York University Press, 2004), 218.

60. Ibid., 221.

61. For an analysis of the common testimony among soldiers that prayer and the sacraments became especially important at quiet, tense moments just before fighting, see Richard Schweitzer, *The Cross and the Trenches* (London: Praeger, 2003), 129–60.

62. For a summary of Sassoon's objection to the war, see Robert Graves, *Good-bye to All That* (New York: Doubleday Anchor, 1967), 260–64. After being injured in France, Sassoon wrote a letter to his commanding officer stating, "I believe that the war is being deliberately prolonged by those who have the power to end it. . . . This war, upon which I entered as a war of defence and liberation, has now become a war of aggression and conquest." Ibid., 260. He was court-martialed and nearly imprisoned, but Graves made sure Sassoon's tribunal found him insane (though Graves comically insists they were probably the only two sane men at the trial).

63. Duff Crerar, *Padres in No Man's Land: Canadian Chaplains in the Field, 1885–1945* (Montreal: McGill-Queen's Press, 1995), 7–8, quoted in Schweitzer, *Cross and Trenches*, 166. Schweitzer cites statistics that show the percentage of Anglican chaplain casualties at the front actually was comparable to the percentage suffered by the Catholic priests. Ibid., 172.

64. Graves, *Good-bye to All That*, 190.

65. For a thorough analysis of the comedic elements in *Good-bye to All That*, see Fussell, *Great War and Modern Memory*, 205–7. Fussell argues that *Good-bye to All That* "is rather a satire, built out of anecdotes heavily influenced by the techniques of stage comedy." Ibid., 207. Graves himself admitted that "the most painful chapters have to be the jokiest." Ibid., 205. Graves's comment reflects my reading of his text as a serious work infused with comedic moments and a sarcastic tone to soften the tragedy.

66. In the November 1914 encyclical *Ad Beatissimi Apostolorum*, Benedict XV appealed for peace and warned of the possibility of a long and senseless war.

67. Ford, *War Prose*, 209.

68. Ibid., 71.

69. Ibid., 73.

70. Ibid.

71. Ford, Madox Ford, *Parade's End*, (New York: Penguin, 1982), 187.

72. Ford never saw Christina after she entered the convent, although he only opposed her decision because she was young, and he did not want her to regret such a drastic step. He later embraced the idea of her vocation. Saunders, *Dual Life, Vol. 1*, 494.

73. Ford, *Parade's End*, 370.

74. Ibid., 680.

75. Ibid., 454.

76. Ibid., 603.

77. Ibid., 491.

78. Ibid., 492.

79. Ford, *Critical Essays*, 215.

80. Ford, *Parade's End*, 39.

81. Ibid., 237.

82. Ibid., 172 (Ford's ellipses).

83. Ibid., 348

84. Ibid., 175.

85. Ibid., 349.

86. Ibid., 164.

87. Ford, Madox Ford, *Your Mirror to My Times* (New York: Holt, Rinehart, and Winston, 1971), 163.

88. Ford, *Parade's End*, 760; 692.

89. Ford, Madox Ford, *It Was the Nightingale* (Philadelphia: J. B. Lippincott Co., 1933), 282.

90. Quoted in Bernard J. Poli, *Ford Madox Ford and the Transatlantic Review* (Syracuse, NY: Syracuse University Press, 1967), 37.

91. Ford, *It Was the Nightingale*, 366.

92. Ford, Madox Ford, *The Transatlantic Review* (New York: Kraus Reprint Corp., 1967), 1, no. 1., 95.

93. Quoted in Poli, *Ford Madox Ford*, 40.

94. Ford, *The Transatlantic Review*, 1, no. 3, 61.

95. Ford, *The Correspondence of Ford Madox Ford and Stella Bowen* (Bloomington, IN: Indiana University Press, 1993), 181; 188 (Ford's italics).

96. Ford, *The Transatlantic Review*, 1, no. 4, 468 (final ellipsis is Ford's).

97. Pound, *Selected Prose*, 463.

CHAPTER 3. T. S. ELIOT

Basil Bunting, "English Poetry Today," *Poetry* 39 (January 1932): 266.

1. Ford, *The Critical Attitude*, 173.

2. Pound, *Selected Prose*, 163.

3. Arthur Mizener, *T. S. Eliot: A Collection of Critical Essays*, ed. Hugh Kenner (Englewood Cliffs, NJ: Prentice-Hall, 1962), 19.

4. Ibid., 33.

5. T. S. Eliot, *For Lancelot Andrewes* (London: Faber & Gwyer, 1928), 11.

6. Rainey believes Eliot willfully attempted to control interpretations of his own early work by citing the fact that his choices of works in *Selected Essays* disregarded essays with a more liberal tone. Rainey also insists that "Eliot's conversion to Christianity . . . constituted a profound change in his thought," a belief I contest in this chapter. Lawrence Rainey, *Revisiting The Waste Land* (New Haven, CT: Yale University Press, 2005), 117.

7. Gordon, *Imperfect Life*, 90.

8. Ibid., 88.

9. This and all subsequent Eliot poetry cited from *T. S. Eliot: Collected Poems 1909–1965* (New York: Harcourt Brace & Co., 1963). Parenthetic citations in the text refer to line numbers.

10. T. S. Eliot, *The Letters of T. S. Eliot: Volume I, 1898–1922*, ed. Valerie Eliot (New York: Harcourt Brace & Co., 1988), 57.

11. Eliot, *Letters*, 173.

12. Chesterton wrote, "Tradition means giving votes to the most obscure of all classes, our ancestors. It is the democracy of the dead. Tradition refuses to

submit to that arrogant oligarchy who merely happen to be walking around."
G. K. Chesterton, *Orthodoxy* (New York: Dodd, Mead & Co., 1936), 251.

13. Quoted in Hugh Kenner, *The Invisible Poet: T. S. Eliot* (New York: Mc-Dowell, Obolensky, 1959), 73 (Pound's italics).

14. Ibid.

15. F. R. Leavis, *New Bearings in English Poetry* (London: Chatto & Windus, 1950), 95; 98.

16. John Peale Bishop to Edmund Wilson, November 1922, Yale University, Beinecke Library, Edmund Wilson Papers, quoted in Rainey, *Revisiting The Waste Land*, 103. For a similar "secular" reading that draws on Leavis, see Ronald Bush's essay "Modern/Postmodern: Eliot, Perse, Mallarmé, and the Future of the Barbarians," in *Modernism Reconsidered*, ed. Robert Kiley and John Hildebride (Cambridge, MA: Harvard University Press, 1983), 191–214.

17. Evelyn Underhill, *Mysticism* (New York; E. P. Dutton & Co., 1948), 176.

18. Jessie L. Weston, *From Ritual to Romance* (Garden City, NY: Doubleday & Co., 1957), 113.

19. Ibid., 12.

20. Ibid., 14.

21. Ezekiel 2:1; Ecclesiastes 12:5. Each of these verses is cited in Eliot's notes to lines 20 and 23, respectively. Quotes are from the Douay-Rheims translation of the Bible that a High Church Anglican in twentieth-century England most likely would have read.

22. Eliot, "The Influence of Mr. James Joyce," in *James Joyce: The Critical Heritage*, vol. 1, ed. Robert H. Deming (New York: Barnes & Noble, 1970), 188.

23. Eliot, "*Ulysses*, Order, Myth" in ibid., 268–71.

24. Eliot, *The Waste Land*, note to line 46.

25. Romans 11:8; Cf. Isaiah 29:10 and Matthew 13:13–15.

26. Leavis, *New Bearings*, 103.

27. Lake Geneva is the actual site, but Eliot probably uses "Leman" because it also means "mistress."

28. Buddha, *The Sacred Laws of the Âryas as Taught in the Schools of Âpastamba, Guatama, Vasishtha, and Baudhâyana* (Delhi, India: M. Banarsidass, 1965), 352–53.

29. See 1 Corinthians 3:13, 15: "Every man's work shall be . . . revealed in fire; and the fire shall try very man's work, of what sort it is. . . . If any man's work burn, he shall suffer loss, but he himself shall be saved, yet so as by fire."

30. Eliot, *The Waste Land*, note to line 309.

31. For extended discussion of the archetype of the drowned-revived God, see Weston's chapter "The Fisher King" in *From Ritual to Romance*, 113–36. In Romans 6:4, Paul exclaims, "For we are buried together with him by baptism unto death; that as Christ is risen from the dead by the glory of the Father, so we also may make in newness of life."

32. Ezekiel 37:1–14.

33. Eliot, *The Waste Land*, note to line 402.

34. Revelation 10:4

35. Weston, *From Ritual to Romance*, 182.

36. Ibid., 57.

37. Despite the line describing "a damp gust / Bringing rain" near the close of the last section, Leavis curiously argues, "The thunder brings no rain to revive the Waste Land, and the poem ends where it began." Leavis, *New Bearings*, 103.

38. Underhill, *Mysticism*, 176.

39. Eliot, *Letters*, 596.

40. Eliot, "Isolated Superiority," *Dial* 84 (January 1928): 4, quoted in Michael Levenson, *Genealogy of Modernism*, 216.

41. T. S. Eliot, *To Criticize the Critic and Other Writings* (New York: Farrar, Straus, and Giroux, 1965), 184.

42. Pound, *Selected Prose*, 53.

43. Ibid., 321

44. See Pound's essay, "Provincialism the Enemy" in ibid., 189–203. Pound defines *provincialism* as "ignorance of the manners, customs and nature of the people living outside one's own village, parish or nation" and "a desire to coerce others into uniformity." Ibid., 189. Anglicans were guilty of violating both tenets, while Catholics primarily the latter.

45. Ibid., 317.

46. Richard Hooker, *The Folger Library Edition of the Works of Richard Hooker*, ed. W. Speed Hill (London: Belknap Press, 1977), 280. Hooker's classic text helped delineate the Anglican Church's theology during the reign of Elizabeth. Hooker distanced the Anglican communion from the Puritans and other Reformers, citing the need for apostolic succession and traditional liturgical ceremonies. He warned that excessive fear of Catholicism might endanger the sacramental validity of Anglicanism: "Wee have framed our selves to the customes of the Church of Rome: our orders and ceremonies are papisticall." Ibid. Nonetheless, Hooker refused any formal association with Rome, rejected the core Catholic doctrine of transubstantiation, and never used the term "Anglo-Catholic" to describe the newly formed Anglican Church.

47. Eliot, *For Lancelot Andrewes*, 14.

48. Ibid.

49. Pope Leo XIII, *Apostolicae Curae*. Papal Encyclicals Online, www.papalencyclicals.net/Leo13/l13curae.htm, 1.

50. Vernon Staley, *The Catholic Religion: A Manual of Instruction for Members of the Anglican Church* (London: A. R. Mowbray & Co., 1903), 79.

51. Ibid., 80.

52. Ibid., 97.

53. Frank Weston, *Report of the Anglo-Catholic Congress of 1923* (London: Society of SS Peter and Paul, 1923), 85–86.

54. Eliot, *Selected Essays* (New York: Harcourt Brace, 1960), 325.

55. Ibid., 252.

56. Ibid., 301.

57. Ibid., 300.

58. Eliot, *For Lancelot Andrewes*, 18.

59. Eliot, *Selected Essays*, 322.

60. Ibid., 339.

61. T. S. Eliot, *Essays Ancient and Modern* (London: Faber & Faber Limited, 1936), 117.

62. Eliot, *Selected Essays*, 338.

63. Ibid., 337.

64. Ibid., 338.

65. John Henry Newman, *Lectures on the Present Position of Catholics in England* (1851) (Notre Dame, IN: University of Notre Dame Press, 2000), 55–56.

66. Eliot, *Selected Essay*, 336–37.

67. Allen Tate, *T. S. Eliot: A Collection of Critical Essays*, 135.

68. T. S. Eliot, *The Sacred Wood* (London: Methuen & Co., 1948), 162.

69. Eliot, *Selected Essays*, 203.

70. Underhill, *Mysticism*, 199.

71. William Shakespeare, "Sonnet 29" in *The Complete Works of Shakespeare*, ed. David Bevington (New York: Longman, 1997), 1670.

72. Eliot, *Selected Essays*, 364.

73. Ibid., 217 (Eliot's italics).

74. T. S. Eliot, *After Strange Gods* (New York: Harcourt Brace & Co., 1933), 9.

75. T. S. Eliot, *Notes Towards the Definition of Culture* (New York: Harcourt Brace & Co., 1949), 51.

76. Eliot, *After Strange Gods*, 29.

77. Eliot, *Notes Towards the Definition of Culture*, 74.

78. Eliot, *After Strange Gods*, 64.

79. Jed Esty, *A Shrinking Island: Modernism and National Culture in England* (Princeton, NJ: Princeton University Press, 2004), 14.

80. Eliot, *Notes Towards the Definition of Culture*, 93.

81. Ibid.

82. Jed Esty's chapter "Insular Time: T. S. Eliot and Modernism's English End" in *A Shrinking Island* offers a comprehensive analysis of Eliot's imperial attitude and demonstrates how it matches the political attitude of many artists of the period. Esty argues that "Eliot's conservatism and especially his anti-Semitism have tended to obscure the fact that antidiasporic thinking ran across the political landscape in 1930s England." Ibid., 109.

83. Eliot, *Selected Essays*, 223 (Eliot's italics).

84. Underhill, *Mysticism*, 233. For evidence that Underhill's mystical outline still influenced Eliot in his late career, see Paul Murray's *T. S. Eliot and Mysticism*. Murray claims that Eliot's side notes from Underhill's *Mysticism* accompany early drafts of "East Coker." Murray, *Eliot and Mysticism* (New York: St. Martin's, 1991), 85.

85. For Gordon's discussion of Emily Hale's influence on *Four Quartets*, see the chapter "Lady of the Silences." Gordon, *Imperfect Life*, 392–435. See also Ronald Schuchard, *Eliot's Dark Angel: Intersections of Life and Art* (New York: Oxford, 1999), 195. Schuchard reveals that after each quartet was published, Eliot sent an inscribed edition to Emily Hale, which further points to her closeness to Eliot at the time of composition. Eliot never could bring himself to marry her in part because Vivien lived until 1947, but he eventually married his secretary, Valerie Fletcher.

86. E. M. Forster, *Abinger Harvest* (London: Edwin Arnold, 1965), 112, quoted in Burton Raffel, *T. S. Eliot* (New York: Continuum, 1991), 111.

87. Kenner claims Eliot's note to his brother, Henry Ware Eliot, Jr., explained the references to saints in these lines, particularly noting, "the isles of Iona and Lindisfarne, associated with St. Columba and St. Cuthbert; St. Kevin's lake of Glandalough; the Thebaid of St. Anthony (who is also the tempted 'word in the desert' of *Burnt Norton*); and the Paudua of the other St. Anthony." Kenner, *Invisible Poet*, 319.

88. Eliot, *Murder in the Cathedral* in ibid., 41.

89. T. S. Eliot, *The Cocktail Party* in *The Complete Plays of T. S. Eliot* (New York: Harcourt, Brace and World, 1969), 135.

90. T. S. Eliot, *Affectionately, T. S. Eliot*, ed. William Turner Levy and Victor Scherle (New York: Lippincott, 1968), quoted in Gordon, *Imperfect Life*, 390.

91. See also Ranen Omer-Sherman, "'It Is I Who Have Been Defending a Religion Called Judaism': The T. S. Eliot and Horace M. Kallen Correspondence," *Texas Studies in Literature and Language* 39, no. 4 (Winter 1997): 321–56. Omer-Sherman argues that allegations of Eliot's anti-Semitism have been exaggerated (most notably by Anthony Julius in *T. S. Eliot, Anti-Semitism, and Literary Form* (Cambridge: Cambridge University Press, 1995) by focusing on Eliot's relationship with the Jewish American philosopher Horace M. Kallen. Omer-Sherman discusses Eliot's and Kallen's conversations concerning broad religious, political, and social topics in which Eliot treats the Jewish people with fairness and respect.

92. Eliot, *Selected Essays*, 342.

CHAPTER 4. EVELYN WAUGH

Graham Greene, *Ways of Escape* (New York: Simon and Schuster, 1980), 267.

1. Arthur Waugh, *Quarterly Review* (1916), quoted in Humphrey Carpenter, *The Brideshead Generation: Evelyn Waugh and His Friends* (Boston: Houghton Mifflin, 1990), 47.

2. G. K. Chesterton, "We Will End with a Bang" BBC Broadcast (March 15, 1936), quoted in Joseph Pearce, *Literary Converts: Spiritual Inspiration in an Age of Unbelief* (San Francisco: Ignatius Press, 1999), 128 (Chesterton's italics).

3. Walter Hooper, *C. S. Lewis: A Companion and Guide* (London: Harper Collins, 1998), quoted in Pearce, *Literary Converts*, 124.

4. Graham Greene, *Oxford Outlook* (February 1924), quoted in Pearce, *Literary Converts*, 138.

5. Carpenter notes that Waugh listened to Chesterton's speech at an Oxford Newman Society meeting. At the same gathering, Waugh met Harold Acton, a Catholic who inspired Waugh's portrayal of Sebastian Flyte in *Brideshead Revisited*. Carpenter, *Brideshead Generation*, 70.

6. For Belloc's discussion of the evils of capitalism, see Hilaire Belloc, *Crisis of Civilization* (New York: Fordham University Press, 1937).

7. Lewis writes in his characteristically noncommittal tone, "There is one bit of advice given to us by the ancient heathen Greeks, and by the Jews in the Old Testament, and by the great Christian teachers of the Middle Ages, which the modern economic system has completely disobeyed. All these people told us not

to lend money at interest: and lending money at interest—what we call invest-ment—is the basis of our whole system. Now it may not absolutely follow that we are wrong. . . . But I should not have been honest if I had not told you that three great civilizations had agreed (or so it seems at first sight) in condemning the very thing on which we have based our whole life." C. S. Lewis, *Mere Christianity* (New York: Macmillan, 1960), 66.

8. T. S. Eliot, *The Idea of a Christian Society* (London: Faber and Faber, 1939), 97–98. Recent studies such as John Xiros Cooper's *Modernism and the Culture of Market Society* (Cambridge: Cambridge University Press, 2004) and Ann Ardis's *Modernism and Cultural Conflict: 1880–1922* (London: Oxford, 2002) have connected modernism to the growth of capitalism, but both of their works rely much more closely on artists who I consider members of the historical avant-garde rather than the more conservative modernists who converted to Catholicism.

9. Evelyn Waugh, *The Essays, Articles and Reviews,* ed. Donat Gallagher (Boston: Little, Brown & Co., 1983), 539.

10. Ibid., 367.

11. Evelyn Waugh, *A Little Learning* (Little, Brown & Co., 1964), 182.

12. Ibid., 68.

13. Ibid., 92

14. Ibid., 122.

15. Eliot, *Idea of a Christian Society,* 22.

16. Waugh, *A Little Learning,* 229–30. Waugh does admit, "I cannot tell how much real despair and act of will, how much play-acting, prompted the excur-sion." Ibid., 230.

17. Ibid., 36 (Waugh's italics).

18. Ibid., 39.

19. Evelyn Waugh, *The Diaries of Evelyn Waugh,* ed. Michael Davie (Boston: Little, Brown & Co., 1976), 127.

20. Waugh, *A Little* Learning, 143.

21. Evelyn Waugh, *Decline and Fall* (Boston: Little, Brown & Co., 1946), 216.

22. Ibid., 229.

23. Evelyn Waugh, *Vile Bodies* (New York: Penguin, 1930), 112.

24. Ibid., 112.

25. Waugh, *Decline and Fall,* 159.

26. Waugh, *Vile Bodies,* 81.

27. Ibid., 132 (Waugh's italics).

28. Ibid., 219.

29. Waugh, *Essays,* 21.

30. Waugh, *Vile Bodies,* 68–76.

31. Max Weber, *The Protestant Ethic and the Spirit of Capitalism,* trans. Talcott Parsons (London: George Allen & Unwin Ltd., 1948), 104 (Weber's italics).

32. Weber frames his text with his theory of "The rule of Calvinism," which extends from Geneva and Scotland in the sixteenth century to England and New England in the seventeenth century. According to Weber, Calvinism comprises "the most absolutely unbearable form of ecclesiastical control of the individual which could possibly exist." Ibid., 37.

33. For an influential criticism of Weber, see R. H. Tawney, *Religion and the Rise of Capitalism: A Historical Study* 1929; repr., (New York: Harcourt, Brace and Co., 1952).

34. Waugh, *Essays*, 103.

35. Ibid., 103.

36. Ibid., 104.

37. Quoted in Selina Hastings, *Evelyn Waugh: A Biography* (Boston: Houghton Mifflin Co., 1994), 227. Cf. Christopher Sykes, *Evelyn Waugh: A Biography* (Boston: Little, Brown & Co., 1975), 107.

38. Evelyn Waugh, *Black Mischief* (London: Chapman and Hall Ltd., 1932), 152.

39. Ibid., 242.

40. Ibid., 241; 242.

41. Ibid., 243.

42. Evelyn Waugh, *The Letters of Evelyn Waugh*, ed. Mark Amory (New Haven, CT: Ticknor & Fields, 1980), 76; 74.

43. For example, see Waugh's review of Greene's controversial *The Heart of the Matter* (*Essays*, 360–65). Waugh's opinion of Greene's intentions as a Catholic novelist is empathetic but critical: "Many Catholics, I am sure, will gravely misunderstand [the book], particularly in the United States of America, where its selection as the Book of the Month will bring it to a much larger public than can profitably read it. There are loyal Catholics here and in America who think it the function of the Catholic writer to produce only advertising brochures setting out in attractive terms the advantages of Church membership. To them this profoundly reverent book will seem a scandal. For it not only portrays Catholics as unlikeable human beings but shows them as tortured by their Faith. . . . Thousands of heathen will read it with innocent excitement, quite unaware that they are intruding among the innermost mysteries of faith. There is a third class who will see what this book intends and yet be troubled by doubt of its theological propriety." Ibid., 361. Waugh implicitly places himself in this third class.

44. In "The Same Again Please," Waugh lists the slow procedures of the Ecclesiastical Court in matters of annulment, the Index of Prohibited Books, and the unclear "limits of the personal authority held by the bishop over the laity" as the key issues needing reformation just after the announcement of the Second Vatican Council. Waugh, *Essays*, 665.

45. Evelyn Waugh, *A Handful of Dust* (Boston: Little, Brown & Co., 1944), 35–36.

46. Evelyn Waugh, *Edmund Campion* (Boston: Little, Brown and Co., 1946), 18.

47. Waugh, *A Handful of Dust*, 222.

48. Ibid., 288.

49. For statistics regarding the dwindling of the landowning class, see W. L. Guttsman, *The English Ruling Class* (London: Wiedenfeld and Nicolson, 1969), 7. The reason for the decimation of the English landowning class lies in the technological advances, especially in agriculture, stemming from the Industrial Revolution. For example, agricultural income accounted for 14% of England's GDP in 1867, but only 6% in 1900. Ibid.

50. Michael Gorra, *The English Novel at Mid-Century: From the Leaning Tower* (New York: St. Martin's, 1990), 175.

51. Waugh, *Essays,* 539.

52. For an in-depth analysis of the role of the upper class in Waugh's early satirical novels, see Terry Eagleton, "Waugh and the Upper Class Novel," *Critical Essays on Evelyn Waugh,* ed. James F. Carens (Boston: G. K. Hall, 1987), 106–15. Eagleton claims that in Waugh's novels "upper class values are satirised but not dismissed; they are fraudulent and hollow, but there is really nowhere else to turn." Ibid., 108. In Waugh's more somber later novels, his affection for the upper classes is evident more demonstrably than in his earlier satirical works.

53. See my Introduction for a discussion of the history of English Catholic families.

54. Waugh, *Campion,* 231.

55. Evelyn Waugh, *Brideshead Revisited* (Boston: Little, Brown & Co., 1972), 9.

56. Weber, *Protestant Ethic,* 70.

57. Waugh, *Brideshead Revisited,* 139.

58. Oddly enough, Waugh is surprisingly silent about England's colonization of Catholic Ireland. Even when he later considered moving to Ireland, he says almost nothing about the political situation.

59. Quoted in Hastings, *A Biography,* 482. These two phrases are taken from Waugh's description of the novel on the dust jacket of the novel's first edition.

60. Quoted in Carpenter, *The Brideshead Generation,* 370. These phrases are taken from the Preface to the 1960 edition of the novel.

61. Waugh, *Letters,* 439.

62. Waugh, *Brideshead Revisited,* 151.

63. Ibid., 127; 128.

64. Ibid., 173.

65. Ibid., 308–9.

66. Ibid., 309.

67. Although many critics simply ignore Ryder's implicit acceptance of Catholicism, Stephen Spender justly criticizes Waugh's portrayal of this important conversion narrative. In "The World of Evelyn Waugh," Spender argues, "For Charles Ryder to be brought to see that Lord Marchmain received spiritual comfort from Extreme Unction does not therefore convince the reader of the transcendence of God's Catholic plan." However, Spender misreads Waugh's intentions slightly when he states, "If you are, like Sebastian, a hopeless drunkard, God according to Brideshead (who despite his wooden pomposity is an authority on these matters) particularly loves you." Spender, in Carens, *Critical Essays on Evelyn Waugh,* 70. Yet it is not Sebastian's drunkenness but his Catholicism that endears him to God in Brideshead's eyes. Furthermore, only Ryder's conversion makes him tolerable from this perspective.

68. Waugh, *Brideshead Revisited,* 85.

69. Ibid., 329.

70. Ibid., 338.

71. Ibid., 340.

72. Ibid., 341.

73. Ibid., 351.

74. In "Splendors and Miseries of Evelyn Waugh," Edmund Wilson condemns Waugh's portrayal of both Lord Marchmain's and Ryder's conversions. Wilson asserts, "The last scenes are extravagantly absurd, with an absurdity that would be worthy of Waugh at his best if it were not—painful to say—meant quite seriously." Wilson, in Carens, *Critical Essays on Evelyn Waugh,* 118.

75. For example, in Waugh's assessment of the American Catholic Church, he compares the old Catholic families in Baltimore to the recusant English Catholic families in Lancashire. His language is excessively romanticized in describing these Catholic strongholds: "The countryside . . . has the same tradition of Jesuit missionaries moving in disguise from family to family, celebrating Mass in remote plantations, inculcating the same austere devotional habits, the same tenacious, unobtrusive fidelity." Waugh, *Essays,* 382–83.

76. Ibid., 161.

77. Waugh, *Diaries,* 662.

78. Because he remained so conscious of Communism's threat to his faith and nation, Waugh was sometimes portrayed unfairly as a supporter of Fascism. He was forced to respond to such criticism during the Spanish Civil War; when asked whether he sided with the Fascists or Communists in Spain, he retorted, "As an Englishman I am not in the predicament of choosing between two evils. I am not a Fascist nor shall I become one unless it were the only alternative to Marxism." Waugh, *Essays,* 187.

79. Evelyn Waugh, *Sword of Honour* (Boston: Little, Brown, & Co., 1961), 741.

80. Waugh, *Essays,* 237.

81. Evelyn Waugh, *Mr. Wu and Mrs. Stich: The Letters of Evelyn Waugh and Diana Cooper,* ed. Artemis Cooper (London: Hodder & Stoughton, 1991), 82, quoted in Hastings, *A Biography,* 527.

82. According to Carpenter, Waugh's superiors judged him unfit for commanding a battalion because of his "total incapacity for establishing any sort of human relations with his men." Carpenter, *Brideshead Generation,* 347.

83. For a thorough discussion of Waugh's relationship with his men in the war and his experience throughout the war years, see Martin Green's chapter "1939–1945: The War," in *The Children of the Sun: A Narrative of 'Decadence' in England after 1918* (New York: Basic Books, 1976), 309–45.

84. Originally published in three volumes: *Men at Arms* (1952), *Officers and Gentlemen* (1955), and *The End of the Battle* (1962), the one-volume *Sword of Honour* trilogy was published in 1964. Because Waugh claims in his preface to the 1964 edition, "The product is intended (as it was originally) to be read as a single story," I will cite from the single-volume edition without distinguishing between the three initial publications. Waugh, *Sword of Honour,* 9.

85. Ibid., 300 (Waugh's italics).

86. Ibid., 546.

87. In his Preface to the 1964 publication of *Sword of Honour,* Waugh explains his depiction of Apthorpe, Col. McTavish, and Col. Ritchie-Hook, the three most ostentatious Halberdiers: "I invented three clowns who have prominent parts in the structure of the story, but not in its theme." Ibid., 9.

88. Waugh, *Letters*, 443.
89. Waugh, *Sword of Honour*, 719.
90. Mme. Kani, one of the handful of minor Catholic characters in the novel, offers Guy her own assessment of the war's beginnings: "It seems to me there was a will to war, a death wish, everywhere. Even good men thought their private honour would be satisfied by the war. They could assert their manhood by killing and being killed. They would accept hardships as recompense for being selfish and lazy. Danger justified privilege." Ibid., 788. Guy admits that he had thought in such a manner before the war.
91. Ibid., 699.
92. Waugh, *Letters*, 579.
93. Ibid.
94. Waugh, *Sword of Honour*, 9.
95. Waugh, *Essays*, 606.
96. Waugh, *Letters*, 303.
97. Greene, *The Times* (April 15, 1966), 15, quoted in Carpenter, *Brideshead Generation*, 468.

CHAPTER 5. GRAHAM GREENE

Thomas Merton, *The Sign of Jonas* (San Diego, CA: Harvest, 1981), 236.

1. Graham Greene, "Waugh Trilogy," BBC Broadcast (1987), quoted in Humphrey Carpenter, *The Brideshead Generation: Evelyn Waugh and His Friends* (Boston: Houghton Mifflin, 1990), 220.
2. Quoted in Vincent Sherry, *The Life of Graham Greene*, vol. 2 (New York: Viking, 1996), 196.
3. Graham Greene, *A Sort of Life* (New York: Simon and Schuster, 1971), 167.
4. Although the comparison might initially strike one as surprising, Greene greatly admired Chesterton. Greene enjoyed Chesterton's "prose fantasies" and his "cosmic optimism, the passionately held belief that 'it is good to be here'" even if Greene found it impossible to maintain such a perspective on life and faith. Graham Greene, *Graham Greene: Collected Essays* (New York: Viking, 1969), 137.
5. Graham Greene, *The Man Within* (New York: Penguin, 2005), 165.
6. Greene, *A Sort of Life*, 133.
7. Marie-Françoise Allain, *The Other Man: Conversations with Graham Greene* (New York: Simon and Schuster, 1983), 20.
8. Graham Greene, *Another Mexico* (New York: Viking, 1939), 144. By the time Greene arrived in Mexico, the enforcement of anti-Catholic policies had softened in the northern part of the country, causing Greene to seek action in the more dangerous southern states of Tabasco and Chiapas where the government continued to persecute Catholics.
9. Graham Greene, *Power and the Glory* (New York: Penguin, 2001), 135.
10. Ibid., 50.
11. Ibid., 94.

12. Ibid., 219.

13. Ibid., 220.

14. Greene admired the emotion and drama that pervaded Latin Catholicism. Although Latin expressions of faith sometimes pushed the line of ridiculousness, after returning home Greene felt English Catholic services "seemed curiously fictitious; no peon knelt with his arms out in the attitude of the cross, no woman dragged herself up the aisle on her knees. It would have seemed shocking, like the Agony itself." Greene, *Another Mexico*, 278.

15. Greene, *Power and Glory*, 58.

16. Ibid., 91.

17. See Luke 23: 39–43. In Matthew and Mark, neither thief is repentant. In John, all that is revealed is that two others are crucified with him.

18. Greene, *Another Mexico*, 80.

19. Greene, *Collected Essays*, 463.

20. Greene explains his dislike for the term *Greeneland:* "Some critics have referred to a strange violent 'seedy' region of the mind (why did I ever popularize that last adjective?) which they call Greeneland, and I have sometimes wondered whether they go round the world blinkered. 'This is Indochina,' I want to exclaim, 'this is Mexico, this is Sierra Leone carefully and accurately described.' . . . They won't believe the world they haven't noticed is like that." Graham Greene, *Ways of Escape* (New York: Simon and Schuster, 1980), 80.

21. Graham Greene, *Brighton Rock* (New York: Penguin, 1977), 268.

22. Graham Greene, *The Heart of the Matter* (New York: Penguin, 1991), 242.

23. Greene, *Power and Glory*, 210.

24. Alan Warren Friedman, "'The Dangerous Edge'; Beginning with Death'" in *Graham Greene: A Revaluation,* ed. Jeffrey Meyers (New York: St. Martin's 1989), 154.

25. Elizabeth Bowen, Graham Greene, and V. S. Pritchett, *Why Do I Write? An Exchange of Views Between Elizabeth Bowen, Graham Greene & V. S. Pritchett* (Folcroft, PA: Folcroft Press, 1969), 31.

26. Allain, *Conversations*, 161.

27. Greene, *Ways of Escape*, 267.

28. Unlike Waugh, Greene consistently maintained, "My books only reflect faith or lack of faith, with every possible nuance in between. I don't see why people insist on labeling me a Catholic writer. I'm simply a Catholic who happens to write." Allain, *Conversations*, 149. There is an amount of disingenuousness in this answer, however, because there is nothing compelling a "Catholic who happens to write" to consistently employ Catholic themes.

29. Quoted in Sherry, *Graham Greene,* vol. 2, 274.

30. Greene, *A Sort of Life*, 168.

31. Allain, *Conversations*, 154.

32. Frank Kermode, "Mr. Greene's Eggs and Crosses," in *Graham Greene,* ed. Harold Bloom (New York: Chelsea House, 1987), 41.

33. Graham Greene, *The End of the Affair* (New York: Penguin, 2004), 160.

34. Irving Howe, *The Decline of the New* (New York: Harcourt, Brace & Co., 1970), 22. Howe's emphasis on modernist "exhaustion" should be distinguished from John Barth's use of the idea in his seminal essay on postmodern literature,

"The Literature of Exhaustion." Barth prefaces his essay by clarifying that "exhaustion" does not refer to "anything so tired as the subject of physical, moral, or intellectual decadence" but instead "the exhaustion, or attempted exhaustion, of possibilities." John Barth, *The Friday Book: Essays and Other Nonfiction* (New York: G. P. Putnam's Sons, 1984), 64; 73. Barth employs the term in praise of postmodern novelists like Borges, who explore various aesthetic possibilities in the novel, whereas Howe focuses specifically on the modernist's exhaustion with promoting or exploring belief through art.

35. Jean-François Lyotard, *The Postmodern Condition: A Report on Knowledge* (Minneapolis: University of Minnesota Press, 2002), xxiv. Lyotard develops this term in the context of examining the role of scientific knowledge in the twentieth century, although he contends the renunciation of metanarratives has "altered the game rules for science, literature and the arts." Ibid., xxiii. To complement his definition of postmodernism, Lyotard "uses the term *modern* to describe any science that legitimates itself with reference to a metadiscourse of this kind making an explicit appeal to some grand narrative, such as the dialects of Spirit, the hermeneutics of meaning, the emancipation of the rational or working subject, or the creation of wealth." Ibid., xxiii (Lyotard's italics). A similar definition can be applied to literature with overtly spiritual, philosophical, or socioeconomic/political assumptions or objectives, whose adherents sometimes aggressively promote their system of belief, as might be the case with Hopkins, Eliot, and Waugh with regard to liturgical Christianity.

36. It is important to note that Lyotard's distinction does not draw the modernist-postmodernist divide strictly according to aesthetic difference, but primarily by how artists give credence to political, social, and spiritual systems and narratives. Lyotard also explains that the line between modernism and postmodernism in any given culture or era remains inexact. He even insists that postmodernism "is undoubtedly part of the Modern." Ibid., 79.

37. From a strictly formal standpoint, *The End of the Affair* might be considered Greene's most representative high modernist work, for in it Greene employs a pastiche of literary techniques, including stream of consciousness, a running diary, and the use of flashbacks and discordant chronology. Greene's subsequent novels rely less on these techniques (with exceptions, such as in *The Comedians*), although they are still used by many postmodernist novelists, such as Salman Rushdie and Thomas Pynchon. For this reason, I believe defining the difference between modernism and postmodernism along aesthetic lines is less exact than Lyotard's and Jameson's distinctions. Furthermore, I would argue that the qualities of postmodern fiction listed by John Barth, which includes "disjunction, simultaneity, irrationalism, anti-illusionism, self-reflexiveness, medium-as-message, political olympianism, and moral pluralism approaching moral entropy" are all contingent upon the postmodern artists' abandonment of metanarrative and not on an aesthetic break with modernism. Barth, *Friday Book*, 203.

38. Greene, *End of the Affair*, 54.

39. Ibid., 73.

40. Ibid., 1

41. Lyotard, *Postmodern Condition*, 23.

42. Greene, *End of the Affair,* 153; 122.

43. Ibid., 89.

44. Ibid., 104.

45. Ibid., 11.

46. Ibid., 158.

47. Ibid., 128

48. Ibid., 154.

49. Ibid.

50. Ibid., 152.

51. A handful of critics believes that Bendrix will eventually convert to Catholicism like Sarah. For example, K. C. Joseph Kurismmootil argues that Bendrix's wrestling with God is "a prelude to surrender." Kurismmootil, *Heaven and Hell on Earth: An Appreciation of Five Graham Greene Novels* (Chicago: Loyola University Press, 1982), 164. Robert Hoskins insists "the novel's structural irony suggests that he has already been drawn toward God and divine love against his will." Hoskins, *Graham Greene: An Approach to the Novels* (New York: Garland Publishing, 1999), 155.

52. Lyotard, *Postmodern Condition,* 22.

53. Greene, *End of the Affair,* 36.

54. Ibid., 137.

55. Ibid., 52; 53; 59.

56. Ibid., 72.

57. Lyotard, *Postmodern Condition,* 15; 60 (Lyotard's italics).

58. Greene, *End of the Affair,* 76.

59. Lytoard, *Postmodern Condition,* 15.

60. Ibid., 82.

61. Graham Greene, *The Quiet American* (London: Penguin, 1973), 124.

62. Ibid., 12.

63. Lyotard, *Postmodern Condition,* 5. Lyotard develops this notion to articulate his prophetic assertion that "new forms of the circulation of capital that go by the generic name of *multi-national corporations*" will enact political and economic power "beyond the control of nation-states." Ibid., 5 (Lyotard's italics).

64. Greene, *Quiet American,* 94.

65. Ibid., 37.

66. Ibid., 20.

67. Ibid., 163.

68. In Jameson's influential Foreword to a 1984 reprinting of Lyotard's *The Postmodern Condition,* he emphasizes the resilience of metanarratives in the postmodern world. In a later interview, Jameson underscores this belief: "All one has to do is to look at the reemergence of religious paradigms, whether it is Iran, or liberation theology, or American fundamentalism. There are all kinds of master narratives in this world which is was supposed to be beyond narrative." Frederic Jameson, "Regarding Postmodernism: A Conversation with Frederic Jameson," ed. Anders Stephason, *Social Text,* no. 17 (August 1987): 47. This point alone does not disprove Lyotard's theory—for Lyotard did not argue that metanarrative would cease to exist, but that no "Postmodernist" turns to metanarrative for a comprehensive answer to the world's problems.

69. Frederic Jameson, *Postmodernism, or The Cultural Logic of Late Capitalism* (Durham, NC: Duke University Press, 1991), 84.

70. Frederic Jameson, *The Jameson Reader* (Oxford: Blackwell, 2000), 316–17.

71. Jameson, *Postmodernism*, 65.

72. Ibid., 64 (Jameson's italics).

73. Ibid., 107; 28.

74. Jameson, "Regarding Postmodernism," 34.

75. Greene, *Quiet American*, 88.

76. Ibid., 36. As Norman Sherry notes in his biography of Greene, some political thinkers believed "Catholics were the true Third Force in Vietnam" because they straddled the lines of conflict. Sherry, *Graham Greene*, vol. 2, 485.

77. Greene, *Quiet American*, 49.

78. Ibid., 122.

79. Quoted in Sherry, *Graham Greene*, vol. 2, 437.

80. Allain, *Conversations*, 72. Although American authorities made much of Greene's membership in a Communist organization while at Oxford, Greene asserted that he and the university friend who joined with him had "no scrap of Marxist belief between us" and "joined only with the farfetched idea of gaining control and perhaps winning a free trip to Moscow and Leningrad." Greene, *A Sort of Life*, 134. Greene's explanation is verified by his conduct during a Socialist strike of *The London Times* while he worked as a copy editor, when he crossed the picket line and made sure some form of the paper reached the presses. Greene felt that the Communist-instigated strike against the paper was preposterous. Sherry, *Graham Greene*, vol. 1, 302.

81. Greene complains, "Like many English writers I have royalties awaiting me in the Soviet Union," but "I have no desire to make use myself of my royalties by revisiting the Soviet Union so long as these authors [who protested the Soviet government's behavior] remain in prison, however happy my memory of past visits." Sherry, *Graham Greene*, vol. 3, 460.

82. Greene, *Collected Essays*, 410.

83. Allain, *Conversations*, 160.

84. Alan Wilde, *Horizons of Assent: Modernism, Postmodernism, and the Ironic Imagination* (Baltimore, MD: Johns Hopkins University Press, 1981), 44. Wilde later adds that, when postmodernism replaces modernism, "a world in need of mending is superseded by one beyond repair. Modernism . . . reaches toward the heroic in the intensity of its desire and of its disillusion. Postmodernism, skeptical of such efforts, presents itself deliberately, consciously antiheroic." Ibid., 131–32. I would contend further that metanarratives inspire modernists to move toward the heroic, as they romantically try to defend systems rendered increasingly anachronistic by modernity.

85. Greene, *Ways of Escape*, 266.

86. Graham Greene, *Our Man in Havana* (New York: Viking, 1981), 13–14.

87. Ibid., 33.

88. Ibid., 28.

89. Ibid., 210.

90. Ibid., 214.

91. Greene, *Ways of Escape*, 261.

92. After Waugh noted the sometimes transparent autobiographical depictions of Querry in the novel, Greene responded, "With a writer of your genius and insight I certainly would not attempt to hide behind the time-old gag that an author can never be identified with his characters. Of course in some of Querry's reactions there are reactions of mine, just as in some of Fowler's reactions in *The Quiet American* there are reactions of mine." Ibid., 263.

93. Graham Greene, *A Burnt-Out Case* (New York: Viking, 1961), 50.

94. Ibid.

95. Ibid., 141.

96. Ibid., 111 (Greene's ellipsis).

97. Ibid., 225.

98. Ibid., 233.

99. Waugh, *Diaries of Evelyn Waugh*, 775.

100. Ibid.

101. Greene, *Ways of Escape*, 259.

102. Graham Greene, *The Comedians* (New York: Viking, 1966), 300.

103. Ibid., 241.

104. Ibid., 289.

105. Ibid., 307–8. Critics almost invariably quote Dr. Magiot's more dubious statement later in the letter as a supposedly definitive reflection of Greene's politics: "Catholics and Communists have committed great crimes, but at least they have not stood aside, like an established society, and been indifferent. I would rather have blood on my hands than water like Pilate." Ibid., 308. This claim, however, certainly does not befit Greene's criticism of American-authored violence as depicted in *The Quiet American*. The Americans certainly have "not stood aside," and Greene does not apologize for their behavior. Therefore, I believe using the quote as a summary of Greene's attitude to violent conflict is problematic.

106. Ibid., 154.

107. Ibid., 155.

108. Ibid., 17.

109. Ibid., 141.

110. Ibid., 153.

111. Ibid., 28.

112. Ibid.

113. Greene, *Ways of Escape*, 271.

114. Allain, *Conversations*, 39.

115. Quoted in Neil Sinyard, *Graham Greene: A Literary Life* (New York: Palgrave Macmillan, 2003), 58.

116. Sherry, *Graham Greene*, vol. 3, 741.

117. Graham Greene, *Monsignor Quixote* (New York: Simon and Schuster, 1982), 179.

118. Ibid., 220.

119. Sherry, *Graham Greene*, vol. 3, 691.

120. Ibid.

121. Ibid., 797.

122. Greene, *Collected Essays*, 396.

CONCLUSION

Cardinal Joseph Rutzinger, *Salt of the Earth: The Church at the End of the Millennium* trans. Adrian Walker (San Francisco, CA: Ignatius Press, 1926), 272.

1. Greene, *Essays*, 349–50.
2. Lyotard, *Postmodern Condition*, 51.
3. Ford, *Parade's End*, 812.
4. Arthur Mizener, *The Saddest Story: A Biography of Ford Madox Ford* (New York: World Publishing Co., 1971), 451.
5. Max Saunders, *Ford Madox Ford, vol. 2*, 488.
6. Mizener, *Saddest Story*, 431.
7. Waugh, *Essays*, 629.
8. Ibid., 630.
9. Waugh, "To Ruth McQuillan" (February 19, 1964, National Library of Scotland); Waugh, *Mr. Wu and Mrs. Stich*, 316; quoted in Hastings, *Evelyn Waugh: A Biography*, 619; 620 (my italics).
10. Hopkins, *Gerard Manley Hopkins*, 301.
11. Eliot, *Essays Ancient and Modern*, 114 (Eliot's italics).
12. Eliot, *Murder in the Cathedral*, in *Complete Plays of T. S. Eliot*, 20.
13. Lyndall Gordon, *Eliot's New Life* (Oxford: Oxford University Press, 1988), 255; 260.

Bibliography

Allain, Marie-Françoise. *The Other Man: Conversations with Graham Greene.* New York: Simon and Schuster, 1983.

Altholz, Josef. "The Political Behavior of the English Catholics, 1850–1867." *Journal of British Studies* 4, no. 1 (November 1964): 89–103.

Anderson, Benedict. *Imagined Communities: Reflections on the Origin and Spread of Nationalism.* New York: Verso, 1983.

Ardis, Ann. *Modernism and Cultural Conflict: 1880–1922.* London: Oxford, 2002.

Atkin, Nicholas and Frank Tallett. *Priests, Prelates and People: A History of European Catholicism Since 1750.* Oxford: Oxford University Press, 2003.

Barth, John. *The Friday Book: Essays and Other Nonfiction.* New York: G. P. Putnam's Sons, 1984.

Beer, John. *Romantic Influences.* New York: St. Martin's Press, 1993.

Belloc, Hilaire. *Crisis of Civilization.* New York: Fordham University Press, 1937.

———. *Europe and the Faith.* London: Burns & Oates, 1962.

Blalock, Susan E. *Guide to the Secular Poetry of T. S. Eliot.* New York: G. K. Hall & Co., 1996.

Bloom, Harold, ed. *Graham Greene.* New York: Chelsea House, 1987.

Bossy, John. *The English Catholic Community 1570–1850.* New York: Oxford University Press, 1976.

Bowen, Elizabeth, Graham Greene, and V. S. Pritchett. *Why Do I Write? An Exchange of Views Between Elizabeth Bowen, Graham Greene & V.S. Pritchett.* Folcroft, PA: Folcroft Press, 1969.

Brooke, Rupert. *The Collected Poems of Rupert Brooke.* London: Kessinger Publishing, 2005.

Brooks, Cleanth. *Modern Poetry and the Tradition.* Chapel Hill, NC: University of North Carolina Press, 1979.

Buddha. *The Sacred Laws of the Âryas as Taught in the Schools of Âpastamba, Guatama, Vasishtha, and Baudhâyana.* Delhi, India: M. Banarsidass, 1965.

Bunting, Basil. "English Poetry Today." *Poetry* 39 (January 1932): 228.

Bush, Ronald. "Modern/Postmodern: Eliot, Perse, Mallarmé, and the Future of the Barbarians." In *Modernism Reconsidered,* edited by Robert Kiley and John Hildebride, 191–214. Cambridge, MA: Harvard University Press, 1983.

Carens, James F., ed. *Critical Essays on Evelyn Waugh.* Boston: G. K. Hall, 1987.

Carpenter, Humphrey. *The Brideshead Generation: Evelyn Waugh and His Friends*. Boston: Houghton Mifflin, 1990.

Chesterton, G. K. *Orthodoxy*. New York: Dodd, Mead & Co., 1936.

Cooper, John Xiros. *Modernism and the Culture of Market Society*. Cambridge: Cambridge University Press, 2004.

Eagleton, Terry. "Waugh and the Upper Class Novel." In Carens, *Critical Essays*, 106–15.

Eliot, T. S. *After Strange Gods*. New York: Harcourt Brace & Co., 1933.

———. *Collected Poems 1909–1962*. New York: Harcourt Brace & Co., 1963.

———. *The Complete Plays of T. S. Eliot*. New York: Harcourt, Brace and World, 1969.

———. *Essays Ancient and Modern*. London: Faber & Faber Limited, 1936.

———. *For Lancelot Andrewes*. London: Faber & Gwyer, 1928.

———. *The Idea of a Christian Society*. London: Faber and Faber, 1939.

———. *The Letters of T. S. Eliot: 1898–1922*. Edited by Valerie Eliot. New York: Harcourt Brace & Co., 1988.

———. *Notes Towards the Definition of Culture*. New York. Harcourt Brace & Co., 1949.

———. *The Sacred Wood*. London, Methuen & Co., 1948.

———. *Selected Essays*. New York: Harcourt Brace & Co., 1960.

———. *To Criticize the Critic and Other Writings*. New York: Farrar, Straus, and Giroux, 1965.

———. "*Ulysses*, Order, Myth." In *James Joyce: The Critical Heritage*, vol. 1, 268–71. Edited by Robert H. Deming. New York: Barnes & Noble, 1970.

———. "The Influence of Mr. James Joyce." In ibid., 186–89.

Esty, Jed. *A Shrinking Island: Modernism and National Culture in England*. Princeton, NJ: Princeton University Press, 2004.

Feeney S. J., Joseph. "Four Newfound Hopkins Letters." *Hopkins Quarterly* 23, no. 1–2 (Winter–Spring, 1996): 3–40.

———. "Hopkins' Frequent Reassignments." *Hopkins Quarterly* 11, no. 3 & 4 (Fall 1984–Winter 1985): 101–18.

Ford (Hueffer), Ford Madox. *The Correspondence of Ford Madox Ford and Stella Bowen*. (Bloomington, IN: Indiana University Press, 1993.

———. *The Critical Attitude*. London: Duckworth & Co., 1911.

———. *England and the English: An Interpretation*. New York: McClure, Phillips & Co., 1907.

———. *Ford Madox Ford: Critical Essays*. Edited by Max Saunders and Richard Stang. Manchester, UK: Carcanet, 2002.

———. *The Good Soldier*. Oxford: Oxford University Press, 1999.

———. *It was the Nightingale*. Philadelphia: J. B. Lippincott Co., 1933.

———. *Memories and Impressions*. London: Harper, 1911.

———. "On Impressionism," reprinted in *The Good* Soldier, 260–80. Ontario, Canada: Broadview, 2003.

————. "On a Notice of Blast." *Outlook.* 36 (July 31, 1915).

————. *Parade's End.* New York: Penguin, 1982.

————. *Return to Yesterday.* New York: Horace Liverright, Inc., 1932.

————. *The Transatlantic Review,* vols. 1 & 2. New York: Kraus Reprint Corp., 1967.

————. *War Prose.* Edited by Max Saunders. New York: New York University Press, 2004.

————. *Your Mirror to My Times.* New York: Holt, Rinehart, and Winston, 1971.

Forster, E. M. *Aspects of the Novel.* New York: Harcourt, Brace & Co., 1927.

Fussell, Paul. *The Great War and Modern Memory.* New York: Oxford University Press, 1975.

Gordon, Lyndall. *Eliot's New Life.* Oxford: Oxford University Press, 1988.

————. *T. S. Eliot: An Imperfect Life.* New York: Norton, 1998.

Gorra, Michael Edward. *The English Novel at Mid-Century: From the Leaning Tower.* New York: St. Martin's, 1990.

Graves, Robert. *Good-bye to All That.* New York: Doubleday Anchor, 1967.

Green, Martin. *The Children of the Sun: A Narrative of 'Decadence' in England after 1918.* New York: Basic Books, 1976.

Greene, Graham. *Another Mexico.* New York: Viking, 1939.

————. *Brighton Rock.* New York: Penguin, 1977.

————. *A Burnt-Out Case.* New York: Viking, 1961.

————. *Collected Essays.* New York: Viking, 1969.

————. *The Comedians.* New York: Viking, 1966.

————. *The End of the Affair.* London: Penguin, 2004.

————. *The Heart of the Matter.* New York: Penguin, 1991.

————. *The Man Within.* New York: Penguin, 2005.

————. *Monsignor Quixote.* New York: Simon and Schuster, 1982.

————. *Our Man in Havana.* New York: Viking, 1981.

————. *The Power and the Glory.* New York: Penguin, 2001.

————. *The Quiet American.* London: Penguin, 1973.

————. *A Sort of Life.* New York: Simon and Schuster, 1971.

————. *Ways of Escape.* New York: Simon and Schuster, 1980.

Griffin, Susan M. *Anti-Catholicism and Nineteenth-Century Fiction.* Cambridge: Cambridge University Press, 2004.

Guttsman, W. L. *The English Ruling Class.* London: Wiedenfeld and Nicolson, 1969.

Hassan, Ihab. *The Postmodern Turn: Essays in Postmodern Theory and Culture.* Columbus: Ohio State University Press, 1987.

Hastings, Selina. *Evelyn Waugh: A Biography.* Boston: Houghton Mifflin Co., 1994.

Heimann, Mary. *Catholic Devotion in Victorian England.* Oxford: Clarendon Press, 1995.

Hollis, Christopher. *Newman and the Modern World.* Garden City, NY: Doubleday, 1968.

Hooker, Richard. *The Folger Library Edition of the Works of Richard Hooker.* Edited by W. Speed Hill. London: Belknap Press, 1977.

Hopkins, Gerard Manley. *Further Letters of Gerard Manley Hopkins.* London: Oxford University Press, 1956.

———. *Gerard Manley Hopkins.* Edited by Catherine Phillips. Oxford: Oxford University Press, 1986.

———. *Gerard Manley Hopkins: Selected Prose.* Oxford: Oxford University Press, 1980.

Hornsby-Smith, Michael. *Roman Catholics in England.* London: Cambridge University Press, 1987.

Hoskins, Robert. *Graham Greene: An Approach to the Novels.* New York: Garland Publishing, 1999.

Howe, Irving. *The Decline of the New.* New York: Harcourt, Brace & World, 1970.

Huyssen, Andreas. *After the Great Divide: Modernism, Mass Culture, Postmodernism.* Bloomington: Indiana University Press, 1986.

Jameson, Fredric. *The Jameson Reader.* Oxford: Blackwell, 2000.

———. *Postmodernism, or The Cultural Logic of Late Capitalism.* Durham, NC: Duke University Press, 1991.

———. "Regarding Postmodernism: A Conversation with Frederic Jameson," edited by Anders *Social Text,* no. 17 (August 1987):29–54.

Jodock, Darrell, ed. *Catholicism Contending with Modernity: Roman Catholic Modernism and Anti-Modernism in Historical Context.* Cambridge: Cambridge University Press, 2000.

Joyce, James. *The Critical Writings of James Joyce,* vol. 1. Edited by Ellsworth Mason and Richard Ellmann. New York: Viking, 1959.

Julius, Anthony. *T. S. Eliot, Anti-Semitism and Literary Form.* Cambridge: Cambridge University Press, 1995.

Kenner, Hugh. *The Invisible Poet: T. S. Eliot.* New York: McDowell, Obolensky, 1959.

———. *Paradox in Chesterton.* New York: Sheed & Ward, 1947.

———. *A Sinking Island.* London: Barrie & Jenkins, 1988.

Ker, Ian. *The Catholic Revival in English Literature 1845–1961.* Notre Dame, IN: University of Notre Dame Press, 2003.

———. *John Henry Newman: A Biography.* Oxford: Oxford University Press, 1988.

Kurismmootil, S. J., K. C. Joseph. *Heaven and Hell on Earth: An Appreciation of Five Graham Greene Novels.* Chicago: Loyola University Press, 1982.

Leavis, F. R. *New Bearings in English Poetry.* London: Chatto & Windus, 1950.

Levenson, Michael H. *A Genealogy of Modernism: A Study of English Literary Doctrine 1908–1922.* Cambridge: Cambridge University Press, 1984.

Lewis, C. S. *Mere Christianity.* New York: Macmillan, 1960.

Loyola, St. Ignatius. *The Spiritual Exercises.* Translated by Louis J. Puhl, S. J. Westminster, MD: The Newman Press, 1954.

Lyotard, Jean-François. *The Postmodern Condition: A Report on Knowledge.* Minneapolis: University of Minnesota Press, 2002.

Martin, Robert Bernard. *Gerard Manley Hopkins: A Very Private Life.* New York: G. P. Putnam's Sons, 1991.

McClelland, Alan. V. and Michael Hodgetts, eds. *From Without the Flaminian Gate: 150 Years of Roman Catholicism in England and Wales, 1850–2000.* London: Darton, Longman, & Todd, 1999.

Meixner, John A. *Ford Madox Ford's Novels: A Critical Study.* Minneapolis: University of Minnesota Press, 1962.

Merton, Thomas. *The Sign of Jonas.* San Diego, CA: Harvest Books, 1981.

Meyers, Jeffrey, ed. *Graham Greene: A Revaluation.* New York: St. Martin's, 1989.

Miller, J. Hillis. "The Linguistic Moment." In *Gerard Manley Hopkins,* edited by Harold Bloom, 147–162. New York: Chelsea House Publishers, 1986.

Mizener, Arthur. *T. S. Eliot: A Collection of Critical Essays.* Edited by Hugh Kenner. Englewood Cliffs, NJ: Prentice-Hall, 1962.

———. *The Saddest Story: A Biography of Ford Madox Ford.* New York: World Publishing Co., 1971.

Morgan, Kenneth O., ed. *The Oxford History of Britain.* Oxford: Oxford University Press, 2001.

Muller, Jill. *Gerard Manley Hopkins and Victorian Catholicism: A Heart in Hiding.* New York: Routledge, 2003.

Murray, Paul. *T. S. Eliot and Mysticism.* New York: St. Martin's, 1991.

Newman, John Henry. *Lectures on the Present Position of Catholics in England (1851).* Notre Dame, IN: University of Notre Dame Press, 2000.

———. *The Letters and Diaries of John Henry Newman,* Vols. 1 & 2. Oxford: Clarendon Press, 2006.

———. *Second Spring: A Sermon.* London: Thomas Richardson and Son, 1852.

Norman, Edward. *Roman Catholicism in England.* Oxford: Oxford University Press, 1985.

Omer-Sherman, Ranen. " 'It Is I Who Have Been Defending a Religion Called Judaism': The T.S. Eliot and Horace M. Kallen Correspondence." *Texas Studies in Literature and Language* 39, no. 4 (Winter 1997): 321–56.

Pearce, Joseph. *Literary Converts: Spiritual Inspiration in an Age of Unbelief.* San Francisco: Ignatius Press, 1999.

Peppis, Paul. *Literature, Politics, and the English Avant-Garde: Nation and Empire, 1901–1918.* Cambridge: Cambridge University Press, 2000.

Poli, Bernard J. *Ford Madox Ford and the Transatlantic Review.* Syracuse, NY: Syracuse University Press, 1967.

Pope Benedict XV. *Ad Beatissimi Apostolorum.* Papal Encyclicals Online. www.papalencyclicals.net/Ben15/b15adbea.htm.

Pope Leo XIII. *Apostolicae Curae.* Papal Encyclicals Online. www.papalencycli-
cals.net/Leo13/l13curae.htm.

Pope Pius X. *Pascendi Dominici Gregis.* Papal Encyclicals Online. http://www
.papalencyclicals.net/Pius10/p10pasce.htm.

Pound, Ezra. *Selected Prose 1909–1965.* New York: New Directions, 1973.

Raffel, Burton. *T. S. Eliot.* New York: Continuum, 1991.

Ratzinger, Cardinal. *Salt of the Earth: The Church at the End of the Millennium.*
Translated by Adrian Walker. San Francisco, CA: Ignatius Press, 1996.

Rafferty, Oliver P. *The Church, the State, and the Fenian Threat.* New York: St.
Martin's, 1999.

Rainey, Lawrence. *Institutions of Modernism: Literary Elites and Public Culture.* New Haven, CT: Yale University Press, 1998.

———. *Revisiting The Waste Land.* New Haven, CT: Yale University Press,
2005.

Reed, John Shelton. *Glorious Battle: The Cultural Politics of Victorian Anglo-
Catholicism.* Nashville, TN: Vanderbilt University Press, 1996.

Roberts, Gerald. "Hopkins and the Catholics of England," *Hopkins Quarterly*
14, no. 1–4 (April 1987–January 1988): 113–43.

Said, Edward W. *Culture and Imperialism.* New York: Alfred A. Knopf, 1993.

———. *Reflections on Exile and Other Essays.* Cambridge, MA: Harvard University Press, 2000.

Saunders, Max. *Ford Madox Ford: A Dual Life*, vols. 1 & 2. Oxford: Oxford University Press, 1996.

Schuchard, Ronald. *Eliot's Dark Angel.* New York: Oxford, 1999.

Schweitzer, Richard. *The Cross and the Trenches.* London: Praeger, 2003.

Shakespeare, William. *The Complete Works of Shakespeare.* Edited by David Bevington. New York: Longman, 1997.

Sherry, Norman. *The Life of Graham Greene*, vols. 1–3. New York: Viking, 1989;
1996; 2004.

Sinyard, Neil. *Graham Greene: A Literary Life.* New York: Palgrave Macmillan,
2003.

Spender, Stephen. *The Struggle of the Modern.* Berkeley: University of California
Press, 1963.

———. "'The World of Evelyn Waugh." In Carens, *Critical Essays,* 70–77.

Staley, Vernon. *The Catholic Religion: A Manual of Instruction for Members of
the Anglican Church.* London: A. R. Mowbray & Co., 1903.

Stebbing, C. SS. R., Reverend George. *The Church in England.* London:
Sands & Co., 1921.

Sulloway, Alison G. *Gerard Manley Hopkins and the Victorian Temper.* New
York: Columbia University Press, 1972.

Sykes, Christopher. *Evelyn Waugh: A Biography.* Boston: Little, Brown & Co.,
1975.

Tawney, R. H. *Religion and the Rise of Capitalism: A Historical Study.* New
York: Harcourt, Brace and Co., 1952. First published 1929.

Thomas S. J., Alfred. *Hopkins the Jesuit: The Years of Training.* London: Oxford University Press, 1968.

Underhill, Evelyn. *Mysticism.* New York; E. P. Dutton & Co., 1948.

Vickery, John B. *The Literary Impact of The Golden Bough.* Princeton, NJ: Princeton University Press, 1973.

Waugh, Evelyn. *Black Mischief.* London: Chapman and Hall Ltd., 1932.

———. *Brideshead Revisited.* Boston: Little, Brown & Co., 1972.

———. *Decline and Fall.* Boston: Little, Brown & Co., 1946.

———. *The Diaries of Evelyn Waugh.* Edited by Michael Davie. Boston: Little, Brown & Co., 1976.

———. *Edmund Campion.* Boston: Little, Brown and Co., 1946.

———. *The Essays, Articles and Reviews.* Edited by Donat Gallagher. Boston: Little, Brown & Co., 1983.

———. *A Handful of Dust.* Boston: Little, Brown & Co., 1944.

———. *The Letters of Evelyn Waugh.* Edited by Mark Amory. New Haven: Ticknor & Fields, 1980.

———. *A Little Learning.* Little, Brown & Co., 1964.

———. *Mr. Wu and Mrs. Stich: The Letters of Evelyn Waugh and Diana Cooper.* Edited by Artemis Cooper. London: Hodder & Stoughton, 1991.

———. *Sword of Honour.* Boston: Little, Brown, & Co., 1961.

———. *Vile Bodies.* New York: Penguin, 1930.

Weber, Max. *The Protestant Ethic and the Spirit of Capitalism.* Translated by Talcott Parsons. London, George Allen & Unwin Ltd., 1948.

Weston, Frank. *Report of the Anglo-Catholic Congress of 1923.* London: Society of SS Peter and Paul, 1923.

Weston, Jessie L. *From Ritual to Romance.* Garden City, NY: Doubleday & Co., 1957.

Wilde, Alan. *Horizons of Assent: Modernism, Postmodernism, and the Ironic Imagination.* Baltimore, MD: Johns Hopkins University Press, 1981.

Wilson, Edmund. "Splendors and Miseries of Evelyn Waugh." In Carens, *Critical Essays,* 117–19.

Wordsworth, William. *The Fourteen-Book Prelude.* Edited by W. J. B. Owen. Ithaca, NY: Cornell University Press, 1985.

Yeats, W. B., ed. *The Oxford Book of Modern Verse.* New York: Oxford University Press, 1936.

Zonneveld, Sjaak. *The Random Grim Forge: A Study of Social Ideas in Gerard Manley Hopkins.* Maastricht, Netherlands: Van Gorcem, 1992.

Index